I0004433

Local Governance and ICTs in Africa

Through the voices of the peoples of Africa and the global South, Pambazuka Press and Pambazuka News disseminate analysis and debate on the struggle for freedom and justice.

Pambazuka Press

www.pambazukapress.org

 A Pan-African publisher of progressive books and DVDs on Africa and the global South that aim to stimulate discussion, analysis and engagement. Our publications address issues of human rights, social justice, advocacy, the politics of aid, development and international finance, women's rights, emerging powers and activism. They are primarily written by well-known African academics and activists. Most books are also available as ebooks.

Pambazuka News

www.pambazuka.org

 The award-winning and influential electronic weekly newsletter providing a platform for progressive Pan-African perspectives on politics, development and global affairs. With more than 2,500 contributors across the continent and a readership of more than 660,000, Pambazuka News has become the indispensable source of authentic voices of Africa's social analysts and activists.

Pambazuka Press and **Pambazuka News**
are published by Fahamu (www.fahamu.org)

Local Governance and ICTs in Africa

Case Studies and Guidelines
for Implementation and Evaluation

*Edited by Timothy Mwololo Waema
and Edith Ofwona Adera*

**Pambazuka
Press**

International Development Research Centre
Ottawa · Cairo · Dakar · Montevideo · Nairobi · New Delhi · Singapore

Published 2011 by Pambazuka Press,
the International Development Research Centre and
the African Training and Research Centre in Administration for Development

Pambazuka Press, an imprint of Fahamu
Cape Town, Dakar, Nairobi and Oxford
www.pambazukapress.org   www.fahamubooks.org   www.pambazuka.org

Fahamu, 2nd floor, 51 Cornmarket Street, Oxford OX1 3HA, UK
Fahamu Kenya, PO Box 47158, 00100 GPO, Nairobi, Kenya
Fahamu Senegal, 9 Cité Sonatel 2, POB 25021, Dakar-Fann, Dakar, Senegal
Fahamu South Africa, c/o 19 Nerina Crescent, Fish
Hoek, 7975 Cape Town, South Africa

International Development Research Centre,
PO Box 8500, Ottawa, ON K1G 3H9, Canada
www.idrc.ca / info@idrc.ca

African Training and Research Centre in Administration for Development,
PO Box 310, 9001, Tangier, Morocco

British Library Cataloguing in Publication Data
A catalogue record for this book is available from the British Library

ISBN   978-0-85749-032-2   paperback (Pambazuka)
ISBN   978-1-55250-518-2   e-book (IDRC)

Manufactured on demand by Lightning Source
Designed and typeset in Monotype Garamond
by illuminati, Grosmont, www.illuminatibooks.co.uk

Contents

Figures and tables

Acronyms and abbreviations

A₅H	business process modelling tool
AITI	Advanced Information Technology Institute
ARE	Arab Republic of Egypt
BC	birth certificate
BEC	Bureau État Civil (Register Office)
BPEL	Business Process Execution Language
BPM	business process modelling
BPMN	Business Process Modelling Notation
CAD/CAM	computer aided design/manufacturing
CAFRAD	African Training and Research Centre in Administration for Development
CDA	community development assistant
CGAA	City Government of Addis Ababa
CICs	community information centres
CILOR	contribution in lieu of rates
CIOs	chief information officers
CITRED	Centre for Information Technologies and Research Development
CMCs	community multimedia centres
CSCP	civil service computerisation programme
CSOs	civil society organisations
DAI	Digital Access Index
DDI	Digital Divide Index
DINAGECA	National Directorate of Geography and Cadastre
DOI	Digital Opportunity Index
DPU	District Planning Unit

EICTDA	Ethiopian ICT Development Agency
EISI	Egyptian Information Society Initiative
EMM	Ekurhuleni Metropolitan Municipality
EMS	emergency medical services
EPQ	Eysenck Personality Questionnaire
FGDs	focus group discussions
G2B	government to business
G2C	government to citizen
G2G	government to government
GBC	Ghana Broadcasting Corporation
GDP	gross domestic product
GDS	growth and development strategy
GEMS	Gauteng Emergency Medical Services
GGegovDD	Good Governance egov Development and Deployment Method
GINS	Government Intranet System
GIS	Geographic Information System
GLSS	Ghana Living Standards Surveys
GNI	gross national income
GOC	Government Online Centre
GOK	Government of Kenya
GSS	Ghana Statistical Service
GSSC	Gauteng Shared Services Centre
GT	Ghana Telecom
HA	health assistant
HLG	higher local government
HRDC	Human Resource Development Council
ICTA	Information and Communication Technology Authority
ICT4AD	ICT for Accelerated Development
ICT4D	ICT for Development
ICTs	information and communication technologies
IDEF	Integrated Definition
IDPs	integrated development plans
IDRC	International Development Research Centre
IFMIS	Integrated Financial Management Information System
InQ	style of thinking
IOI	ICT Opportunity Index
IS	information systems
ISPs	Internet service providers

IT	information technology
ITES	information technology enabled services
KLESS	Kebele Life-Event Services System
KLGRP	Kenya Local Government Reform Programme
KPI	key performance indicator
LA	local authority
LAIFOMS	Local Authority Integrated Financial Operations Management System
LAN	local area network
LASDAP	local authority service delivery action plan
LATF	Local Authority Transfer Fund
LC	local council
LFA	logical framework analysis
LG	local government
LGDP	Local Government Development Project
LGFC	Local Government Finance Committee
LGRP	Local Government Reform Programme
LLG	lower local government
LMIS	Land Management Information System
LoGICS	Local Government Information Communication System
LOG-IN Africa	Local Governance and ICTs Research Network for Africa
M&E	monitoring and evaluation
MCIT	Ministry of Communication and Information Technology
MIS	management of information systems
MITT	Ministry of Information Technology and Telecommunications
MMC	Mavoko Municipal Council
MMPI	Minnesota Multiphasic Personality Inventory
MoES	Ministry of Education and Sports
MoH	Ministry of Health
MoLG	Ministry of Local Government
MSAD	Ministry of State for Administrative Development
MSP	Master Systems Plan
NCB	National Computer Board
NGOs	non-governmental organisations
NIMES	National Integrated Monitoring and Evaluation Strategy
NMC	Nyeri Municipal Council

NTRA	National Telecommunications Regulatory Agency
OECD	Organisation for Economic Cooperation and Development
PEAP	Poverty Eradication Action Plan
PMA	Plan for Modernisation of Agriculture
PPT	planned patient transport
PRSP	National Poverty Reduction Strategy Paper
RBM	results-based management
RMLF	Road Maintenance Levy Fund
RMS	revenue management systems
SAPS	South Africa Police Services
SAPs	structural adjustment programmes
SBP	Single Business Permit
SME	small and medium enterprises
SMS	short message service
ST	structuration theory
TUGI	The Urban Governance Initiative
UML	Unified Modeling Language
USAA	Universal Service and Access Agency
W3C	World Wide Web Consortium
WfMC	Workflow Management Coalition

Acknowledgements

The effects of information and communication technologies (ICTs) on governance in both central and local governments are still an under-researched area, especially in Africa. This research was carried out partly to generate cases that would shed more light in this field. First and foremost, the editors would like to express their appreciation of the work done by the authors in undertaking the research and in contributing chapters for this book. We wish to extend our gratitude to the African Training and Research Centre in Administration for Development (CAFRAD) for hosting the research network and diligently managing the administration of the project. We also wish to thank the International Development Research Centre (IDRC), Ottawa, Canada for the generous grant that supported the project and facilitated the documentation of the research findings in this book. Special appreciation goes to Dr Catherine Adeya for her dedication and hard work in carefully editing the draft manuscript to a very tight deadline.

We also wish to thank our scientific advisers, namely: Prof. Mammo Muchie of DIIPER Research Centre on Development Innovation and IPER and NRF/DST SARCHI, Aalborg University, Denmark and Institute of Economic Research on Innovation (IERI), Tshawne University of Technology, South Africa; Prof. Joseph Migga Kizza of the Department of Computer Science, College of Engineering and Computer Science, University of

Tenneessee–Chattanooga, Tennessee, USA; and Dr Mohammed Timoulali. They provided invaluable academic and practical advice to the researchers.

Finally, we would like to thank various national partners in a number of countries who were instrumental in providing information, attending project workshops and validating the findings arising from the studies. They include administrators in the host institutions, policymakers and decision-makers in local and national governments, civil society actors, the private sector and community members. They played very important facilitative roles, without which the various national projects would not have succeeded in the way they did.

Foreword

Mammo Muchie

There is perhaps no continent that requires the application of new technologies, inventions and innovations to help solve its numerous and varied social and economic problems more than Africa. The ICT revolution has opened up vast opportunities to meet the intractable challenges and difficulties that have confronted Africa since the 1960s. One of the thorniest problems in Africa has been a persistent crisis of governance. This has created a context for human rights violations. Sadly, those with the responsibility for protecting people ended up exacerbating the economic and governance difficulties instead of promoting human development and the comprehensive well-being of citizens.

Finding ways to deal with this intractable dilemma has become the priority concern of several internal and external stakeholders. The ICT revolution has been seized upon to help improve the overall governance landscape on the African continent. The usefulness of ICT lies in its complementary relationship with other options that are available for improving human governance (h-governance). This suggests that a stand-alone role for the ICT revolution in fixing intractable problems cannot work.

In Africa, the twin problems of despotism and corruption have not been eradicated. Therefore all necessary means, including the ICT revolution, must be deployed to deal with these forces that have undermined Africa's vast potential and prevented the continent from emerging as a powerful, prosperous, healthy and strong region. It is an embarrassment that after more half a century of political independence, no African state has become a fully developed economy. Most of the reasons for this lack of success can be attributed to the lack of a predictable system of governance able to mobilise citizens' energies, and to the absence of innovations to steer society and the economic foundations of the continent to full prosperity.

Governance in Africa operates from the local community to the continental level. Unfortunately, the crisis of governance persists at all levels, partly because the conscious and deliberate work of overhauling the system has not been done. There is a need, therefore, to deploy all means available to tackle the crisis as the starting point for creating a sustainable system. The main objective is to develop an irreversible system that works to stimulate sustainable human and economic development by eradicating poverty and promoting comprehensive well-being as a key priority.

There are three broad strategies for getting to grips with the issue of governance. One is to continue with what can be described as business as usual, paddling along the 'h-governance route' that has been in place since the wave of African political independence in the early 1960s, which on balance has ended up producing more corruption and despotism than good government and democratic fair dealing.

The second strategy is represented by the important innovation introduced by the onset of the ICT revolution. This has brought considerable potential to initiatives aimed at fighting dictatorship and increasing the participation of citizens in the institutions of governance. To be more specific, ICTs have opened a new e-governance space or route that has huge potential for improving opportunities for the participation of citizens in local and central government structures. This is exemplified in settings that enhance equity, transparency, accountability, responsiveness, responsibility, effectiveness and efficiency in the manifold transactions that link service suppliers and service recipients. In Africa, the full potential of ICTs is yet to be fully realised.

The third strategy is a judicious combination of h-governance and e-governance. ICTs cannot replace h-governance; their job is to improve it. H-governance cannot replace ICTs. The strengths and weaknesses of each must be assessed in order that their virtues can be combined. Such a creative combination is most likely to maximise staff effectiveness and accountability, as well as promote institutional transparency and citizen participation. It is here to stay. Close scrutiny of the weaknesses and strengths of each component of the dual governance structure is needed. The overall objective should be to speed up the process of improving governance across the continent at every level by utilising this socio-technical combination to best effect.

The LOG-IN Africa research programme takes the local and the municipal core of the African experience as pivotal to the improvement of services and as the levels through which decision-making, performance, effectiveness, efficiency, transparency, accountability and the participation of citizens in governance can be enhanced. This choice of the local and the municipality as the settings for the studies in this volume is appropriate for several reasons. First, it provides an opportunity to examine and appreciate the tangible impacts of ICTs on service delivery. This objective was achieved by analysing primary data to determine what changes had actually occurred in the operations of municipal administrative systems as a result of the introduction of new technology. The pan-African thrust of the research also yields fruitful insights on how ICT readiness and uptake are evolving in different local municipalities. The *very local* as research setting, coupled with a pan-African orientation, gives the studies a pioneering dimension. Had the research setting concentrated on the continental level, the micro-details provided by the local municipal sites would easily have been overlooked. Consequently, the decision to use quality governance indicators at the local level was very appropriate as a tool for collecting information on the best practices that apply to Africa's varied governance landscape.

The LOG-IN Africa programme thus deserves support. In this volume the network used the research expertise of those with technical knowledge in ICTs and those with knowledge in local governance through the support of the African Training and Research Centre in Administration for Development (CAFRAD), a pan-African organisation committed to improving public administration. IDRC was also very supportive; over the years, it has been at the forefront in supporting research initiatives on the continent. These stakeholders spent three years working with ten countries, designing studies and research around an active municipal-level issue, in order to learn how the introduction and use of ICTs changed the way both staff and citizens operate in transactions generally carried out at the municipality level. The investigations covered areas such as business process modelling methodology and financial management systems.

In those three years, a number of regional workshops and one stakeholder major conference were convened, and primary data collection was carried out, mostly using UNDP good-governance criteria. This original research produced findings and knowledge that policymakers could not ignore. In at least three cases, the output involved designing prototypes to improve services that had been identified during the course of the research experience and assessed through a peer-reviewed conference. These efforts have finally resulted in this edited collection.

There is an argument that pan-African unity can be better facilitated if there is local self-recognition and active service provision. In fact, the way to overcome the tragedy of failed states in Africa is to promote local-level governance, while simultaneously promoting the 'Africanness' of all the existing states. This is one way that has been suggested to help reconstruct Africa's governance architecture by clearing up post-colonial myopia. The relics of the arbitrary maps of post-colonialism have been a source of governance crisis in Africa. A way out of this crisis is to create cross-border municipal self-governance that permits ease of mobility and effective public service delivery. More widely, a number of analysts have suggested that the best way to get around this dilemma is to improve participation and provide effective services at the local level. The idea is to make municipal governance the core engine for service delivery. Analysts suggest that the more effective municipal governance becomes, the easier it will be to forge stronger pan-African unity. In support of this position is the argument that a municipal government is easier to define and has fewer opportunities for expanding the corruption networks that have been a key feature in many states that emerged after decolonisation, where the elite competed to capture the booty.

Given this background, ICTs and e-governance at the local level, promoted by research initiatives like those of LOG-IN Africa, become a critical means for spreading pan-African unity by promoting functioning decentralisation at the municipal government level.

The LOG-IN Africa research output on e-local governance is a timely and important contribution to pan-African research as it creates space for the interaction of the dual world of ICTs and governance to address the problems that persist in Africa. What the researchers addressed together is the application of ICTs, not only to improve governance by addressing the good governance criteria outlined by the UNDP (i.e. participation, rule of law, transparency, responsiveness, consensus orientation, equity, effectiveness and efficiency), but also to arrive at a novel conception of what it means to govern, and to be governed and managed. The objective is to make those who manage accountable to the managed, and those who are managed to participate in decision-making in contexts where responsiveness, responsibility, efficiency and effectiveness determine work ethic.

This objective implies that those who govern must view the governed as consensual partners in a network where hierarchical relationships are there to facilitate rather than to hinder the best form of governing. The E-governance Assessment Framework developed by Professor Timothy Mwololo Waema brings to the fore the distinctive contribution of the LOG-IN Africa research programme in providing concrete empirical evidence of the effects of ICT on governance, whilst clarifying and reviewing the relevant conceptual linkages between ICTs and governance. An important conceptual innovation is the distinction between *government* and *governance*, on the one hand, and *good governance*, on the other. Waema redefines good governance in terms of its 'quality'. Quality of governance is in turn shown to refer to the achievement of tangible improvements in the lives of citizens through the introduction and utilisation of ICT applications in society, in business and infrastructure initiatives. The main requirement is the need to improve the quality of service transactions between those who supply and those who receive services.

The specific country cases deal with a range of different issues, but they represent a common research effort to highlight improvements in governance following the application of ICTs. Significantly the volume has a roadmap for future research.

The Egyptian case study on business process mapping for e-local governance looks at the local municipal government's service provision to citizens. Specifically, it examines how local government staff and citizens interact by using ICT to request and receive information in an atmosphere that generates satisfaction by eliminating administrative hurdles. In the process of studying the local government development project, the researchers recognised the significance of using common business process modelling (BPM) for those receiving and providing information, knowledge, services and communication.

In comparison, the Ethiopian case study carries out an assessment of local *kebeles*, the lowest level in the country's administrative system. The research explores life-event service provision at the *kebele* level by targeting the following: the level of ICT usage; the status of e-readiness; the availability of an ICT policy and strategy; the nature of citizen participation; the quality of service provision to citizens.

In Kenya, attention shifts to a study of the application of ICTs in financial management in the two municipal councils of Mavoko and Nyeri by examining how the qualities of participation, effectiveness, efficiency, responsiveness, transparency and accountability play out in the municipalities' Integrated Financial Management Information System. The findings are striking in that the staff and the councils were responsive to billing errors that had been captured by using ICTs. Citizens also thought that on the whole the councils had become more accountable due to the ICTs. The study reveals nevertheless that certain weaknesses persist in the two councils, despite the introduction of ICTs.

The Mauritius case study relates to the Kenyan one in that it also focuses on revenue management in municipal and district councils. The study concludes that the revenue management system of three municipal councils, whilst currently working well, needs additional improvements, which could be achieved by using a more user-friendly approach to promote the roll-out of services.

The Mozambique case study directs attention to the Land Management Information System. This was potentially a critical study, involving as it did the introduction of ICTs in rural municipalities, establishing a setting for the possible co-evolution of rural and urban communities within a community for which what matters is the quality of service transaction, and not the dynamics of transforming a rural community into an urban one.

The other studies from Uganda, South Africa and Ghana deal more or less with the value and importance of ICTs for local governance. The Ugandan case targets communication; in the South Africa study the area of interetst is local economic and social development; the Ghana study broadly addresses the issue of political inclusion. Taken together, they indicate the range of application of ICTs.

A number of benefits can be derived from the LOG-IN Africa research programme. First, it can contribute to the use of *quality* as a measure for generating a toolkit for pan-African governance indicators. Second, it has the potential to apply lessons from the country-specific case studies in order to establish nationally a system for indicating local e-governance quality. It is also possible to expand further the programme's empirical research foundation, by including monitoring and evaluation as significant components of the research process. Through this orientation, it would be possible to use the empirical case studies to assess the costs and benefits of e-governance from both short- and long-term perspectives.

In conclusion, in addition to developing the stock of knowledge on the African e-governance experience, this volume provides information on and analyses of e-governance at the municipal and the local level in Africa, thereby opening up the possibility of further research on how new technologies can be used to change the governance architecture in Africa.

This volume presents important original research that must not be ignored by public policymakers – at municipal, regional, national and continental levels – in the respective countries in Africa. It is strongly recommended that this work be used and debated.

Congratulations are due to the research teams in the participating nations and to the team leader for the arduous task of coordinating the complex research process that resulted in the publication of this volume. It will undoubtedly influence the governance landscape of the continent.

I

Introduction

Edith Ofwona Adera
and Timothy Mwololo Waema

Background

In June 2004 the International Development Research Centre
(IDRC) and the United Nations Economic Commission for Africa
(UNECA), in collaboration with the United Nations Capital Development Fund (UNCDF), convened in Addis Ababa an 'International Workshop on Innovative Applications of ICTs for Local
Governance in Africa'. The main output of the workshop, attended
by some 60 participants from Africa and elsewhere, was a proposal
to set up a regional research network, coordinated by the African
Training and Research Centre in Administration for Development
(CAFRAD) to design and undertake applied research on the
impact of e-government and e-governance in Africa.

E-government and e-governance are different concepts, although
people often use the two terms interchangeably. While the study
of 'government' is primarily concerned with understanding the
institutional means through which public management is realised,
'governance' is concerned with the broader relationships between
citizens and those institutions.[1] These matters are brought into
additional relief when seen through the prism of ICT applications,
where e-government is concerned with the service delivery and
transactions undertaken by institutions in support of the variety of
public management activities, while e-governance is more broadly

concerned with the outcomes that may be enabled through the use of ICTs to support public involvement in public management, as well as the relationships among all the stakeholders involved in the governance process. As a concept and in practice, e-governance[2] seeks to realise processes and structures for harnessing the potentialities of ICTs for including citizens in democratic processes of public-sector management, service design and delivery and towards achieving good governance at the local level.[3]

Good governance is high on Africa's development agenda, premissed on the belief that it is a prerequisite for improved socio-economic performance. As a result, in Africa, there is movement towards making institutional changes in public administration and in governance systems. The capacity and autonomy of local governments are attracting specific consideration in Africa's governance agenda, because they are closest to the rural communities. This is where over 80 per cent of the continent's population lives and where it is easier to address community interests and needs. Increased emphasis on local governance has generated greater demands from citizens for effective participatory governance structures, for transparency and accountability, and for the efficient delivery of services. In response, African governments are attempting to revitalise their public administration to be more proactive, efficient and service-oriented.

To achieve this transformation, governments are introducing innovations in their organisational structures, practices and capacities, and in the ways they mobilise, deploy and utilise human capital. In addition, they are also using their information, technological and financial resources to deliver services to citizens (United Nations, 2008). This trend has resulted in increasing demands for access to public information, which has implications for information and communications technology applications in this digital era. According to the UN e-government index[4] (United Nations, 2008), the world average of the global e-government index continues to increase, but Africa lags behind. Central and West Africa are far below the world average, while Eastern and Southern Africa show little improvement. North Africa, on the other hand,

FIGURE 1.1   e-Government readiness of Africa

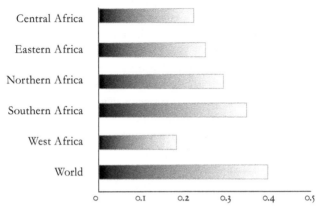

Source: United Nations, 2008.

has shown a marked improvement, in contrast to the region's ranking in the 2005 survey. Figure 1.1 shows the performance of the regions in Africa, compared to the world average.

The e-readiness index shows, however, that South Africa continued to lead the Southern Africa region, due to the country's strong online presence. Mauritius also continued to lead the Eastern African countries, largely because of the island nation's e-government readiness. The UN report notes that, with the exception of Mauritius and Seychelles, all the other countries in this region had low infrastructure scores, which reduced their overall e-government index.

Egypt, which is a lower middle-income country, performed well (in the top 80) and continued to lead the North African countries. The country also scored high in the web measure index (0.6054), ranking 28th globally (United Nations, 2008). However, Morocco, which is in the same league as Egypt from the perspective of the GNI and ICT Opportunity Index, performed rather poorly on the e-government ranking, much like the low income countries.

The West African region had the lowest regional index in the survey, as reflected in Figure 1.1. Ghana was ranked third after

Cape Verde and Nigeria. The UN report notes that a majority of the countries in this region continue to lag at the bottom because of low scores on education, infrastructure and web measurement indices.

Although the results of the survey indicate that governments have been moving forward in e-government development in Africa, progress has been slow in implementing e-government services, since it requires infrastructure improvement as well as enactment of appropriate laws and policies, capacity development, content development and use of ICT applications. So far, a few governments have made the necessary investment to move from the stage of utilising e-government applications to that of having an integrated connected governance framework.

Decentralisation and locally controlled administration are increasingly recognised as basic components of democratic governance and provide an enabling environment in which decision-making and service delivery can be brought closer to the people, especially to the poor and the marginalised. Community participation in decision-making, planning, implementation and monitoring – especially when supported by appropriate institutions, resources and effective decentralisation – can create local services that are more efficient, equitable, sustainable and cost-effective (UN DESA, 2003). This can be done by ensuring there is greater accountability and responsiveness.

The integration of ICTs in these processes (in essence e-governance) can enhance the delivery of public services to all citizens. It is therefore a key factor in improving performance in governance systems at one level. At another level, it can be the basis for improving the democratic governance framework of a society. The potential for e-governance in developing countries, however, remains largely unexploited (Ndou, 2004). This may be due to the following reasons: the difficulty of developing revised organisational structures and the skills needed to manage them; problems associated with determining the degree of decentralisation that applies to decision-making (Aliyu, 2003); the implications of emerging new forms of leadership; challenges linked to the shift towards public–private partnerships; and the necessity of involving stakeholders.

Local governance receives little attention in national e-governance policies and strategies. One possible reason for this tendency is the lack of evidence to show that decentralisation policies can influence good local governance. To date, there has been little empirical evidence of the 'multidimensional' effects of ICTs on local governance to inform national e-governance policies. While there are some examples of linkages between ICTs and local governance, the causal connection between ICTs and innovation in local governance for socio-economic development is little understood.

In view of these factors, the project idea of e-government and e-governance was presented for discussion at the 2004 PICTA meeting, as well as at the African Development Forum 2004 and the African preparatory meetings for WSIS-II, which all endorsed the idea. In addition, during an Acacia/CA team meeting in Dakar, the project idea was officially earmarked for support. Following the team meeting, IDRC funded pre-project development activity to support the collaborative development of this proposal, including the identification of appropriate institutions and researchers, who eventually participated in the 'LOG-IN Africa Pre-Project Consultative Workshop', which was held in Nairobi on 3–5 September 2005.

The selection of the research institutions was done on a competitive basis, resulting in the identification of nine research institutions from nine African countries, from almost all of Africa's major subregions. Thirteen institutional applications had been submitted for this exercise, with each participating institution required to prepare a preliminary analysis of 'The Current State of ICTs and Local Governance' in their respective countries, in order to identify knowledge and information gaps and research priorities for discussion at the Consultative Workshop. During the workshop, researchers agreed on common research issues and on methodological approaches, and prepared, with the support of CAFRAD and IDRC, draft documents that underpinned the 'LOG-IN Africa Project Proposal'.

Why the research?

In order to address this research gap, the International Development Research Centre (IDRC) supported a regional research project – the Local Governance and ICT Research Network for Africa (LOG-IN Africa) – from 2006 to 2009. This project set out to find answers to the following related research questions:

- What progress has been made and what are the outcomes in the provision of e-local governance in Africa?
- What are the challenges and threats?
- What are the good-practice strategies and solutions that are emerging?

The network conducted studies to assess the current state and outcomes of e-local governance initiatives in selected African countries. More specifically, it looked at how ICTs are being used to achieve good local governance based on the following parameters: the internal organisational processes of local governance; the provision of information and the delivery of services; the promotion of the principles of good governance; the degree of public participation and consultation.

LOG-IN Africa is a network of research teams from nine African countries. Each national team had a specific project area, looking at how e-government applications and their implementation have affected good governance. The projects were as follows:[5]

- *Egypt* (Faculty of Computers and Information, Cairo University). Development of a methodology and software tool for documenting service delivery business processes, based on past e-government implementation experiences.
- *Ethiopia* (Department of Computer Science, Addis Ababa University). Application of ICTs to life-event services provision in two *kebeles* of the city government of Addis Ababa, and development of a prototype system to showcase the application of ICTs in local governance.
- *Kenya* (Institute for Development Studies, University of Nairobi). Assessing the effect on local governance of implementing an

Integrated Financial Management Information System (IFMIS) in two local authorities.

- *Mauritius* (School of Public Sector Policy and Management, University of Technology). Assessing the effects of implementing a revenue management system on e-administration and e-service delivery.
- *Morocco* (School of Science and Engineering, Alakhawayn University). Implementing a citizen registration system in Larache city (medium-size city municipality) and observing the effects on governance through action research and drawing lessons.
- *Mozambique* (Department of Mathematics and Informatics, University Eduardo Mondlane). Assessing the effects of an electronic Land Management Information System (LMIS) and an electronic government network on local governance.
- *South Africa* (WITS University Graduate School of Public and Development Management). Assessing the relationship between e-government initiatives and social and local economic development in six local governments in Gauteng Province.
- *Uganda* (Faculty of Social Sciences, Makerere University). Assessing the effects of an e-government application (LoGICS) on participation, transparency, efficiency, effectiveness and strategic vision.
- *Ghana* (Centre for Information Technologies and Research Development, CITRED). Analysing examples of how e-local governance can be utilised in two local government areas, with a focus on the use of ICTs for political inclusion and good governance.

Summary of findings

Enabling effects of national context

The researchers found that national context was generally enabling to e-local governance in all countries. In this regard, all countries recognised the importance of local government in national socio-economic development and had developed, or were in the process

7

of developing, a governance policy enshrined in particular laws and regulations, including national constitutions. However, the implementation of the policy was generally slow and incomplete in all countries, except in Kenya where it had stalled (Waema and Mitullah, 2008). Nevertheless, considerable power, resources and responsibilities were still vested in central government. Despite this incomplete implementation of governance policies, local governments in the various countries were still able to implement ICT initiatives, with some achieving relative success in impacting on governance. This success was due to the existence of an enabling context for e-local governance, as illustrated in the case of Kenya (Waema and Mitullah, 2008).

Countries with an enabling context for e-local governance had recognised that ICT is a critical or strategic resource in national development, and had prepared a national ICT policy and e-government strategy. This was the case in all countries except Ethiopia, where both documents remained in draft form. It was also evident that in most countries planning and/or implementation of the e-governance policy and strategy was vested in an agency or unit in an appropriate ministry. The relevant ministry varied from country to country.

A further enabler of e-local governance in most countries was explicit alignment between the national ICT policy and governance. In addition, the link between e-government strategy and governance was clear across the board.

The role of infrastructure provision, as an enabler of e-local governance, stands out in this research, especially in the context of isolated cases of successful implementation of e-government projects. One of the key projects in this connection involved developing an ICT backbone infrastructure to link central government ministries, effectively creating a government intranet. However, no country had rolled out this infrastructure in all ministries or at all levels of local government.

Notwithstanding these observations, ministries and government departments in all the countries had created websites to provide public information and online services. In addition, senior officers had been assigned email accounts. It also emerged – depending on the priority concerns of each country – that all had started to use ICTs in the following sectors:

- processing of priority business applications;
- customs clearance;
- citizen and electoral registration;
- tax, financial, land and human resource management.

However, these initiatives tended to create isolated sectoral systems or databases. Nevertheless, work had started in some countries, for example Egypt, to integrate systems.

One can deduce that the initiatives had generated an awareness of the role of ICT in development and spurred interest in the use of ICTs in government. This had the effect of setting a foundation for e-local governance. There are also useful lessons to be drawn from the initiatives on the implementation of e-local governance.

Constraining effects of national context

Despite the positive aspects of the national enabling context, the researchers found a number of problems at the national level that constrained or could constrain the realisation of e-local govern-ance. These are outlined below, with examples from the various research projects:

- *Ineffective or poor coordination* in e-government implementation. For example, in South Africa, the researchers noted the lack of support from institutions that have been set up to address and facilitate ICT penetration and, by implication, e-government. An example is the Universal Service and Access Agency (USAA) (Abrahams and Newton-Reid, 2008).
- *Poor quality and limited penetration of the ICT infrastructure* in central and local governments, as well as at the household level. Mauri-tius has one of the highest ICT ratings in the region, according to the ITU (2007). Yet less than 18 per cent of the population could access the Internet from their homes by 2006. A further example is that of South Africa, another regional ICT giant,

where only about 4 per cent in Gauteng province had a working Internet connection at home (Abrahams and Newton-Reid, 2008).

- *Absence of local government* as an area of focus in the e-government strategies of most countries, resulting in lack of e-government policies/strategies at the local government level.[6] For instance, in South Africa there was no e-government policy framework at either national or provincial government level (Abrahams and Newton-Reid, 2008).
- *Vesting a lot of power in the central government* in most of the countries. In Egypt, for example, although local authorities have a certain degree of administrative authority, they are still financially and politically managed by the central government (Atnafu et al., 2008). On the other hand, in Morocco financial management is highly centralised (Kettani and Asmae, 2008).
- *Inadequacy of the budgetary allocation to local governments* in many of the countries. As an example, the Kenya government allocates only 5 per cent of national income tax to local authorities. The research also noted the tendency to allocate insufficient financial resources to ICT at the national level in all the countries. By way of illustration, Morocco is a lower middle-income country, according to World Bank classification; the ICT budget is less than 1 per cent of the total government operational budget (Kettani and Asmae, 2008). This inadequacy in national financial resource allocation has a negative impact on budgetary allocations to ICT at local government level.

The widespread lack of ICT infrastructure and the high cost of ICT equipment and services also constitute key constraining factors. Thus, although most countries, such as Kenya and Uganda, have ICT universal access/services policies and/or strategies to enable marginalised communities to have easily accessible, available and affordable ICT infrastructure and services, this goal is yet to be achieved. In fact, a number of countries have poor ICT infrastructure and relatively unaffordable ICT equipment and services. This means that local governments cannot provide e-services, because citizens lack online access to this level of government whereby they might obtain important information and services, or consider participating in online interactions.

The cost factor has been cited as a key impediment in the study. In Kenya, for example, the cost of dial-up Internet services was projected at 233 per cent of gross national income (GNI) (Waema et al., 2007). In response, certain municipalities, like some in South Africa, have acquired a class licence from the regulator to operate electronic communication networks for commercial purposes that would make it possible to provide universal access/service to underserved areas and to disadvantaged households (Abrahams and Reid, 2008). It remains to be seen whether these municipalities will be able to provide local communities with affordable broadband ICT infrastructure and services and readily provide e-services.

Other challenges identified in the research concerned:

- the lack of adequate basic ICT skills at all levels of government;
- the problem of uncoordinated ICT investment;
- the slow pace of integrating existing systems;
- the lack of political will for e-government;
- the shortage of relevant local research and human capacity in e-governance.

E-local governance context

The results indicate that local governments in most of the countries had started to implement ICT applications, but often lag behind efforts to implement e-government in central government. Of crucial importance, however, is the fact that in almost all countries where e-government applications had been implemented, local governments had created the necessary local area networks, Internet connectivity and web presence. In spite of this observation, from an e-government perspective, the emphasis had predominantly been on improving the internal administrative processes of local authorities, which is simply e-administration.

Evidence from the research also showed that in Kenya, Uganda and Mozambique e-government implementation at the local government level was still largely driven or championed by the central government. In addition, the technical quality of the implemented e-local government systems was largely unsatisfactory, because of poor systems implementation or the inability of the systems to interface with other e-government systems.

It was also the case that although a few local governments were able to provide services and information to key stakeholders electronically (e-services) through web portals, this achievement encountered difficulties in most countries. In Morocco, for example, the government portals did not take into account the implications of the socio-economic and cultural characteristics of the targeted users. These characteristics include linguistic background, level of literacy and level of ICT knowledge. The oversight indirectly tended to enhance e-exclusion.

In South Africa, the study concluded that the web content was generally presented in English in a context where one of the country's provinces, Gauteng, has four official languages. To magnify the problem, it was found that some of the content was not only difficult to understand and out of date, but also poorly written and irrelevant (Abrahams and Newton-Reid, 2008).

Furthermore, the research findings revealed that in local governments that had web presence the websites were at the publishing stage of the e-service content development model (Chan et al., 2007) or at stage 1 (emerging) of the United Nations in e-government readiness (United Nations, 2008).

Not surprisingly, therefore, in most countries the provision of information through the web portals tended to be frustrated by the poor state of the e-readiness of most local governments and the local community. This status was characterised by, among other things, poor penetration of the ICT infrastructure, limited access to the Internet at the household level, and a low level of ICT literacy among the local community members.

Other constraining factors at the local government level included the observation that the e-readiness of most local governments in the research was low. It was also clear that measures were needed to address a number of other limiting factors. For instance, the inclusion of e-government strategies in relevant documents at the national level did not adequately address expectations at the local government level. In fact, in almost all the countries where e-government systems had been or were being implemented at the local government level, there was no guiding e-governance or e-government strategy at the local government level. Only at the highest levels of local government – such as large city directorates in South Africa and Egypt – were there e-governance strategies in place.

Noticeably, there was also an inadequate financial resource allocation to ICTs in most countries. A further problem concerned a lack of the technical ICT skills necessary for e-readiness. This explains why most local governments lacked essential in-house managerial ICT skills, and even training programmes to create a sustainable pool of staff with basic ICT literacy or technical and managerial skills. The main consequence of this problem was the tendency to use external consultants and contractors, which makes e-governance roll-out very expensive.

Added to these limitations, the researchers found that most local governments lacked institutional governance structures. It can be concluded, therefore, that the status of ICT staffing and governance structures in local authorities in the various countries reflects the embryonic stage of ICT development at that level of government.

Moreover, in almost all the countries, business processes had not been redesigned to ready them for implementation of e-local governance systems. This is why Egypt, one of the leading states in Africa with respect to e-government, chose a business process mapping project in LOG-IN Africa. The purpose was to help develop a methodology and tools for re-engineering business processes before embarking on ICT implementation in government.

E-local governance outcomes

The effects of ICT systems on good governance were found to vary from country to country depending on local and national contexts. Table 1.1 shows a synthesis of the effects of ICTs on

TABLE I.IA   Effects of ICTs on good local governance

	Participation
Kenya	*No effect*
Mozambique	*No effect* Focus was on improving internal processes related to land management, overlooking the importance of improving external processes which link the system to citizens and other stakeholders
Uganda	*No effect* A faulty system design: lack of useful reports and did not take account of all the requirements of the sectors; lack of appropriate LAN infrastructure; prevalent perceptions that the system was appropriate for techies and low-level data entry staff, and very few *political leaders* at the LG level were aware of LoGICS
Mauritius	n/a
South Africa	*Small positive* Some citizens could use ICTs to interact with LGs through the websites
	No change Lack of access to the Internet by the majority of citizens; the total cost of ownership of a mobile phone was beyond most citizens
Ghana	*Positive* Enhanced effective participation of illiterate citizens in the decision-making processes of LGs

Responsiveness	Efficiency and effectiveness
Positive Improved quality of service; reduced turnaround in preparing financial reports and in issuing business licences; fewer complaints and increased customer satisfaction	*Positive* Increased revenue collection; increased business registrations; increased staff productivity; reduced turnaround time for payments, and increased payroll accuracy
Small positive Better organised land information and reduced time for searching specific data *No effect* Incomplete roll-out: most procedures on land registration were performed manually; surveyors had to deal with both electronic and manual systems	*No effect* Incomplete system roll-out – system had been developed and partially implemented by foreign consultants, who left when resources ran out
n/a	*No effect* Low usage of the system, due for example, to poor technical system design and poor system implementation
Small positive Improved quality of service, wider choice of payment modes, improved personalised attention and improved interactive communication *No effect* Limited level of education of some citizens prevented them understanding documents given to them	*Small positive* Reduced customer turnaround time; increased staff productivity *No effect* Lack of regulations on resource allocation, poor technical performance (outdated software and platform), lack of integration of revenue management system (RMS) with other systems, users' resistance to change
n/a	n/a
n/a	n/a

	Participation
Morocco	n/a [rule of law][7]
	Positive Enhanced application of rule of law (citizens served in a timely/real time manner and motives to tip or beg to be served disappeared)

TABLE I.IB   Effects of ICTs on good local governance

	Transparency
Kenya	*Positive* All payments are receipted; issuance of business permits are transparent, consistent and straightforward; reduction in corrupt practices
Mozambique	n/a
Uganda	*No effect* Inter-operability challenges that severely compromised the attainment of transparency in monitoring the performance of local authorities.
Mauritius	*Small positive* Availability of detailed information on claims and reminders, and increased public access to information on revenue collection procedures and on specific rates
	No effect Lack of adequate and up-to-date information on local government websites; limited level of education of some citizens; obsolete software and platform
South Africa	n/a
Ghana	n/a
Morocco	*Positive* Increased visibility of workflows (the principle of first come, first served became respected as various sub-processes of certificate issuance were merged into one process)

Responsiveness	Efficiency and effectiveness
Positive Improved service quality (automated certificate served citizens in a timely/real time manner) and reduced dependency on bureaucracy (employees no longer controlled the workflow)	*Positive* Increased time/money/effort savings in requesting and obtaining birth certificates by citizens

Accountability	Equity
Positive Ease of tracking business permit licences; more accurate records of all properties; more effective monitoring of revenue collection; effective payroll tracking	n/a
n/a	n/a
n/a	n/a
n/a	*No effect* *Negative* Enhanced discrimination between educated and less educated citizens, low income earners and high income earners, and young and old citizens
n/a	n/a
n/a	n/a
Positive Existence of standards to hold individuals accountable (birth certificate issuance system no longer opaque, becoming increasingly predictable)	*Positive* More equitable service provision (citizens started being served in a timely manner and ICT noticeably eliminated the need for citizens to tip or beg in order to be served)

different characteristics of good governance. The table summarises the effects as positive, no effect or negative, and provides either the outcomes when the effect is positive or the reasons when the effect is negative or non-existent.

In all cases it was possible to explain these mixed effects of e-local governance by reference to contextual information of the application system design and its implementation. Explanations are to be found in the individual chapters and are synthesised in Chapter 12.

In addition to the above – good governance outcomes brought about by implementation of ICTs – there were also other developmental outcomes achieved by researchers using e-local governance implementation to influence policy and practice. The following is a summary of key developmental outcomes:

1. In *Ethiopia*, the city government of Addis Ababa launched a programme called 'ICT for Community' which organised and sponsored the training of employees representing 55 *kebeles*, the smallest administrative unit of the Ethiopian government. The research team had conducted three major awareness campaigns, targeting both decision-makers and *kebele* officials, and convinced them that the computerisation of life-event services needed to be preceded by training on ICTs. In addition, the city government requested the researchers to provide the source code and manuals so that they could start implementing the system. They also asked the research team to upgrade the prototype into an operational system ready for implementation, which they agreed to do. By the end of the research, the system had been installed in one of the *kebeles*. This is evidence that the research team had been successful in raising awareness that computerisation was important, that effects on governance after computerisation of life events were a worthwhile justification for automation, and that ICT training needed to precede the computerisation.

2. In *Morocco*, the municipal governments of Fez and Larache voted in favour of budgets to implement an electronic civil registration system. As a consequence, they received further support from

the respective municipal governments for ICTs in general. They obtained an increased budget for ICTs, which was to support the implementation of the registration system as well as the development of ICT in the municipalities. No budget had been allocated for ICTs before the introduction of the civil registration system. The implementation of a civil registration e-governance system in both Fez and Larache has achieved phenomenal success. It convinced Morocco's decision-makers of the need to replicate it in several local governments, including Marrakech, Essaouira, Midelt, Casa, Taza, Jerada, Mekness and Sefrou.

3. In *Kenya*, the researcher was requested to lead a team to review the existing national e-government strategy and develop the next five-year strategy. This strategy borrowed heavily from the LOG-IN e-local governance roadmap and had a very strong component of e-local governance. This issue was discussed and agreed by top e-government and public-sector reform officials in Kenya during the June 2008 international e-governance conference organised by LOG-IN Africa.

4. In *South Africa*, the LINK Centre designed a one-week course entitled 'Information and Communications Technologies for Development: ICT for Managers in Local Government (IT for non IT managers)', following a request by the Ekurhuleni metropolitan municipality. The course was presented to 20 municipal officials on 11–19 June 2008. The course curriculum included some of the key literature relating to e-local governance, as well as a full session on e-governance for social and local economic development. The design and presentation of such new courses contribute to the long-term sustainability of the research organisation, namely the LINK Centre, which hosted the LOG-IN Africa South African research project.

5. In *Mauritius*, a member of the research team was invited to participate in the e-regulation project committee, a key national e-government project enabling online applications for 117 business permits. So far as business facilitation is concerned, the following components of the project have been identified: simplifying business licensing procedures; improving access to

commercial justice; improving land title registration services; extending the credit reference bureau to improve access to finance; and streamlining the legal framework for business.

6. In *Egypt*, the business process mapping methodology (BPM) and tool developed by LOG-IN Africa's Egyptian team was adopted by the government. This means that the Ministry of State for Administrative Development (MSAD) plans to use the BPM tool to model business functions of other e-government projects. The ministry in charge of local government agreeed to test the BPM methodology and tool in e-government projects. MSAD committed to provide funds for further development of the methodology and tool as long as IDRC provided additional funding for the second phase of LOG-IN Africa. This commitment was made publicly by the minister when he opened the International Conference on e-governance organised by LOG-IN Africa in Cairo in June 2008.

7. *Publications* The LOG-IN Africa team leader was invited to share the network's research findings at high-level policy and research meetings between 2007 and 2009. The key meetings included:
   - *Egypt* as a presenter in the international INFOS conference organised at Cairo University in 2007.
   - *China* as a paper presenter in the first international conference on e-governance in 2007.
   - *Canada* to present LOG-IN research work to a visiting Haitian ministerial delegation to Canada in Ottawa in 2007.
   - *Kenya* as a presenter in an East African e-government forum for local governments in 2007.
   - *Ethiopia* as a presenter in the IFIP World IT Forum 2007 (WITFOR 2007) in 2007;
   - *Uganda* as a presenter in a Commonwealth Telecommunications Organization (CTO) e-government forum held in conjunction with Uganda's Ministry of ICT in 2008.
   - *South Africa* as an external keynote speaker in the GovTech conference organised by the State Information Technology Agency (SITA) in 2008.

- *Brazil* as a keynote speaker in the V South American Conference in Science and Technology applied to Electronic Government – CONeGOV in 2009.

In addition, LOG-IN Africa researchers have published in peer-reviewed journals and had papers accepted, through a peer review process, for presentation at respected international conferences such as those listed above. In total, there have been over 30 peer-reviewed journal and conference papers from LOG-IN research work.

E-local governance roadmap

The key findings from this study became the basis for a proposed roadmap that has the following activities as key requirements:
- Develop an e-governance strategic goal aligned to a wider governance reform programme and a national development plan capable of cascading to the local government level.
- Develop good governance outcome indicators for e-governance projects to be implemented as part of project planning, using the framework shown in Chapter 12.
- Re-engineer the business processes for the priority e-governance projects to be implemented, using a specific business process mapping methodology, such as that outlined in Chapter 3.
- Roll out the e-governance projects, using the four-stage framework described in Chapter 12.
- Use the good governance outcome indicators to monitor and evaluate the implementation of the e-governance projects.
- Ensure participation of policymakers and citizens in all these activities.

Limitations of the research

Although the study has important findings, it has a number of limitations, which include its focus on a wide spectrum of e-local governance issues. The focus was useful in bringing out a rich understanding of e-local governance in Africa. However, the approach made it difficult to collate the finer details in a selected set of governance indicators. The research also faced difficulties because of the diversity in the level of research experience within country teams. While some teams had strong research expertise, others included relatively inexperienced members. An attempt to pair stronger and weaker teams to address this shortfall, to facilitate peer review and learn from each other, did not work as anticipated. This necessitated greater involvement on the part of the project team leader to ensure quality control. Apart from these limitations, some of the country teams took an inordinately long period of time to engage central and local government stakeholders. This delay affected the impact the research could have had on policymakers.

Outline of the book

This research on the analysis of the relationship between ICTs and local governance provides empirical evidence of the dynamics, outcomes and implications of the integration of ICTs in local governance systems in Africa for policy formulation and for practice. The evidence is rooted in the case studies of the country members of LOG-IN Africa in Chapters 3 to 11. It is to be noted that certain chapters do not follow the framework described in Chapter 2: namely, Chapters 3 and 4, which focus on development of e-governance tools and applications, and Chapters 10 and 11; Chapter 10 examines the relationship between e-governance and social and local economic development, and Chapter 11 focuses on the nature of the relationship between ICTs and the issue of political inclusion and other aspects of good governance.

The conceptual and methodological frameworks for the type of research in this book are in the process of development, even in developed countries. Unfortunately, there has been very little work done to adapt any existing frameworks to make them suitable for application in the less developed countries and the African context in particular. Consequently, the nine case studies are preceded by the presentation of such a framework that was developed jointly by the network team members (Chapter 2). This framework guided five of the case studies (the four exceptions are indicated above). The volume has thus succeeded in making a contribution to the shaping and development of a conceptual and methodological framework for studies on e-government and e-governance in Africa. Its significance lies, therefore, in being part of an evolving research area that is still largely underdeveloped, or even given inadequate attention, in Africa.

The research also provides an e-local governance 'roadmap', which is presented in the last chapter of the book. This final chapter also synthesises the findings of the research.

Notes

1. S. Cheema and L. Maguire, 'Democracy, Governance and Development: A Conceptual Framework', 4th Global Forum on Re-inventing Government – Citizens, Businesses and Governments: Dialogue and partnerships for Development and Democracy, Marrakech, Morocco, 10–13 December 2002, United Nations, New York 2002. www.unpan.org.

2. K.B.C. Saxena, 'Towards Excellence in e-Governance', *International Journal of Public Sector Management*, vol. 18, no. 6, 2005.

3. The theoretical and conceptual framework of LOG-IN Africa is mainly based upon the preliminary findings of the 'Research on ICTs for Local Governance in Africa' conducted by Gianluca Misuraca for IDRC and UNECA (currently being finalised for publication). It will be further developed during the execution of the research. See also Misuraca Gianluca, 'E-Africa Initiative for Good Governance: Building e-Governance Capacity in Africa', *Encyclopedia of Developing Regional Communities with ICTs*, IDEA Group, Hershey PA, 2005.

4. The e-government readiness index is a composite index comprising the web measure index, the telecommunication infrastructure index and the human capital index. This survey focuses mainly on the 'government to citizen' (G2C) and 'government to government' (G2G) aspects of e-government. Although this current survey captures some elements of 'government to business' (G2B), it is a relatively small part of the survey.

5. Ghana was not part of the original LOG-IN Africa network. The

Ghanaian research team had a self-sponsored stand-alone project on e-local governance. They later became part of the network and their research results were accepted as part of this book.

6. The only exceptions were the large city councils in the more developed economies of South Africa and Egypt. These tended to have council-specific e-government strategies.

7. 'Rule of law' is included in the box for 'Participation' for information.

2

E-governance assessment framework

Timothy Mwololo Waema

Researchers on e-governance are from a variety of disciplines, such as Computer Science, Information Systems, Political Science and Public Administration. These often have discipline-specific theoretical foundations or frameworks, which leads to divergent perspectives on the nature of *governance*. Whilst the body of knowledge is increasing in this area, there has been no attempt to integrate it into a solid set of theories or frameworks that others can draw upon, for instance to evaluate the outcomes or impacts of e-governance. In fact, very little has been produced at the way of a guiding theory or framework.

Instead statements about the benefits of e-government and e-governance dominate the literature. There are claims, for example, that e-government can lead to the following outcomes: saving costs while improving quality, response times and access to services (ADB, 2003); improving the efficiency and effectiveness of public administration (Pacific Council, 2002); increasing transparency in administration, reducing corruption and increasing political participation (Seifert and Bonham, 2003); making governments more competitive (OECD, 2003). Most of these benefits are actually e-governance outcomes.

The situation on the ground is not quite so rosy, however, as most e-government projects or initiatives have not achieved the often quoted outcomes. In 2002, for example, the Gartner

Group reported that 'more than 60 percent of all e-government initiatives either fail or fall short of expected outcomes.'[1] Saxena (2005) subsequently argued that in spite of the worldwide diffusion of e-government initiatives, achieving the claimed benefits of e-governance has not been easy due to various technological and organisational reasons. Heeks (2003) noted, in support of this proposition, that e-government projects often fail either totally or partially to achieve their objectives, despite their initial successes. Statements or conclusions on the benefits of e-government and e-governance initiatives, therefore, have largely been based on studies that lack the essential serious research framework needed to assess associated benefits or outcomes.

The research framework reported in this chapter was developed in an attempt to establish a guiding model for assessing the good governance outcomes of ICTs at the local government level in nine African countries as an initiative of the Local Governance and ICTs Research Network for Africa (LOG-IN Africa).

The next section of the chapter reviews the various definitions of *governance* and *good governance*. It also has an outline of the characteristics of good governance, as defined by UNDP. This is followed by an overview of the definition of *e-government* and *e-governance*. In the next section the focus shifts to a description of results-based management, with special emphasis on the conceptual senses of *results chain* and *results-based outcome monitoring and evaluation*. There follows a description of the chapter's research framework for evaluating the outcomes of e-governance. The final section provides some recommendations.

Governance and good governance

In most developing countries, the concepts of *governance* and *good governance* have taken root as part of the conditions imposed by 'donor' institutions before providing development assistance. The concepts are also part of a wider public-sector reform programme that is often externally driven through the World Bank and other donor institutions. They have a tendency, nevertheless, of carrying different senses depending on the interests of a given 'donor'.

UNDP defines *governance* as the exercise of economic, political and administrative authority to manage a country's affairs at all levels. It comprises mechanisms, processes and institutions through which citizens and groups articulate their interests, exercise their legal rights, meet their obligations and mediate their differences.[2] This definition indicates that for governance to exist there has to be the interplay of a country and its citizens in a relationship. In that relationship, governance attains a reality, in this case in the form of a political entity (that is, the state) to exercise power by organising and by administering its functions through relevant establishments. This process brings to the foreground the role of procedures, actions and entities that make it possible for citizens to communicate concerns, exercise rights, undertake responsibilities and arbitrate in disputes.

Weiss (2000), GDRC (2004a, 2004b, 2004c) and Kettani et al. (2005) provide different conceptual senses of the term, based on their preference for one element or a set of elements that appeal to their interest. They all agree, however, that governance is not synonymous with government. Saxena (2005) points out that governance concerns longer-term processes rather than immediate decisions that are the concern of government. Thereafter, whereas government focuses on *outputs* by expending *effort*, governance focuses on *outcomes* or the *effects* produced over a longer time perspective.

Like governance, *good governance* has different interpretations depending on who is defining or describing it. For example, the World Bank highlights four elements that constitute good governance,[3] namely:

- openness and predictability in policymaking;
- professionalism in bureaucracy;
- accountability of government and participation of civil society;
- adherence to the rule of law.

Elsewhere, the World Bank (World Bank, 2003) contends that inclusiveness, in terms of equal participation and equal treatment, and accountability, in terms of transparency and contestability, are the values that underpin good governance. However, the World Bank definition of good governance is inadequate in handling certain issues in e-governance implementation, for a number of reasons. First, openness refers only to policymaking, although it is true that policy formulation and implementation are highly interrelated. This makes it difficult to separate the two. However, in e-governance implementation, one has to be concerned about the transparency of implementation processes and the openness with which key stakeholders have access to information and knowledge.

Second, it is doubtful whether professionalism in bureaucracy does necessarily ensure the efficient utilisation of resources in serving stakeholders, which is an important good governance consideration. Finally, the World Bank definition of good governance excludes connotative senses that are important, such as responsiveness in providing services and information.

According to the UNDP, the defining properties of good governance include, among other things, the fact that it is participatory, *transparent* and *accountable*. It is also *effective* and *equitable*. In addition, it *promotes the rule of law fairly* and ensures that the voices of the poorest and the most vulnerable are heard in decision-making over the allocation of development resources. In addition, political, social and economic priorities are based on broad consensus among the three stakeholders – the state, the private sector and civil society.[4]

Here, the concept of good governance has these attributes:

- adoption of a participatory approach;
- transparency and openness;
- accountability by assuming responsibilities for actions;
- effectiveness, equity and fairness;
- endorsement of the rule of law;
- openness in decision-making;

TABLE 2.1   UNDP's nine underlying characteristics of good governance and their meanings

Characteristics of good governance	UNDP's definition	Interpreted meaning
Participation	'All men and women should have a voice in decision-making, either directly or through legitimate intermediate institutions that represent their interests. Such broad participation is built on freedom of association and speech, as well as on capacities to participate constructively.'	The act of involving people, regardless of gender, to voice their interests in the decision-making processes. This involvement can be direct or indirect, e.g. the public participating through institutions that articulate their interests.
Rule of law	'Legal frameworks should be fair and enforced impartially, particularly the laws on human rights.'	The act of justly and objectively putting laws in place.
Transparency	'Transparency is built on the free flow of information. Processes, institutions and information are directly accessible to those concerned with them, and enough information is provided to understand and monitor them.'	The full release of information and providing stakeholders with free access to institutions, operations and information.
Responsiveness	'Institutions and processes try to serve all stakeholders.'	Institutions and operations answer the requests of stakeholders.
Consensus orientation	'Good governance mediates differing interests to reach a broad consensus on what is in the best interest of the group and, where possible, on policies and procedures.'	Arbitration of the clash of interests in order to establish agreements based on the optimal interests of stakeholders.

Characteristics of good governance	UNDP's definition	Interpreted meaning
Equity	'All men and women have opportunities to improve or maintain their well-being.'	The act of providing people, irrespective of gender or other factors of possible discrimination, with equal chances to foster the quality of their welfare.
Effectiveness and efficiency	'Processes and institutions produce results that meet needs while making the best use of resources.'	Achievement of optimal use of resources while serving stakeholders.
Accountability	'Decision-makers in government, the private sector and civil society organisations are accountable to the public, as well as to institutional stakeholders. This accountability differs depending on the organisation and whether the decision is internal or external to an organisation.'	Managers and decision-makers are held liable to the community.
Strategic vision	'Leaders and the public have a broad and long-term perspective on good governance and human development, along with a sense of what is needed for such development. There is also an understanding of the historical, cultural and social complexities in which that perspective is grounded.'	Managers and the public have a long-term view with regard to governance and are aware of contextual obstacles related to history, culture and society.

Source: UNDP, 2002.

- formulation of the national agenda through a consensus between the state, the private sector and the civil society, all of which serve as stakeholders in governance.

Most of the definitions of good governance tend to focus on the quality as well as on the characteristics of the processes of *governance*. One such definition is that of UNDP in its *Handbook on Monitoring and Evaluation of Results* (2002) in which the characteristics of good governance, together with interpreted meanings, are outlined (see Table 2.1).

It is often the case that the list of the characteristics of good governance changes according to the institution defining them. This factor demonstrates that defining the principles of good governance can be difficult and controversial. In this chapter, UNDP's (2002) interpretation of good governance, as presented in Table 2.1, is a good starting point in tackling the conceptual senses of the term for two main reasons. First, the interpretation has a comprehensive coverage of all key characteristics of good governance. Second, the characteristics of good governance as presented have a level of generality that creates room for the inclusion of other senses of the term because of its generic nature. The term can therefore be customised to function in a specific governance context. Consequently, this chapter has adopted this definition of good governance and regards it as most appropriate for its framework.

E-government and e-governance

E-government attracts different interpretations. Misuraca (2006) states that e-government focuses on the use of ICTs for public service delivery only. More specifically, he says that e-government refers to the use of ICTs as a 'facilitator' that is capable of 'reshaping' the role of governments, apart from providing tools to support public service reforms, or even of enhancing public administration management and public-sector performance in comparison with the private sector and citizens. Kumar and Best (2006) define e-government as the use of information and communications technologies (ICTs) in the public sector to improve operations and delivery of services.

Although Misuraca's definition is useful, it only focuses on service delivery to the public and ignores the back-end systems that facilitate that service delivery. The second definition by Kumar and Best goes beyond service delivery and mentions operations, pointing to the importance of back-office or administrative systems. Neither definition provides an explicit categorisation of e-government that would be useful in a framework.

Ndou (2004: 6) provides a slightly broader conceptualisation of e-government and lists the following as three of its key applications:

- *E-administration* through which an administration or a government office can use ICT to interrelate its various departments and digitise its internal operations via 'automation and computerisation of administrative tasks'.
- *E-citizens and e-services*, which are e-government applications that enable online access to government information, knowledge and 'deliver automated services'.
- *E-society*, which provides a platform that facilitates interactions between government actors and civil society.

On the whole, there are as many definitions of e-government as there are individuals, organisations or forums defining it. As a result, e-government scholars and practitioners often lack clarity as to the precise meaning of e-government (Misra, 2006). A distinction, however, can be drawn between what e-government means to industrialised countries (the 'North') and what it means in economically developing countries (the 'South'). In most countries in the 'North', e-government was triggered by developments in the Internet and other communications technologies, making it possible to access government agencies and the services from a distance and without much expense.

Internally, government institutions had already computerised operations and services. However, government institutions in the 'South' have to move from largely manual processes and service provision to computerised and highly networked situations. They have to develop the required ICT infrastructure, computerise operations and services, and ensure that the public and other stakeholders can readily access information and services electronically. The notion of e-government in such a context would slightly differ from the one ordinarily assumed in the 'North'. That is why, for example, it is possible to have an effective e-government system that only focuses on computerising internal business processes, with no Internet connection or even a wide area network.

It would therefore be inappropriate to adopt an e-government definition that only focuses on service delivery and ignores back-office computerisation, which has been the focus of many government departments in Africa. This factor makes Ndou's (2004) broad definition of e-government the best option for this chapter because it is closest to the realities found in most countries in Africa. A further refinement of this definition is described in the research framework presented in this chapter.

As is the case for definitions of e-government, the definitions of e-governance vary greatly, sometimes depending on contextual considerations. Gordon (2004) defines e-governance as the use of ICTs to improve the quality and efficiency of all phases of the life cycle of legislation, while Gurstein and Misuraca (2006) define it as the use of ICTs to enhance the role of citizens in relation to their capacity and opportunity for effective participation in the broad structures of governance. These definitions of e-governance are very narrow, with the former focusing on legislation, while the latter emphasises the participation of citizens as the basis for e-governance.

Sheridan and Riley (2006) distinguish the concepts of e-governance and e-government by emphasising that they are two very distinct terms. E-governance is more encompassing, focusing on the relationship within government, especially with reference to the use of ICTs. E-government, therefore, is narrower, with a focus on development of online services to the citizen. Therefore, in their view e-governance includes stages for government agencies to ensure successful implementation of e-government services to the public.

It is evident that there is a spectrum of positions informing attempts to define e-governance. A key limitation of most definitions or conceptualisations of e-governance is the tendency of authors to define the concept based on the methodological or discipline-specific foundations of their work. Others define it to suit their own interests or research agendas. Furthermore, and most importantly, the definitions given by most researchers are limited by their views on governance or e-government, or indeed on both concepts. The implication is that the assessment of e-governance can be limited by being subject to narrow definitions and uses of the terms.

For the purposes of this chapter, e-government refers to the application of ICTs to automate specific aspects of government. The chapter recognises nevertheless that e-governance is a concept that goes beyond e-government. In this regard, it is concerned with the impacts of e-government on governance. From this perspective, e-governance deals not only with the mere application of ICTs, but also with how these ICTs are used to achieve governance outcomes.

Results-based management

For a long time, development practitioners have been using a number of frameworks to try to evaluate the outcomes of development projects. One popular and relevant framework, results-based management (RBM), is a relatively new management approach that is often used interchangeably with the terms 'strategic management', 'performance-based management', 'outcome management' and 'new public management' (Swiss, 2005). Despite these different labels, almost all of these results-based management approaches are marked by their tendency to emphasise the following:

- strategic planning;
- performance measurement, especially the measurement of programme outcomes;
- customer satisfaction as one of the desired outcomes;
- setting of results-oriented objectives, as well as long-range and
  shorter-range goals;
- delivery of many of those outcomes through cross-functional
  teams and empowered front-line employees;
- use of business-like process-improvement tools (Osborne and
  Plastrik, 1997).

This chapter prefers RBM. UNDP (2002: 19), states that:

> Results-based management provides a coherent framework for strategic
> planning and management by improving learning and accountability.
> It is also a broad management strategy aimed at achieving important
> changes in the way agencies operate.

The RBM approach, which makes the achievement of expected
results the underlying driver for project management and assessment, is currently preferred by many international institutions.
UNDP, for instance, justifies its adoption of the approach through
the following argument:

> There is growing demand for development effectiveness [that] is largely
> based on the realization that producing good 'deliverables' is not
> enough. Efficient or well-managed projects and outputs will lose their
> relevance if they yield no discernible improvement in development
> conditions and ultimately in peoples' lives. (UNDP, 2002:5)

This chapter consequently has several good reasons for choos-
ing the results-based management approach over other approaches.
First, the approach is able to direct attention to the results of
e-governance initiatives. Furthermore, RBM is a better tool for
monitoring and evaluating results than traditional management
tools such as logical framework analysis (LFA), which is objective-
oriented, and largely focuses on the assessment of inputs, on
implementation processes and on outputs. A description of RBM

FIGURE 2.1   The internal logic of RBM

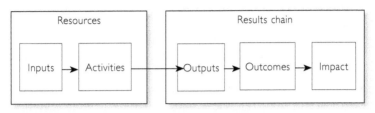

would be incomplete without an account of the *results chain* aspect of the approach. This aspect has a fundamental role to play in the proposed framework in this chapter.

Results chain

The internal logic of RBM is based on cause–effect relationships between inputs, activities and results, as illustrated in Figure 2.1. In the results chain, results are linked by virtue of a chain of cause–effect relationships in which each level of results is related to the next higher one by means of achievement. The cause–effect linkages can be expressed with 'if... then' phrases, representing the internal logic of a program/project, such as: 'if' the outputs are achieved as expected, 'then' we should achieve the outcomes, and 'if' the outcomes are achieved as expected, 'then' we should get the impact.

Inputs are the organisational, intellectual, human, ICT and other resources that are brought together in time and space and transformed by certain management or implementation activities, such as the implementation of e-government projects. In turn, these activities generate a chain of results. This chain is composed of outputs, outcomes and impact-level results.

Outputs are at the lowest level of the results chain and are related to both resources and outcomes, as shown in Figure 2.1. Outputs, which are sometimes referred to as 'deliverables', are the immediate, visible, concrete and tangible consequences of inputs that can be exemplified by the number of people served by an implemented e-government service, the number of research papers, the number of seminars organised or the number of people trained.

Outcomes, which are results in the medium term, are effects or consequences of the achievement of a set of planned outputs. Establishing outcomes illustrates what success looks like (Kusek and Rist, 2004), and assessing outcomes demonstrates whether success has been achieved or not. Impact refers to ultimate long-term desired results and is a consequence of the achievement of planned outcomes. It represents widespread changes in society, the economy or the environment of a targeted population.

In this chapter the focus is on outcomes, because impacts take a relatively long time to be realised. Focus on impacts is inappropriate, given the timeframe in the LOG-IN Africa projects, most of which last only a few years. In any case, the chapter is mainly interested in the evaluation of outcomes, although in practice it is difficult to separate monitoring from the evaluation process. The reality accounts for the interest in the outcome monitoring and evaluation of e-governance projects.

Outcome monitoring and evaluation

According to UNDP (2002: 20) outcome monitoring refers to

> a continual and systematic process of collecting and analyzing data to measure the performance of UNDP interventions towards achievement of outcomes at country level. While the process of outcome monitoring is continual in the sense that it is not a time-bound activity, outcome monitoring must be periodic, so that change can be perceived. In other words, country offices will accumulate information on an ongoing basis regarding progress towards an outcome, and then will periodically compare the current situation against the baseline for outcome indicators and assess and analyze the situation.

How should outcome monitoring be carried out? From the UNDP perspective, to monitor outcomes 'managers need to track the outputs and measure their contributions to outcomes by assessing the change from baseline conditions'. Further, to conduct effective outcome monitoring, managers need 'to establish baseline data, select outcome indicators of performance, and design mechanisms that include planned actions such as field visits, stakeholder meetings and systematic analysis or reports' (UNDP 2002: 20). Monitoring outputs, therefore, is an integral part of outcome monitoring. According to the same source, outcome evaluation covers a set of related projects, programmes and strategies intended to bring about a certain outcome. These evaluations assess how and why outcomes are or are not being achieved and could help to clarify underlying factors affecting the situation, recommend actions to improve performance in future programming, and generate lessons learned.

Monitoring and evaluations of results are performed through performance indicators. Each of the results levels has associated indicators. These are qualitative or quantitative 'pointers' that can be measured or described and that help determine progress towards achieving planned results. It is through the regular measurement or observation of these key outcome indicators that one can determine if outcomes are being achieved.

Kusek and Rist (2004) have developed a ten-step approach to designing, building and sustaining a results-based monitoring and evaluation system. In the framework proposed in this chapter, a subset of these steps was used to put forward a framework for monitoring and evaluating the good governance outcomes of e-government projects. The purpose of monitoring and evaluating the outcomes in the case of LOG-IN Africa is to test the usefulness of the proposed research framework, learn some lessons regarding the effects of e-government initiatives or projects on good governance, and create knowledge that can be used to build a roadmap on e-local governance in Africa. This framework is the focus of the next section.

Towards an integrated e-governance outcome evaluation framework

Kettani et al. (2005) created a methodological framework for assessing the impact of e-government systems and governance. The framework does this by assessing the impact of e-government on good governance outcomes, among other major outcome categories like technology, organisation, citizen and regulation. The researchers used the UNDP definition of the attributes of good governance, but customised the definitions to fit the e-government project that they were working on, in this case a system for providing citizen-related services. They then developed a measurable set of indicators for the identified project outcomes. The idea was to assess how project activities and outputs generate project-defined good governance outcomes, using defined indicators, and compare these with values of indicators that were in existence before the e-government system was introduced (in what is commonly referred to as reference or baseline status).

The work of Kettani et al. (2005) was this chapter's starting point for developing the e-governance outcome evaluation framework reported here[5] because it also borrowed UNDP's definition of good governance, which is inclusive and contains comprehensive coverage of the key characteristics of good governance. The chapter also took the position that it is important to create 'working' or contextualised definitions of good governance. Based on this understanding, the proposed research framework has two notable differences from the work of Kettani et al.

The first point of departure lies in the fact that the conceptual framework for this study considers the various dimensions of e-government. In the framework being proposed, the three applications of Ndou (2004) are taken to reflect the key dimensions of e-government. In the context of this chapter, the three applications have been redefined to give them the following senses:

- *E-administration*: the computerisation of internal government business processes, including business process re-engineering and the development of the required ICT infrastructure.
- *E-services*: the electronic delivery of government information, knowledge and services to citizens, businesses and other government units through wide area network infrastructure and Internet connectivity, as may be required.
- *E-society*: the electronic interactions between government

actors and citizens, businesses and other government actors. This interaction can be through a number of communication facilities, including mobile phones, cyber cafés and public access facilities.

The key reason for incorporating these changes in the proposed framework is the conviction that good governance outcome indicators vary depending on the phase in which an e-government project finds itself. For example, the good governance indicators for participation in the e-administration phase of an e-government project are different from the indicators in the e-services phase of the project.

The framework being proposed is also different from those already discussed because of its utilisation of a results-based outcome monitoring and evaluation approach to create, monitor and evaluate the good governance outcomes. More specifically, the framework has borrowed from Kusek and Rist's (2004) monitoring and evaluation steps, as outlined earlier. It entails a *five-step iterative process* as a methodological tool for evaluating good governance outcomes, as outlined below:

1. *Assessment of context*   Conduct an assessment of the context of the e-government project to gain a deeper understanding of the implementation for the e-government intervention being studied. The context may include the e-government/e-governance policy environment, the business and ICT environment, political commitment, ICT infrastructure and connectivity, human resource skills and budget allocation. This context is critical in explaining why certain outcomes were realised or failed to be realised.

2. *Working definitions of 'good governance'*   Create contextualised or 'working' definitions of each of UNDP's broad constructs of 'good governance' that the research will focus on. These localised definitions would inevitably be linked to the national government and/or local government concepts of good governance, as well as to the specific context of the e-government project.

3. *Outcome indicators* Translate the working definitions of good governance into identifiable and measurable (or at least observable) outcome indicators. This translation is carried out for each of the three dimensions of e-government. Outcome indicators can be further specified or associated with identifiable and measurable output indicators that are meaningful in the specific context and directly linked to the e-government project-based intervention.

4. *Baseline data on indicators* Collect baseline data on the chosen indicators to establish the status of the various outcome indicators before the implementation of the e-government intervention. This status sets the reference point against which future changes can be assessed.

5. *Evaluate the outcomes* This is the assessment of the status of the chosen indicators to establish the effects of the completed e-government intervention on good governance. In general, outcome measurement is a challenge (Mayne, 2005). In fact, this is where the greatest challenge lies. In particular, determining the extent to which an e-government intervention can be associated with observed outcomes is quite a challenge, largely because of the attribution problem. Furthermore, the long periods from the times outputs are produced to the time 'allegedly' associated outcomes are realised creates an additional problem of attribution. In order to deal with these challenges, the chapter proposes that researchers should focus on the degree to which an e-government system under investigation has *contributed* to the status of the outcomes in question, and, at the same time, establish *other factors* that have contributed to the realisation of the outcomes.

The proposed approach is necessary as the basis for a sound methodological framework for monitoring and evaluating e-governance outcomes.

Table 2.2 is a representation of the proposed conceptual framework. It combines the constructs or characteristics of good governance, the components of e-government and the concept outcome

TABLE 2.2   Proposed research methodology

Good governance constructs	Working definitions of good governance	Outcome indicators		
		e-admin	e-services	e-society
1. Participation				
2. Transparency				
3. Responsiveness				
4. Equity				
5. Effectiveness & efficiency				
6. Accountability				
7. Rule of law				
8. Consensus orientation				
9. Strategic vision				

indicators. It does this across the three aspects of e-government that are essential for outcome monitoring and evaluation. Outcomes are bound to vary from one project to another. Thus the constructs of good governance may require some fine tuning to make them more relevant for a project context. This implies the need for a working definition that is not only more functional and more precise, but also context-sensitive for project evaluation.

Illustration of the framework

At a generic level, the LOG-IN researchers collectively developed a set of generic good governance outcome indicators. These are illustrated in Table 2.3. Each country project team was then expected to translate these generic indicators into the relevant project-level outcome indicators for that country, in line with the methodological framework as outlined in this section. Other illustrations will be made in the various chapters for the LOG-IN Africa research teams that adopted this framework.

Conclusions and recommendations

This chapter has viewed good governance as the quality of governance. It adopted UNDP's (2002) definitions of the various qualities of governance as a starting point in defining the concept of good governance. In the process of doing so, it identified and defined three main components of e-government, namely:

- the computerisation of internal government business processes;
- the electronic delivery of government information, knowledge and services to citizens, businesses and other government units through wide area network infrastructure and Internet connectivity, as may be required;
- the electronic interactions between government actors and citizens, businesses and other government actors.

In addition, the chapter conceptualised e-governance as the relationship between the various components of e-government and a well-defined concept of good governance to produce governance outcomes. With these definitions, it succeeded in presenting a results-based monitoring and evaluation approach as a good basis for investigating the effects of e-government on good governance. At the same time, it went further and integrated the defined concepts and proposed a research framework for assessing the good governance outcomes of e-government projects. At a fundamental level, the chapter demonstrated how its proposed framework can be used at levels other than the pan-African. Some of the following chapters further demonstrate how the proposed framework can be used.

The proposed research framework helped LOG-IN Africa to define a set of e-local good governance outcome indicators. This was done through a process of aggregating, integrating and generalising outcome indicators from the various national projects to refine the good governance outcome indicators.

In conclusion, the proposed framework represents a relatively sound research approach that is able to act as an effective starting

TABLE 2.3 Generic good governance outcome indicators

Good governance constructs	Working good governance definitions	Outcome indicators		
		e-administration	e-services	e-society
Participation	Stakeholders participate in local government decision-making processes and activities	Participation in staff decision-making at different levels	Involvement of customers, politicians, private sector and civil society in LG e-governance processes Availability of electronic delivery enabling citizens to serve themselves without being dependent on employee intermediaries and their 'good will' to do their job	Improvement in interactions with central government, businesses, citizens and other key stakeholders Joint planning between LG and civil society Participation of less privileged in LG decision-making
Transparency	Full disclosure of information, accessible information and free access to LG operations and information by stakeholders	Access to and understanding of e-governance policy by stakeholders Extent to which LG processes and information are clear and accessible to stakeholders Visibility and 'trackability' of LG internal operations	Improvement of public access to information and services Ease of access to services Information and services are presented in everyday language Ease of comments, questions and complaints on services	n/a

Responsiveness	Two-way communication between LG officials and stakeholders	Extent to which government institutions exchange and share information	Response rate to comments, questions and complaints	Not applicable
		Enhancement of feedback and response to feedback from staff	Availability of government official documents as electronic resources	
		Staff satisfaction with computerised service	Availability of public servants' profiles	
		Reduction in response time for internal transactions	Extent of enhancement of feedback from customers, central government, private sector, public and civil society	
		Degree to which peer or hierarchical communication is enhanced	Effectiveness of complaints resolution from external stakeholders	
			Extent of customer satisfaction with service provision	
			Increase in access to LG services and information	
			Reduction in turnaround for citizens to request and receive services	
			Improvement in the quality of services delivered	
			Extent to which citizens can check progress of service requests	

Good governance constructs	Working good governance definitions	Outcome indicators		
		e-administration	e-services	e-society
Equity	Services provision or access on equal basis irrespective of gender, disability, socio-economic status or other forms of possible discrimination	Degree of equity in computerised service access by staff without discrimination Degree of equity in staff ICT training without discrimination	Degree of equity in service delivery irrespective of gender, country's geographical location and other forms of marginalisation Reduction in 'favouritism' in serving customers Availability of 'self-service technology' (e.g. touch-screen kiosks) to enable citizens to serve themselves without being dependent on employee intermediaries, as a way to fight favouritism and endorse the principle of 'first come, first served'	n/a
Accountability	LG managers and employees are accountable to citizens and other key stakeholders	Accountability of LG managers and employees for their actions Availability of ways to monitor and trace LG personnel activities (i.e. know who does what and when)	Extent to which LG staff can be held responsible for their actions in service delivery Degree to which public servants and local governors are accountable to citizens	n/a
Effectiveness and efficiency	Optimal use of resources to achieve LG objectives	Increased efficiency and effectiveness of internal business processes Enhancement of institutional performance	Increase in effectiveness of service delivery Improvement in quality of services and information	n/a

	Integration of e-governance applications Reduction in effort needed by LG employees in accomplishing internal business processes Improvement in quality of services Reduction in persons required to carry out internal operations	Increased customer satisfaction Increase in access to public services and information Reduction in waiting time for the delivery of services Reduction in effort to request and receive needed services (e.g. time of queuing)	n/a
Rule of law Laws and administrative procedures are applied fairly and objectively	Increase in objectivity in applying legal instruments, policies and administrative procedures Increased visibility and traceability of violations of rule of law, due to back-office routinisation and automation Decrease unruliness of staff in shouldering their responsibilities	Increase in objectivity in applying legal instruments, policies and administrative procedures	n/a
Consensus orientation Conflicts of interest of stakeholders are resolved	Reduction in internal conflicts of interest Reduction in staff alienation caused by minority versus majority of votes	Reduction in conflicts of interest in service delivery	n/a
Strategic vision Managers and public have long-term view of LG aware of obstacles and their solutions	Enhancement of long-term view of governance Existence of e-governance strategy Alignment of e-governance strategy to national socio-economic development priorities	Enhancement in long-term view of governance Existence of e-governance strategy Alignment of e-governance strategy to national socio-economic development priorities	n/a

point for empirical studies aimed at assessing the effects or benefits of e-governance. It has been used and tested by LOG-IN Africa researchers. Given the limited knowledge in this area, we invite other researchers to use and test the proposed outcome assessment framework, through case studies, in order to build the required knowledge in this area.

Notes

1. Gartner Symposium/ITxpo, 29 April–2 May, San Diego Convention Center, USA, www.gartner.com/5_about/press_releases/2002_04/pr 20020430b.jsp.
2. The Urban Governance Initiative (TUGI), 'Good Governance Issues Report Card: Solid Waste', www.tugi.org/reportcards/solidwaste.pdf.
3. World Bank Group (WBG), 'What is Governance? Arriving at a common understanding of "governance"', www1.worldbank.org/mena/ governance/issues-keyQuestion.htm.
4. The Urban Governance Initiative (TUGI), 'Good Governance Issues Report Card: Solid Waste', www.tugi.org/reportcards/solidwaste.pdf.
5. The research work done by Kettani et al. (2005) at Fez City in Morocco was a key basis for the LOG-IN Africa project. The work by the same researchers in the City of Larache in Morocco, based on the work in Fez, is one of the projects being carried out under LOG-IN Africa.

3

Business process mapping for
e-local governance projects in Egypt

Aly A. Fahmy, Hatem M. Elkadi
and Hisham M. Abdelsalam

The need to modernise by introducing enhanced business models to replace traditional ones has been recognised by governments in many countries (Ho, 2002; Moon, 2002; West, 2002a; West, 2002b). For a government to deliver in a cost-effective manner the growing number of services it is required to provide, costs have to be reduced as services increase. One of the greatest opportunities for accomplishing this is to increase the efficiency of the delivery of services to the citizen (Aicholzer and Schmutzer, 2000). Technology allows governments to serve citizens in a timely, effective and cost-efficient way (Kraemer and Dedrick, 1997). This can be done through e-government, which broadly defined is the use of information and communications technology (ICT) to: promote more efficient and effective government; facilitate more accessible government services; allow greater public access to information; make a government more accountable to citizens (Pacific Council on International Development, 2002).

Egypt recognised the importance of ICT relatively early and started an ambitious e-government project in 2001. The Egyptian e-government programme covers both central and local government and operates with the following as its main goals: first, to provide services through new and easy channels; second, to update the systems of governmental work. One of the main projects that exemplifies this commitment is the Local Government Development

Project (LGDP). It aims to support local government at different levels in cities, small towns and districts. The project will ensure services can be provided to citizens speedily and accurately in a technologically work-friendly environment for employees.

This programme was preceded by the Government of Egypt's decision in October 1999 to establish a Ministry of Communication and Information Technology (MCIT). This was followed by the publication in 2001 of the *Egyptian Information Society Initiative* (EISI) (Government of Egypt, 2008a) policy document. The initiative identified the following areas as crucial for ICT development and its role in the country: 'e-readiness [to bring about] equal access for all'; 'e-learning [to ensure the] nurturing of human capital'; 'e-government [to ensure the] government now delivers'; 'e-business [as a] a new way of doing business'; 'e-health [as a way of] increasing health services availability'; 'e-culture [as a way of] promoting egyptian culture'; 'ICT export initiative [to spur] industry development'.

The third area of focus, namely e-government, was later given the status of a programme to cover numerous projects before being transferred to the Ministry of State for Administrative Development (MSAD) in 2004 (Government of Egypt, 2008b). Significantly, EISI and the e-government programme are all components within the larger national framework aimed at achieving better governance, at both central and local government levels. Developments of this nature contributed to the granting of observer status to the country's MSAD in the Public Governance Committee of the Organisation for Economic Cooperation and Development (OECD).

Background

Local governments provide many different types of service to citizens. The interactions between a local government and its clients are mostly process-based and can be categorised as consisting of the following: structured procedures or routines; semi-structured decision processes; negotiation-based case-solving

(Lenk and Traunmueller, 1999). Typically, government services are characterised by complex multi-step – possibly fuzzy – business processes, involving the exchange of administrative information and documents. In this context, a business process can be defined as a set of one or more interconnected activities needed to achieve a business objective or policy goal, normally within the context of an organisational structure that defines functional roles and relationships (Verginadis and Mentzas, 2004).

E-government projects normally target specific products and/or services, rather than an organisational unit, to bring about a customer-oriented government. To have effective and efficient services requires a careful and thorough analysis of the service delivery process, not only to identify the best way to do it, but also to determine the areas with a high chance of success (Davenport, 1993). Unlike functional or task-oriented analyses, process-oriented analysis offers good opportunities for continual improvement.

Efforts to deploy e-government applications are always faced with the complexity of trying to improve government processes. These involve a large number of people, with a complicated network of relationships that link actors, organisations, documents and regulations.

In local government – as in any other organisation – *processes* constitute a key building block (Davenport, 1993; Hammer and Champy, 1993). A business process can be seen as a 'generative structure' that is not fixed but varies according to type of input, personnel involved in execution, and so on. Variety in a business process can be looked at in three dimensions: the range of tasks performed, the order in which these tasks are performed, and the inputs and outputs of the process (Pentland, 2003a, 2003b).

This suggests that the modelling of processes for electronic administration has major demands. In this regard, it is not enough to use traditional modelling tools for business process management in e-government. Before engaging in the task, it is necessary to identify flaws, marshal the resources needed to address them, specify the roles to go with responsibilities and consider the competencies of authorities (Karagiannis and Palkovits, 2003).

Research in the field of business process modelling is extensive, since there are many reasons for using process models. They include: facilitating human understanding; enhancing communication; improving learning in organisations; supporting process improvement; benchmarking process performance; contributing to the integration of technical aspects (Wyssusek et al., 2001).

A large number of process modelling languages have been developed over the years, including data flow diagrams (Yourdon, 1989), event-driven process chains (Keller and Teufel, 1998), Petri nets (Gordijn and van Vliet, 2000) and process maps (Rummler and Brache, 1995). These are used to produce tightly defined models of a process in terms of specific task sequences – and illustrate how the process should be performed and not what outcome should be achieved (King and Johnson, 2006). Brain et al. (2005) analysed five of the most commonly used and widely accepted generic process modelling notations from the parameter of their suitability in an e-government context, namely IDEFØ, LOVEM-E, ARIS, BPMS and BPMN. While almost all are adequate for activity modelling requirements, they are significantly weak in handling document/ information modelling requirements. For this reason, the focus of this research was to develop a methodology that supports proper documentation of all aspects of service delivery processes at the local government level in Egypt.

The next section outlines the work that has been done through Egypt's local government development project. There follows an overview of the study's research approach, and then a description of the proposed methodology that was the target of this work. A test case on the methodology takes up the subsequent section. This is followed by conclusions and recommendations.

Administrative structure of local government in Egypt

The Arab Republic of Egypt (ARE or Egypt) is a unitary country comprising 26 administrative units, called governorates, of various sizes, populations and resources (as shown in Figure 3.1).

FIGURE 3.1   Map of Egypt

Governorates are, in addition, administratively divided into cities and districts, which are in turn divided into smaller entities called neighbourhoods in districts, and villages in cities (as shown in Figure 3.2). Some villages are further subdivided into boroughs.

The governors are appointed and sworn in by the Egyptian president and they report to the prime minister. The local entities have a certain degree of administrative freedom; however, they are financially and politically managed by the central government. Central ministries have 'antennae' at the governorate level,

FIGURE 3.2   Administrative structure of Egypt

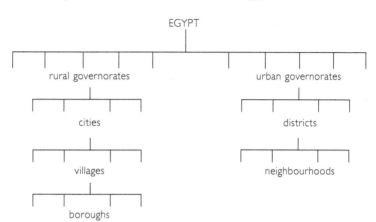

called directorates. Directorates are technically managed by an undersecretary from a corresponding ministry, while the entire directorate reports to the local administration. The Ministry of Local Development overlooks the activities of the local entities, but has no power over them.

Local governments – represented in governorates – manage their operations based on rules, regulations and legal requirements created by the central government. However, they have autonomy in how they provide service to citizens and in how they manage processes. Consequently, governorates might be organised in different ways. If properly used, the degree of autonomy can result in a good administration, although this depends on the personality and abilities of the governor. As an example, the governor of Alexandria succeeded in rallying the enthusiasm of Alexandrians (4.8 million inhabitants) to enhance the living standards of the governorate and attract many investments.

The organisational structure of a governorate (as shown in Figure 3.3) consists of four major departments: the top management, internal services, external services, and administration.

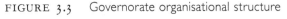

FIGURE 3.3   Governorate organisational structure

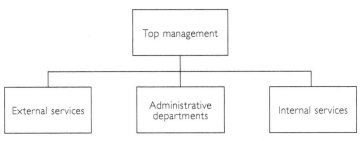

They provide services directly to citizens. The internal services department handles services associated with municipalities, such as the provision of housing and the granting of construction permits and commercial licences. In most cases, the tasks are directly managed by the mayor or by the district council director. In comparison, the external services department provides specialised services on education, health, social security and agriculture. It reports administratively to the mayor, but technically it is under a relevant ministry. In general, it is common for the city or district councils to exert authority over the four departments through committees in which all the departments are members and not via direct management.

Local government development project (LGDP)

The LGDP employs modern information technologies and state-of-the-art management systems to enhance both the quality and the efficiency of government systems and to reduce time wastage. The technologies and systems can be used to overcome corruption at the workplace and contribute to the overall development of the country. However, because Egypt is a developing country, salaries of government employees are relatively low, which discourages some qualified people from applying for jobs. However, local governments need to retain them as part of employment creation. For this reason, LGDP projects do not aim to automate services fully. Instead, they try to enhance the quality of operations through ICT to reduce delivery time and establish a monitoring and control system that provides better transparency and equity.

LGDP project work involves three main stakeholders, namely: governorate management and employees; an outsourced contractor who is responsible for systems analysis, design, development and deployment; the Ministry of State for Administrative Development as a mediator between the first two stakeholders and responsible for project quality.

A successful milestone in the programme was the e-Alexandria initiative in which the seven councils/districts of Alexandria – one of the largest governorates of Egypt – were automated. However, during the programme, the project as well as the MSAD teams faced many challenges, particularly in understanding and documenting service delivery in different sites. A contributory factor was the absence of a proper common modelling methodology that was understood by the project team, local government staff and the software development companies. This weakness affected the systems that had been developed and user acceptance.

Enhancement of services in local governments

Since 2003, championing of the Egyptian e-government programme has been the responsibility of the Ministry of State for Administrative Development. This reflects the understanding that e-government is a natural component of administrative development and reform in the country. The programme's vision is to establish an effective government institution that can adapt to change, manage resources and provide world-class services to its citizens. To realise this vision, a number of target objectives were specified. These include:

- Providing excellent services to citizens, foreigners, business people and investors quickly, accurately and efficiently.
- Enhancing government performance by using ICTs to develop work systems, simplify work procedures and quicken the exchange of documents and information.

- Providing accurate, updated information for decision-makers and investors to help them plan for the future and follow up the implementation of development projects.

The enhancement of services in local government has several benefits. For instance, since they are closer to citizens; they are best placed to encourage interactions between citizens and various levels of government. Second, given their unique position, they can inform the public on policy matters and explain the government's new vision and the strategy required for it to be realised. These factors are crucial in understanding how local government initiatives gained momentum in Egypt, leading to measures aimed at automating work systems and reorganising management systems in different ministries and government agencies.

Research approach

The main objectives of this research were to develop a methodology that supports proper documentation of all aspects of service delivery processes in local government in Egypt, and to build a prototype software tool that facilitates the use of this methodology. Figure 3.4 illustrates the phases the research went through to achieve the following objectives:

1. Identifying and reviewing the literature on business process modelling methodologies.
2. Reviewing field cases from Egypt and identifying hidden business elements and modelling pitfalls.
3. Developing a proper methodology.
4. Building the software tool.
5. Testing the methodology in real-life situations in the country.

In the first phase, the researchers used semi-structured interviews with project stakeholders and document analysis to collect data. This phase of the research had four specific objectives: (i) to act as a foundation for creating a better understanding of work

FIGURE 3.4   Research approach

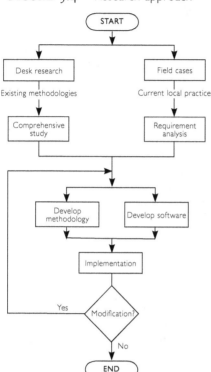

that had been carried out through the LGDP; (ii) to evaluate the business modelling methodology that had shaped the project's activities; (iii) to determine the obstacles and challenges that had been faced; and (iv) to determine user requirements of the developed methodology.

Semi-structured interviews were useful in allowing the researchers to compare and contrast specific information with information that had been gained in other interviews. Apart from this, they also provided the flexibility that was needed for other important information to emerge. Other salient aspects of the interviews included these requirements:

- Development of an interview schedule with a list of specific questions or topics to be discussed. The list was used in each interview to ensure consistency. It was updated and revised after each interview by incorporating into it topics that had arisen in previous interviews.
- Completion of an interview summary form after each interview had taken place.
- Analysis of data as an ongoing process, with content analysis being the chosen tool. It entailed having to read and reread transcripts to identify similarities and differences that portray perspectives on important issues.

In the second phase, there was a comprehensive study of nine business process modelling methodologies: flowcharting and W3C (World Wide Web Consortium); WfMC (Workflow Management Coalition) and BPMN (Business Process Modelling Notation); BPEL (Business Process Execution Language) and UML (Unified Modeling Language); SIPOC (Suppliers, Inputs, Process, Outputs and Customers); IDEF (Integrated Definition); and Swimlane. Studying these methodologies made it possible to assess their advantages and limitations. The results obtained from the assessment were subsequently used in the third phase, in which gaps were tackled by the proposed methodology.

Proposed methodology

Related challenges

Certain contextual realities in the first phase of the research directly affected the design of the proposed methodology. In this regard, it is important to note that in Egypt the role of a municipality is to provide services to citizens, and to have an oversight role in the municipality projects. The major e-government projects that take place in municipalities are mainly concerned with the automation of services being offered to citizens. After reviewing the documents on the development of computerised systems in the e-Alexandria initiative, the research team concluded that the contractor did not follow a clearly unified methodology for process modelling.

It also emerged that the LGDP faced many obstacles. Some were development obstacles and others were managerial. The latter category was mainly financial and contractual in nature and did not constitute an interest area for this research. However, the researcher's interest in development obstacles revealed the following to be the major stumbling blocks:

- Non-cooperation of employees, since they believed the computer would render them jobless.
- Ambiguity of the work cycle as government processes lacked the required documentation.
- Absence of a clear linkage between specific laws to govern specific business processes.
- Conflicting understanding of the nature of different business processes.
- Lack of clarity on the ownership of selected businesses to champion project ideas, resulting in many logistical problems.
- Difficulty in obtaining data.

The proposed methodology in this research tried to overcome these obstacles by avoiding them, or by limiting their effects on e-government project work.

Phases of the proposed methodology

During the study, the researchers developed a detailed comparison between business process modelling in the government context and business process modelling in the private sector. This comparison, as represented in Appendix 1, provided a basis for developing the proposed methodology. Conceptually, in terms of content, the methodology has two segments: a knowledge acquisition (or fact gathering) segment and a knowledge representation (or process modelling) segment. Figure 3.5 illustrates the conceptual basis of the proposed methodology.

As the figure demonstrates, obstacles related to the side of employees (source of knowledge information) are best handled

FIGURE 3.5   Conceptual basis of the methodology

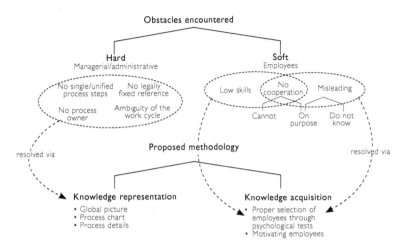

through the proper selection of participating employees and by motivating them. On the other hand, shortcomings related to process modelling can be handled through a three-tier representation approach.

Knowledge acquisition segment

Knowledge is considered to be the most important strategic resource of an enterprise (Spender and Grant, 1996). The way in which knowledge is created, shared and used in an organisation has become an issue that has attracted heated discussion (Ipe, 2003). Research on how human beings share knowledge has been a neglected area of interest. It is known, however, that knowledge is mostly passed on through face-to-face interactions between individuals in an organisation (Cross et al., 2001). In such contexts, the carriers of knowledge are essentially people. Therefore knowledge flow only occurs when individuals are willing to share their knowledge with other individuals who are also willing to receive it (Cheng, 2008).

In this study the knowledge acquisition segment has important implications since one needs to factor in employee informants to help in the analysis of a selected service (business) process. Situations of this nature would require the employee to provide pertinent information and details on the process. The research assumed that in all such cases the selection of participating employees should be based on their personality characteristics. Consequently, the methodology that is proposed in this work examined four psychometric tests to classify candidate employees to ensure the selection of appropriate ones. Such tests can provide varied information on people, ranging from their style of thinking to their level of motivation. However, they should be administered and interpreted by qualified personnel. The following is an overview of the defining characteristics of the tests.

The InQ Instrument   The InQ instrument (Harrison and Bramson, 1988) is one of a number of instruments that measures individual thinking styles and related variables. The styles are evident in the instrument's categorisation of thinkers as synthesists, idealists, pragmatists, analysts and realists. Synthesists supposedly represent a divergent style of thinking, and can reconcile patterns of thought that might be contradictory in the opinion of others. Idealists, on the other hand, exemplify classical 'systems thinkers', who can see the nature of the relationship between the part and the whole. It is argued that idealists often focus on ends and goals, instead of thinking about specific details.

Pragmatists are viewed as thinkers with an orientation for action. They like to get things done and their approach is often flexible and adaptive. Unlike idealists, the solutions provided by pragmatists do not have to be the most elegant. The penultimate category of thinkers, analysts, tend to be logical, structured and prescriptive. They prefer predictability and rationality, and will look for a method, a formula or a procedure to solve a particular problem.

The last category, that of the realists, refers to thinkers who take an empirical view. Their world consists of what can be felt, smelled, touched, seen, heard, and personally observed or experienced. They are interested in concrete results, and at times may appear to be too results-oriented. In terms of thinking style, the realist resembles the analyst. Both focus on the factual, on concrete facts, but unlike the analyst the realist will finally run out of patience and become frustrated with the analyst's endless search for data.

The InQ instrument was developed from responses to 18 questions based on a forced ranking format. The questions represent a variety of hypothetical situations, such as 'When I read a report I am most likely to pay attention to:' Each question is followed by five possible responses, which the individual must rank from five, which is most typical of the individual's style, through to one, which is least typical of the individual's style. Each possible response is linked to one of the five thinking styles, and the values of the responses are added up to give a single score for each style. Scores of 60 or higher on any category indicate a peak or preference for that thinking style. Scores of 48 or below indicate a valley or relative disregard for that thinking style. It is possible to have no peaks or valleys, and end up with a relatively flat profile that may indicate versatility in thinking styles and an ability to adapt one's thinking style to a given situation.

The Eysenck Personality Questionnaire (EPQ) The EPQ has 90 yes/no type questions on ways of feeling and behaving. The questionnaire makes it possible to test personality traits that include: extroversion/introversion; neuroticism/stability; psychoticism/ socialisation. Extroversion is characterised by being outgoing, talkative and in need of external stimulation. Extroverts, according to Eysenck (Eysenck and Eysenck, 1975), are in need of external stimulation to bring them up to an optimal level of performance. In contrast, introverts are supposed to be in need of peace and quiet to bring them up to an optimal level of performance.

The trait of neuroticism or emotionality is characterised by high levels of negative disposition such as depression and anxiety. In most cases, neurotic people cannot inhibit or control their emotional reactions and experience negative feelings quite easily. The final trait of psychoticism is associated not only with the liability of exhibiting psychotic episodes, but also with aggression.

The Minnesota Multiphasic Personality Inventory (MMPI)   This is one of the most frequently used personality tests in the mental health field (Hogan, 2003). It was designed to help identify personal, social and behavioural problems. The original developers of the test were Starke R. Hathaway and J.C. McKinley (McKinley and Hathaway, 1944).

The current standardised version of the test, the MMPI-2, was released in 1989 (Butcher et al., 1989) and is for adults aged over eighteen years. A subsequent revision of certain test elements in the inventory was published in early 2001. Like many standardised tests, scores on the various scales of the MMPI-2 are not representative of either percentile rank or how 'well' or 'badly' someone has done on the test. Rather, raw scores on the scales are transformed into a standardised metric known as T-scores (mean or average equals 50, standard deviation equals 10), making interpretation easier for clinicians.

There are ten main clinical scales on the MMPI-2. In this research, only one scale, the L Scale, was used. The scale was originally called the 'Lie' scale, and was meant to assess naive or unsophisticated respondents' attempts to present themselves in favourable light.

Achievement motivation   One theory of achievement motivation was proposed by Atkinson and Feather (1966), who stated that a person's achievement-oriented behaviour is influenced by three factors: the first is the individual's predisposition to achievement; the second is the probability of success; the third is the individual's perception of the value of the task.

These factors imply that an individual's perception of the probability of being successful in a task would trigger the urge to achieve and a fear of failure. Both are strong emotions that influence an individual's decision on whether or not to attempt the task (Bar-Tal et al., 1974). In this situation, an individual will

TABLE 3.1   Individual differences and knowledge sharing

Individual difference	Test	Effect of knowledge sharing/transfer
Style of thinking	InQ	Analysts tend to be logical, structured and prescriptive.
		Pragmatists have a bias for action; they like to get things done and their approach is often flexible and adaptive.
		Realists tend to be results-oriented and would support the analysis process; unfortunately, they might not withstand long analysis.
Extroversion/ introversion	Eysenck EPQ	Extroverts have quicker retrieval ability from long-term memory and better retention ability over short intervals. However, they have less retention ability over long intervals compared to introverts.
Neuroticism/ stability		Emotionally stable people are calm and collected under pressure.
Psychoticism/ socialisation		Psychoticism is associated with aggression, which might affect the process.
Lies	L Scale from MMPI	Avoid people who try to present themselves in an overly favourable light.
Achievement motivation	Achievement motivation scale	People with high motivation for achievement will have a positive attitude towards success and work hard to ensure they are successful.

find a task easy if there is a high probability of it being success-fully completed. The same individual will find the task hard if the probability of successfully completing it is low.

Some individuals have a need to achieve. They want to be successful at whatever they attempt. They have a strong attitude towards success and work hard to ensure they are successful (Atkinson, 1974). If they are intrinsically motivated, they participate in the activity for the sake of learning that activity or of improving their ability in it. If they are extrinsically motivated, they participate in the activity with the expectation of reward (Eskeles-Gottfried et al., 1998).

Evaluation of the psychometric tests

The InQ was selected instead of the other related instruments for two reasons. First, it looks at how people process informa-tion; second, it does not entail personality measurements. It thus avoids the defensiveness that might result from a discussion of a respondent's personality. Despite this observation, all the instruments have high validity and reliability, and are easy to use with large groups. They also proved suitable for the age range of this study's targeted sample. In addition, all of them could be easily understood by the targeted sample and, most importantly, could be translated into Arabic and tested in the Egyptian context.

After assessing the potential effect of individual differences on knowledge sharing – as illustrated in Table 3.1 – the study selected potential employees to participate in the analysis based on the following criteria. Those who could not finish the tests or who answered wrongly were to be omitted. In this category for omission also were those with high scores in any of the EPQ Tests and those with high scores in the L-Scale. The selection was based on the remaining personnel in the sample. They had high scores in their style of thinking based on the following ranking: analyst, followed by pragmatist and lastly realist.

Knowledge representation (process modelling) segment

This segment is concerned with the representation of knowledge acquired through data/knowledge gathering activities. Its purpose is to serve as a collective process model to satisfy the requirements of different stakeholders. The research proposes representations covering three tiers of views, ranging from compact/summarised to details as shown in Figure 3.6.

Tier 1: Broad spectrum perspective

Tier 1 of the process model is intended to be a one-page compact description of the process model that gives a holistic understanding of the process being analysed. In essence it captures what can be labelled a global representation of the process. From another dimension, Tier 1 can be viewed as an extension of the

FIGURE 3.6   Three levels of detail

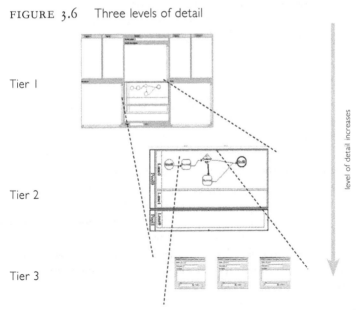

Tier 1

Tier 2

Tier 3

level of detail increases

FIGURE 3.7 Tier I

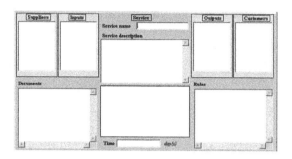

powerful SIPOC tool that helps project teams and stakeholders to understand the 'as is' parameter of a process. It helps to identify and establish the boundaries or scope of a project. In addition, it can assist in analysing proposed deliverable solutions. Last, it has a critical role to play in the documentation of results.

Tier 1 takes multiple elements of a process into consideration, thus providing a 'big picture' perspective that is difficult to achieve with less robust metrics.

Tier 2: Process chart

At this level, more details are listed for analysis and the information obtained can be used to improve the process. The graphical representation system that was used in Tier 2 is BPMN. It has been praised for providing a standard notation that is easy to understand. Normally, modelling in BPMN is achieved through diagrams that have a small set of graphical elements. These include: Flow Objects (for events, activities and gateways); Connecting Objects (to represent sequence flow, message flow and association; Swim Lanes that are visual mechanisms that can be used to organize and categories acts based on cross-functional flowcharting; Artifacts to represent data objects and group annotation). These elements are shown in Figure 3.8.

FIGURE 3.8   Tier 2 Elements

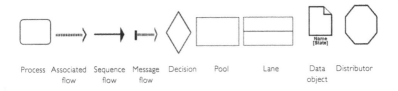

Process Associated Sequence Message Decision   Pool   Lane   Data   Distributor
             flow   flow   flow   object

Tier 3: Process details

This is the level with activity-specific information of the following
kind: (1) general information – name, short name, description,
time; (2) connections to other items; (3) associated documents;
(4) associated business rules and regulations; (5) personnel who
do the activity; and (6) probabilities of branching (for decision
activities only).

Related methodological feature

A business process modelling tool – named A5H – was developed
as part of the methodology. It is a Windows-based menu-driven
software that supports the three-tier representation described
earlier that can facilitate the modelling/analysis process through
the inclusion of these features: process logic validation algorithm;
time calculations algorithm; data aggregation.

Process logic validation ensures that that all relations among different activities are logically valid. For this reason, as an example,
A5H will warn the user when there is a hanging activity (not feeding
another one), an infinite loop, or a no-end event. Time calculation,
by way of comparison, provides a means for in-depth understanding
of a process and supports future process improvement. Process
total time is calculated by using a specific algorithm for each lane,
pool and complete process. The algorithm accommodates different

probabilities associated with different decision branches in the decision node and in the distributor node.

Test case

The methodology (with associated software) was deployed in two different municipalities to validate and evaluate its use. The basic idea was to model a specific service entailing the issuing of a licence in both municipalities and compare the results. Briefly, the process in both municipalities went as follows:

1. An awareness session was held for all employees in different service sectors with the aim of introducing the objectives and the activities of the project.
2. The personality characteristics tests were administered to all relevant employees.
3. A group of employees was selected as the sample for the analysis.
4. An orientation session was held for this group to facilitate the process.
5. The applicable business process was modelled.

To test the effectiveness of the methodology – especially the effect of employee selection – the selection of participating employees in the first municipality (labelled A) was based on the criteria of the proposed methodology, while the participants in the second municipality (labelled B) were selected randomly, to violate these criteria. However, the analysts were not aware of how the process of employee selection had been done. Since the research kept the number of analysts constant in both cases (two analysts), the work in municipality B required more time to complete compared to that in A (four days instead of two). The analysts also sensed significant differences between employees in A and B, from the perspective of their effectiveness and willingness to cooperate.

The service that was modelled involved a moderately intricate collaboration between citizens and government employees of two

FIGURE 3.9   Test Case: Tier 2

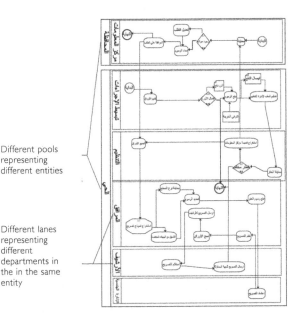

Different pools
representing
different entities

Different lanes
representing
different
departments in
the in the same
entity

entities – a governorate and a municipality. Since the Egyptian e-government context exists in locations in which the manual process has yet to be replaced and requires enhancement, the use of A5H provided application developers, analysts and government staff, as well as managers, with a needed tool to help them analyse existing or proposed processes. This would ensure that they are effectively understood to bring about desired results. A5H made it possible for analysts to articulate organisational processes in a rigorous, precise, complete and clear manner.

Figure 3.9 illustrates a popular method of process modelling. It has flow diagrams that help to identify inconsistencies in process logic and provides the means for process re-engineering. It is important to note that A5H was able to provide analysts with the ability to enhance comparison of processes through explicit

FIGURE 3.10   Test Case: Tier 2

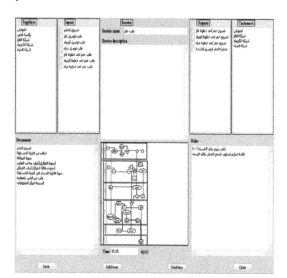

representations via graphical visualisations. Based on the Egyptian e-government experience, this factor can assist in ensuring the standardisation of processes that are intended to be identical in different municipalities. Graphical depiction of a process is a useful step, as it is commonly understood that graphics enhance the communication of complex information (Tufte, 2001). Such use of visualisation could provide government process inspectors with substantially higher confidence in processes, simply because the inspector can absorb more of the complexity through a visual graphic of the process (Osterweil et al., 2004).

It has been noted nevertheless that the visual inspection of graphical representation of processes is typically not sufficient. That is why process details are supported by Tier 3, since it has the means to do the following:

- specify who (a person or position) is responsible for conducting a particular task;
- indicate when the task is to be undertaken;

- highlight the kinds of documents required;
- show the related regulations or rules;
- reveal what other people or processes need to know about the outcomes or about the intermediary stages of the process;
- demonstrate the kinds of outputs produced.

A&H also succeeded in providing, in abstract terms, the ability to view the details of a process at aggregated (Figure 3.10) level to make things simpler to understand. It also managed to provide a breakdown of process activities and details when needed.

Conclusions and recommendations

The process-oriented methodology of this research is consistent with the e-government aspirations of Egypt. The study allows employees to be actively involved in the analysis and possible improvement of the process, as was demonstrated in the case of the licence issuing example. On this occasion, employees were encouraged to consider their work from the point of view of citizens, which created greater mutual understanding and employee satisfaction. The research also illustrated the logical connections between activities in graphic form. Consequently, it was possible to grasp the important sequences and links in actions at a glance. Moreover, different employees could now locate and focus on specific activities, instead of being distracted by the totality of a whole process.

The methodology benefited from insights borrowed from the typology of knowledge in Capurro (2004). According to the typology, in the first category of knowledge there is *know-how knowledge*, which is concerned with how to make things (i.e. technical knowledge). It is also the category that is concerned with knowledge acquired through experience and remembrance (i.e. empirical knowledge). In the second category, there is *know-why* or logical reasoning knowledge (i.e. scientific knowledge). Finally, there is the category of knowledge with the label *what knowledge*, which is about the best means to achieve given goals (the same as practical knowledge).

Through the methodology one can engage in process analysis from the perspectives proposed by Hammer and Champy (1994), whose approach is able to model and analyse e-government processes not only from the perspective of a sequencing of activities, but also from the perspective of the representation of people and organisational structures (Brain et al., 2005).

From the activity perspective, the methodology in this research is able to depict the sequencing of activities and decisions. Thus one is able to analyse the rationale for the sequencing of activities and their combinations (Harrington, 1991). Moreover, all paths (with decision probabilities) in the process are represented, allowing for the assessment of the likelihood and cause of all eventualities. In addition, for each activity, information inputs and outputs are recorded to assess the information given to the performer of the activity. It is certain that resource utilisation will play an important role in any future process improvement. It is also noteworthy that the methodology has room for inclusion of references to governing legislation or to security requirements. This would facilitate an analysis of existing constraints.

To facilitate the analysis of relationships between entities, the organisational perspective of the methodology kept a record of the roles of employees and their requirement in the process activities. In conclusion, although the tool has been tested in two sites, further testing by different users is needed to point out any bugs. The methodology, as a whole, also needs to be tested in other contexts and countries.

4

E-local governance:
a case study on life-event services
in the *kebeles* of Addis Ababa, Ethiopia

Solomon Atnafu, Dessalegn Mequanint and Yigremew Adal

After the change of government in 1991, Ethiopia adopted a federal system of government. According to this system, there are nine regional states and two city administrations. Regional states have a government structure with legislative, executive and judicial branches. They also have presidents, parliaments and flags to mark their status as political entities. In comparison, city administrations are administrative units under the federal government, and not states (Government of Ethiopia, 1994).

The introductory sections provide the necessary background information on the context of the study, especially in relation to the nature of the governance system at national and local levels. The issues and initiatives that dominate the country's national ICT policy and strategy are then highlighted. After this introduction, a detailed account of the study's research design is provided. The next section outlines how the prototype system was developed and validated. The study's findings are then covered at length, while the requirements of e-local governance are the focus of the subsequent section. There follows an account of an information exchange model for the *kebeles*. This logically leads to a description of the study's functional model for *kebeles*. The Kebele Life-Event Services System (KLESS) is presented in the next section. This is followed by concluding remarks.

The city government of Addis Ababa

Addis Ababa, the capital, is one of the city governments of the nation. It has an estimated population of 3 million (Government of Ethiopia, 2005). Addis Ababa is not only the capital city of Ethiopia, but also the largest economic hub of the country. The federal constitution gives it a special status that authorises it to exercise higher level autonomy, unlike other cities, which are under the administration of their respective regional states. Even though the city government of Addis Ababa is accountable to the federal government, it is mainly governed by a charter that ensures its autonomy (Government of Ethiopia, 2003a). In 2004, the government of the city implemented a new structure that divided it into ten sub-cities (called *kifle-ketema*) and about a hundred *kebeles*. The *kebeles* report directly to the sub-city administrations, and the sub-cities to the city government (Government of Ethiopia, 2004).

In essence, the new administrative structure of the country has created federal, regional, zonal, *woreda* and *kebele* government units. Zonal, *woreda* and *kebele* units can be viewed as local government units. However, in Addis Ababa, the structure allows for a city government, a sub-city administration and *kebeles*. The sub-cities and *kebeles* were established through Proclamation No. 1/2003 (Government of Ethiopia, 2003b) and the subsequent amendment Proclamation No. 13/2004 (Government of Ethiopia, 2004). Each sub-city and *kebele* has a council elected by its residents, and that supervises the activities of the executive branch of the sub-city or *kebele*. The two proclamations give powers to the sub-cities and *kebeles*. In particular, according to the charter, the sub-city is expected to 'function as a municipality in accordance with the central leadership of the city'. The sub-city is also expected to 'allocate the budget set it by the city council' and 'approve economic, social development and municipal service plans of the respective sub-city'. *Kebeles* are the last administrative tier below sub-cities.

The Addis Ababa city government revised charter (Government of Ethiopia, 2003a) describes a *kebele* as 'a centre for development and direct popular participation as well as a location for the delivery of basic services'. A *kebele* administration provides services of various types to its estimated 30,000 residents. The administrative activities and services rendered by *kebeles* include those connected to development activities, as well as others intended for small industries and businesses, primary and secondary education, and public relations. Other services focus on resident registration, issuing of identity cards and life-event services such as birth and marriage registration.

Kebeles have powers to provide a wide range of services. On the basis of the directive issued by the city government (Government of Ethiopia, 2006a), the services provided by the *kebeles* include: issuing identity cards to *kebele* residents; registering *kebele* house seekers; supplying documentation verifying eligibility for free health treatment; providing support letters to those who need free education; corroborating marriage status and handling death issues; communicating with utility agencies regarding maintenance and other services that are essential for government and *kebele* houses.

National ICT policy and e-government strategy

Ethiopia's ICT policy aims to create an ICT-driven country and a knowledge based society. It also aims to promote and facilitate the use of ICT in all sectors of the economy to nurture democratic values, good governance, transparency and accountability (Government of Ethiopia, 2006b). The policy outlines its vision, mission, goal and objectives. In this regard, the ICT vision is to 'improve the social and economic well-being of the people of Ethiopia through the exploitation of the opportunities created by ICT'. Its mission is 'to develop Ethiopia into a socially progressive and prosperous nation with a globally competitive, modern, dynamic and robust economy through the development, deployment and exploitation of ICT within the economy and the society at large'.

In order to achieve the goals and objectives of the ICT policy, the government has expressed its commitment to pursue steadfastly strategies that are outlined in the policy (Dzidonu, 2006). These include: designing service network systems that allow citizens and private companies to communicate with public authorities; setting up organisational structures for ICT at different levels of government; developing guidelines, procedures and organisational structures to ensure the integration of ICT in strategic public-sector development programmes; promoting the development of a competitive ICT sector; promoting and facilitating the participation of civil society and communities in ICT development; designing and implementing computerised information systems and applications with emphasis on priority sectors; automating all public service delivery systems; establishing public information gateways; and strengthening institutional capacity in government, educational institutions and in the private sector to deliver ICT services.

There are several ICT projects under implementation. One targets human resource development and has the general aim of building a critical mass of ICT skills and of creating human capacity to meet the fast-changing demands of ICT. The other is the e-government project. This has three sub-projects: content and application development; network expansion; a *woreda* ICT network.

Research design

Research rationale, questions and objectives

Ethiopia has spent millions of dollars to develop a nationwide telecommunications infrastructure. The capital city, Addis Ababa, is also enjoying the benefits of state-of-the-art fibre-optic cables that have improved connectivity (Ethiopia Telecommunications Corporation, 2001). Studies conducted in recent years reveal that there are shortfalls of qualified personnel in the ICT sector in Ethiopia. However, with the increasing number of private and public higher learning institutions with training programmes in ICT fields, the problem is being addressed (Woldehanna et al., 2004).

Public-sector awareness on the use of ICT has also been rising, particularly in the cities. However, hardly any research or survey work has been conducted on the application of ICT in local governance. As a result, little is known about the extent of ICT in this sector. Efforts aimed at using the country's telecommunications infrastructure to support development programmes need to be based on sound research, in order to establish, for instance, the extent to which current ICT interventions can be used to facilitate good governance. To this end, this study targeted the grassroots-level administration units, *kebeles*, as the focus of its investigation. More specifically, it chose the *kebeles* of the city government of Addis Ababa because their status encourages direct interaction between *kebele* administrators and the public.

The main research questions that the study set out to answer are as follows:

- What is the level of ICT usage in *kebele* governance?
- What is the e-local governance readiness status of the *kebeles*?
- How can the application of ICTs in local governance increase the participation of citizens in the affairs of *kebeles*?
- What policies and strategies are needed for effective application of ICTs in local governance, especially in the *kebeles* of the CGAA?
- What are the requirements for the successful implementation of e-local governance in the *kebeles* of the CGAA?
- How would the *kebele* staff and end-users react to the governance implications of applying a prototype system, specifically developed to promote e-local governance in the *kebeles*?

The questions show that the general objective of this research was to influence perspectives on the role of ICTs in local governance. Its specific objectives were to:

- promote the application of ICTs in local governance;
- identify the priority areas of life-event services for the *kebeles* of the CGAA where the intervention of ICTs is required;

TABLE 4.1 Methodological framework

Research areas	Data to be collected	Data sources	Collection instruments	Analysis techniques
Level of ICT usage for local governance purpose at the *kebeles*	ICT awareness; knowledge and skills of *kebele* officials, employees and residents Availability and types of ICT tools in the community and in *kebele* offices	*Kebele* officials *Kebele* residents Documents	Interview of key informants Questionnaire Review of records, files and other documents	Descriptive statistics Thematic analysis Triangulation
e-Local governance readiness of the *kebeles*	ICT literacy level of *kebele* officials, employees and residents ICTs infrastructure Effective demand of ICTs for *kebele* administration and residents	*Kebele* officials *Kebele* residents Documents	Interview of key informants Questionnaire Review of records, files and other documents Focus group discussion	Descriptive statistics Thematic analysis Triangulation
Extent of exercise of good governance constructs in *kebeles*	Constructs applicable to the services considered in the study: participation; rule of law; transparency; responsiveness; equity; effectiveness and efficiency; accountability; strategic vision	*Kebele* officials *Kebele* residents Documents	Interview of key informants Questionnaire Review of records, files and other documents Focus group discussion	Descriptive statistics Thematic analysis Triangulation

Policies and strategies on ICTs tailored to suit *kebeles*	ICT policy and strategy constructs	*Kebele* officials Documents	Interview of key informants Questionnaire Review of records, files and other documents	Thematic analysis
Key factors and drivers of successful implementation of local e-governance in *kebeles*	Potential to acquire and use ICTs Status of ICT infrastructure Needs and requirements for successful use of ICTs for local e-governance	*Kebele* officials *Kebele* residents Documents	Interview of key informants Questionnaire Review of records, files and other documents Focus group discussion	Thematic analysis
Roadmap to e-local governance transformation	Local governance tenets Current governance status and future direction	*Kebele* officials Documents	Interview of key informants Questionnaire Review of records, files and other documents	Thematic analysis

- identify the key factors that can affect the implementation of e-local governance;
- identify the diverse policy and strategy issues required for successful implementation of e-local governance at the *kebele* level;
- propose an appropriate roadmap for an effective transformation of the *kebeles* of the CGAA to e-local governance;
- develop a prototype system to showcase the application of ICT in local governance, in relation to the priority activities of life-event services.

Methodological framework

After assessing the range of activities at the *kebele* level, the research selected life-event services as the most appropriate for the application of ICT. The major life-event services for the study included the registration and issuance of ID cards to residents and the issuance of testimonial letters on a number of issues. Life-event services were chosen because of a number of factors. Of significance is the fact that they represent basic services that are citizen-oriented and that therefore have the potential to satisfy citizens because of their impact. It was also observed that many of the other services rely on the effectiveness of life-event services. However, the most important factor emerged from the study's preliminary investigation: the life-event service category is where usage of ICT can influence the quality of the governance activities of *kebeles*.

Various methods were used to gather the information required for the study, as shown in Table 4.1, which made it necessary to use a variety of analytical techniques.

Through this methodological framework, the study was able to obtain the data it needed to respond to its research questions.

Sampling procedures

Addis Ababa City has 10 sub-cities and 99 *kebeles*, each of which has between 280,000 to 350,000 residents (Government of Ethiopia, 2005). Given the limited time and other resources of the study, it was not practical to select a number of *kebeles* that could be said to constitute a scientifically representative sample. Therefore the study opted for purposive sampling in selecting sub-cities and *kebeles*. Through informal consultations, the researchers identified Bole sub-city as appropriate for investigation as it contains *kebeles* and residents who are relatively better off. However, they lack access to facilities. After that, following consultation with the relevant people in Bole sub-city, the researchers purposively chose two *kebeles* with residents who were relatively better off.

Two hundred residents from both *kebeles* (100 from each) were randomly selected to respond to the survey questionnaire. For this purpose, graduates from the Department of Computer Science at Addis Ababa University were recruited to serve as research assistants. Although the questionnaire that was prepared was in English, training sessions were conducted for the research assistants, so that they could translate the questions into the local language of the residents, Amharic. In addition, the selected key informants and participants in the focus group discussions were either in the *kebele* leadership or were its employees. However, those targeted were *kebele* employees in life-event services.

Data analysis

The quantitative and qualitative data that had been collected from *kebele* residents were analysed using different methods. There were four categories of this data: the first provided information about residents; the second targeted the level of ICT usage; the third focused on the level of e-local governance readiness; the last category had information on citizen-focused life-event services. The statistical tool used to analyse the data collected was CSPro 3.1, which is compatible with SPSS. Editing and coding, data entry and data analysis were managed by a statistician who had been employed for that purpose. Qualitative data were analysed by using thematic analysis and triangulation methods.

Developing and validating the prototype system

The prototype was designed for different purposes. In this respect, it can be used to do the following:

- identify and capture data that are required for future deployment of an automated system;
- demonstrate to the *kebele* employee, the *kebele* authority and the city government authority how a life-event service can be automated;
- motivate employees;
- identify the challenges and opportunities concerning the future deployment of an automated system;
- identify appropriate software tools and systems needed for the deployment of such a system;
- assess the interaction and communication requirements that involve the different units of the *kebele* administration and other administrative units of the city government.

For the purpose of validating the prototype system, the researchers consulted employees of the delivery section of the life-event service that was its target in one of the selected *kebeles*. The prototype can thus be said to be responsive to the current needs, requirements and functioning processes of life-event services. It is significant that after the system was developed, it was presented to more than 80 life-event service delivery employees of some 50 *kebeles* of the CGAA. The response of the employees revealed their high satisfaction with the quality and appropriateness of the system for the current needs of life-event service delivery.

Findings of the study

Respondent characteristics

Two-thirds or 66 per cent of the respondents were male while the rest (one-third) were women. Since the respondents were selected randomly, equal distribution by gender was not attained. This small imbalance did not affect the outcome of the research. The ages of the respondents varied from 18 to 68 years. It could be said that the sampling employed in the study represented the young, the middle-aged, the old, females and males.

Only 12.5 per cent of the respondents had a primary-level educational qualification or lower, while 87.5 per cent had secondary-level educational qualifications or higher. If this mix of randomly selected respondents somehow represents the population, then it could be expected that generally the majority of the *kebele* adult population are adequately qualified for ICT training. The criterion of employment status revealed that about 80 per cent of respondents were employees. Some 22 per cent of these were government employees, while the rest were employed in the private sector.

Kebeles and service delivery to citizens

When respondents were asked to mention the problems they observed during service delivery in *kebeles*, about 41 per cent complained that service delivery took too long. Staff shortages and the incompetence of employees, coupled with ethical concerns, were cited as the key impediments to service delivery.

About 83 per cent of the respondents who use the *kebeles* reported raising their complaints in person, while about 38 per cent said they complained in writing. Both means of complaining require the physical presence of residents and are time-consuming. ICT tools were not used at all to air the complaints of residents, which indicated another important area for the application of ICT. In response to the question of why people do not complain, it was found that complaints did not result in desired solutions, according to 23 per cent of the respondents. This suggested that there was a need to improve services and to design a mechanism for obtaining feedback on the quality of service delivery.

The problems reported by a majority of the respondents can be solved by introducing ICT-based applications for service delivery.

Kebeles and ICT

Discussions with *kebele* officials showed that on average there were four fixed telephones, seven computers, one radio and three televisions in each *kebele* that was studied. It also emerged that the *kebele*

85

offices had no mobile phones and fax machines. The study found, however, that the revenue administration unit used computers that had been automated and networked. The top officials also had computers. The remaining units of the *kebeles*, including life-event services, had none. The provision of a server would be helpful in the future expansion of ICT usage in the *kebeles*.

The study noted furthermore that the *kebeles* did not use ICT equipment for service delivery. It was the case nevertheless that, while fixed telephones were used for administrative tasks, televisions and radio sets were used to entertain the staff. Focus group participants reported that no computer training had been given to *kebele* employees, except for the case of employees in the revenue administration unit. Of greater concern, however, was the study's finding that there was no budgetary provision for the *kebeles* to acquire and use ICT equipment. This shortcoming required attention, since findings revealed that ICT equipment such as fixed phones, mobile phones and computers were rated as very important for the day-to-day activities of the *kebeles*. Though both *kebeles* rated the computer as one of the most important items of equipment for day-to-day activities, it was observed that at the time *kebeles* did not have electronic filing systems, email facilities and other ICT-based applications. Additionally, they did not have Internet connectivity or websites of their own. Furthermore, the computers available in both *kebeles* were not networked.

There are a number of life-event services offered in both *kebeles*. These services need to be updated frequently as they occur. According to the study, the services revealed the following characteristics:

- The registration and updating of life-event related data were initiated by both parties and required physical presence.
- Rules and procedures on life-event services were in place and were accessible to relevant staff.
- Both *kebeles* had mechanisms for staff to register concerns on life-event services and this was being done through direct reporting.

- There were preset standards that both *kebeles* maintained to ensure the quality of life-event services.
- Both *kebeles* had mechanisms to ensure that staff members involved in life-event services were held accountable for wrong-doings. In the event of the occurrence of wrongdoing or detection of malpractice, measures were taken that ranged from a written reprimand to dismissal.
- Both *kebeles* involved residents to some extent in the planning and monitoring of life-event services.
- When a *kebele* office wanted to contact a resident, it was done by letter.

The study concluded that there was no policy on ICTs that had been tailor-made for *kebeles* in a context where both *kebeles* had a short-term plan to offer ICT-based life-event services, particularly over the 2007–08 period. To achieve this goal, they would need to offer computer training to their employees.

In the study, 6 per cent of respondents reported that they communicated with *kebeles* by telephone, while about 92 per cent said they got received services by physically going to *kebele* offices.

Characteristics of ICT usage in *kebeles*

The following table shows the characteristics of ICT usage in the *kebeles* by equipment type, location and percentage.

From Table 4.2 it is evident that about 49 per cent of respondents used computers at home, at the workplace and at service centres. 15 per cent of those who used computers had access through service centres. Some 25 per cent of the respondents used the workplace as their point of access, while another 23 per cent gained access from home. In total, nearly 50 per cent of respondents had access to computers. It can be concluded from the available figures that more than half of the respondents had access to computers either at home, at the workplace or at computer service centres. This rate of computer access was encouraging, since it indicates that respondents possessed an adequate level of awareness that was necessary for the computer-based applications of e-local governance.

TABLE 4.2   Percentage distribution of respondents' access to ICT equipment

	Home		workplace		Service centre		Not used	
	(no.)	(%)	(no.)	(%)	(no.)	(%)	(no.)	(%)
Fixed phone	159	79.5	55	27.5	15	7.5	30	15.0
Mobile phone	152	76.5	38	19.0	2	1.0	42	21.0
Computers	45	22.5	49	24.5	30	15.0	102	51.0
Fax	5	2.5	21	10.5	10	5.0	165	82.5
Radio	188	94.0	2	1.0	—	—	12	6.0
Television	181	90.5	3	1.5	1	0.5	19	9.5

The table shows that access to the phone is more prevalent because 85 per cent and 79 per cent of the respondents had access to fixed and mobile phones, respectively. It is also significant that 94 per cent and 91 per cent of the respondents had access to the radio and to television sets, respectively.

It was also found that 53 per cent of the residents in the sample had taken some sort of training on computer usage. The training courses that were mentioned included MS-Windows, MS-Word, MS-Excel, MS-Access and MS-DOS. The availability of hundreds of computer training and service centres in Addis Ababa must have contributed to this result, as well as the fact that the country's school system had information technology (IT) courses. In fact, computer usage courses were offered in public and in private high schools and also in many of the private elementary schools. The researchers were not surprised, therefore, to find that about 59 per cent of the respondents felt they had either good or very good levels of competence in using computers. About 30 per cent felt that their competence was fair. If those judgements are taken as valid, the implication is that about 90 per cent of the respondents had adequate skills in using computers.

Other findings in the study showed that about 47 per cent of respondents had not taken any computer training courses. There were many reasons for this. The majority of respondents who had not taken computer courses (52 per cent) stated that it was not their priority. This may show the low level of ICT application in the day-to-day activities of residents. However, this may also mean that the introduction of ICT and its practical application could persuade this group of people to enroll for training, depending on certain factors.

In this respect, about one-third of the respondents who had not received any training also indicated that a lack of financial resources had prevented them from being trained in using computer packages. This group could be assisted by introducing free or low-cost training schemes at city government or *kebele* level, through Addis Ababa's NGOs. Creating free access to computers at community centres, as is the case in other developing countries, would be a motivating factor for many people. It would also support efforts aimed at introducing e-local governance applications. The barrier connected to the use of English in applications, as mentioned by some 12 per cent of the respondents, demonstrates the need for localised systems or for the development of systems with local language capabilities.

Status of e-Local governance readiness in *kebeles*

Measuring the e-local governance readiness of the administrative sector of the *kebeles* is very important. This objective was achieved by using the following e-readiness parameters: web presence, access to Internet, the level of ICT literacy of staff members and residents. The availability of telecommunications infrastructure was also considered to be important.

Human resources and access to the Internet are important indicators of e-readiness. The study found, on examining the criterion of qualification, that 8.5 per cent of the respondents in the sample were high-school graduates, while others in this bracket had higher qualifications. Those employed in the resident service unit of the

TABLE 4.3   Employment status distribution of respondents by access to Internet

	Yes		No		Not stated		Total	
	(no.)	(%)	(no.)	(%)	(no.)	(%)	(no.)	(%)
Government employee	23	11.5	12	6.0	10	5.0	45	22.5
Private sector employees	22	11.0	9	4.5	5	2.5	36	18.0
Self-employed	29	14.5	26	13.0	26	13.0	81	40.5
Not employed	14	7.0	12	6.0	9	4.5	35	17.5
Students	–	–	2	1.0	–	–	2	1.0
Retired	–	–	1	0.5	–	–	1	0.5
Total	88	44.0	62	31.0	50	25.0	200	100.0

kebeles had at least a high-school qualification. This suggests many of these employees can be trained in computer usage.

Table 4.3 indicates that 44 per cent of the respondents had access to the Internet. This is encouraging, since it makes it possible to use e-local governance applications: web-based registration of residents, web-based information dissemination and web-based service delivery.

The table also shows that there were no important differences in Internet access between those in public (51 per cent) and those in private (61 per cent) employment. However, those in the category of the self-employed had less access (36 per cent), possibly due to the nature of small businesses as well as to the fact that they probably required less technical knowledge and skills to run their businesses. In the case of the unemployed, 40 per cent had access the Internet, which suggested that young job-seekers had a reasonable level of IT awareness.

TABLE 4.4   Distribution of respondents with access to Internet by place of access

Interet access	no.	%
Home	17	19.3
Workplace	36	40.9
Internet cafés	60	68.2
University/college	2	2.3
School	1	1.1
Friends'/colleagues' workplace	1	1.1

Another important feature of access to Internet services in the case of residents was the contribution of Internet cafés. These had become the most important places for accessing the Internet (Table 4.4) and illustrated the participation of the private sector in creating access to ICTs. It is also encouraging that about 41 per cent of respondents indicated that they accessed the Internet from their workplace. This is a positive trend. It is also significant that about one-fifth of the respondents who had access to the Internet did so from home.

About 90 per cent of respondents used the Internet for email communication, according to Table 4.5, while about 55 per cent used it to access online resources. These are among the important services of Internet technology.

However, what is clearly worrying is the failure to use ICTs to obtain services from *kebeles*, the exception being the insignificant telephone communications. In fact, over 90 per cent of respondents stated that they communicated with the *kebele* through their physical presence, with only 6 per cent stating they used telephones. This shows a very low utilisation of ICT technology and the predominance of a time-consuming physical communication and service delivery method, depending on the distance of the residents from *kebele* offices.

TABLE 4.5 Distribution of respondents with access to Internet by reason for use

Reason for use	no.	%
Email	79	89.8
Online resources	48	54.6
Chatting	27	30.7
Have access, but never used it	4	4.6
To read news	1	1.1
Network marketing	2	2.3

Degree of importance of life-event services

Questionnaire responses show that the issuance of ID cards, the provision of housing information, the provision of unemployment and marital status letters were the most important life-event services that the *kebeles* provided to residents. Table 4.6 supports this conclusion. Most were in favour of automation to improve service delivery.

The frequency of residents' visits to *kebeles* to obtain life-event services was high. A significant proportion of the respondents made between one to four visits per month, although less frequent visits were also common. The significance of such contacts in terms of obtaining services partly depends on how long it takes. Frequent visits and long waiting times to receive the services are indicators of the inefficiency of the services. The percentage distribution of respondents by the average time it takes to obtain services shows that a majority of the services required at least one hour or more. Although mentioned by a smaller number of respondents, occasions arose that required waiting for days to receive services.

TABLE 4.6   Distribution of respondents by type of event service

Life-event service	no.	%
Issuance of ID card	195	97.5
Testimony on marital status	96	48.0
Testimony on unemployment	90	45.0
Housing	141	70.5
Tax services	1	0.5
Testimony on health fee exemption	2	1.0
Testimony on low income earner	2	1.0
Testimony on contributions	1	0.5
Testimony on school fee exemption	1	0.5
Money borrowing	1	0.5

Waiting can be reduced by using ICT to improve service delivery. For this to happen, life-event data on *kebele* residents will require updating. Respondents revealed in their response to a question on how long it took to effect a change in a life-event-related issue affecting a family that it takes up to a year or more. This was the case in 95 per cent of responses. The delay illustrates the difficulty in updating the records of residents to enhance reaction to a given problem on the basis of new information. It also appears that there is a great deal of resident data that is not known to the administrators in the *kebeles*. A number of factors may contribute to the presence of such gaps in the information chain between the residents and the *kebeles*. The absence of an established system for the exchange of such information might be one. The inadequacy of the system of reporting could be another.

Residents' level of participation in governance

Participation in governance structures is increasingly becoming an important issue. In the *kebeles*, committees represent a key decision-making governance organ. About 44 per cent of the respondents indicated that they did participate in decision-making at this level, while a similar percentage said they did not. In general, the figures show a high degree of participation, since it was not necessary for all people to become committee members. Overriding this observation is the fact that the important issue is whether or not the decision-making process in the *kebele* was generally participatory. There was scope for improving the level of participation in the *kebeles*' decision-making structures.

Responsiveness can also be viewed as another important measure of governance, since it indicates the readiness of the *kebele* administration to handle the demands of citizens speedily and sympathetically. The reaction speed of the *kebeles* in dealing with concerns needs to be improved. In fact, only 17 per cent of respondents felt that the *kebeles* reacted immediately. A quarter of respondents said they attended to concerns within a week, while a quarter indicated they did so within a month. 27 per cent of respondents held the view that the *kebeles* never attended to their concerns. On being asked to state how they communicated their concerns to the *kebeles*, 60 per cent of respondents indicated that they used suggestion boxes, while 50 per cent said that meetings were mechanisms through which they were able to forward their views. The study found that, on the whole, no ICT tools were used to express the views of residents on life-event services.

Requirements for e-local governance transformation in the *kebeles*

The following are the key factors for the successful implementation of e-local governance in the *kebeles*. The factors apply to different levels – the national, city government, *kebele* and residents' levels. The city government of Addis Ababa, due to its important national position, should take the lead in using ICT for good governance. In this regard, it should:

- facilitate use of ICT in line with national policy and strategy;
- support the *kebeles* to enhance their human capacity in the use of ICT for local governance and allocate the budgetary resources for ICT infrastructure and facilities;
- ensure that employees of *kebeles* have the required level of education and the basic knowledge on the use of ICT tools and computer applications;
- use a strategic approach and help to develop an ICT-based communication system in the administrative hierarchies of the city government;
- Promote the application of ICT-based service delivery to city residents.

The major requirements at the *kebele* administration level include:

- *Availability of trained service delivery personnel* who would be able to adapt to new technologies for effective delivery of services.
- *Employing staff with skills in using ICT* to improve efficiency and productivity. The study noted in this regard that the employment requirements for life-event service delivery did not include skills or experience in computer usage. As a result, almost all of the *kebele* employees had no training in the use of computers. This is a key factor in the effective implementation of e-governance. It should thus be an employment requirement.
- *Availability of ICT tools* to improve service delivery. The study has shown the inadequacy of ICT tools that can be used to provide services to citizens at the *kebele* or at local governance centres. Since they are key factors for e-local governance transformation, means should be found to acquire them.
- *Improvements in ICT infrastructure* to spur growth in the ICT sector. The poor ICT infrastructure at *kebele* level is a major hindrance to e-local governance since it requires the availability of Internet access, an adequate number of fixed telephone lines and a local area network.

- *Digital content development* Documents, rules, regulations and information needed by residents were found to be in paper format. Since computer-based applications require that these materials be presented electronically, digital content development is a critical requirement for an effective e-governance system.
- *Updating of basic data on residents* It was observed that most of the data on the residents are not up-to-date. In addition, there was no effective mechanism for acquiring reliable, correct and recent information (Atnafu et al., 2008). Since any incorrect information can lead to bad decision-making, establishing mechanisms for gathering up-to-date information on the residents is a major priority.
- *Business processing plans and guidelines* These should indicate avenues for achieving the following: increased participation of residents in the affairs of *kebeles*; strategies on the effective use of ICT for e-governance; policy on ICT usage; and training of *kebele* administrators on the use of ICT for e-governance.

At the *kebele* residents' level, the transformation to e-local governance would depend on the following requirements:

- motivation and awareness creation on the benefits of using ICT for service delivery;
- provision of community-based training on the use of ICT and ICT-based applications;
- identification and development of applications, after considering the most accessible ICT tools (such as mobile phones, fixed line phones, radio and television);
- identification of the most usable systems (email/mailing lists, web-based systems, SMS, WAP, etc.);
- creation of schemes for affordable access to ICT (computer, Internet, email, etc.);
- effective use of trained residents to champion the utilisation of e-local governance applications;
- using awareness-creation activities to highlight the value and importance of *kebele* offices to the lives of residents.

Towards an e-local governance functional model for *kebeles*

E-government model

A number of e-government models have been proposed in the available literature. These include the Israeli government's Merkava Project (Cresswell and Burke, 2006). This e-government model is aimed at enhancing or improving inter-ministerial communication in the Israeli government. The model needs to be made context-sensitive for it to be effective in other countries. The hybrid model proposed by Zhang et al. (2007) examines issues related to developing hybrid e-government projects that entail leveraging both online and offline channels to maximise impacts. Recently, the Ethiopian ICT Development Agency (EICTDA), in its national e-government implementation strategy, proposed a high-level e-government functional model (Dzidonu, 2006).

Proposed e-government functional model

The proposed e-government functional model for life-event services that are offered at the *kebele* offices has provisions for Ethiopian alphabets or for the Amharic language. It is in general designed to fit local needs and environments. It can also be viewed as a reference model that can be adapted to a particular e-government system by adding new layers (or features) or by enhancing the potential of the existing layers.

The two main target groups that can be distinguished in the proposed e-government functional model are the administration units of the *kebeles* and the residents. The proposed model is not limited to internal concerns of the *kebele* offices, since it also caters for external interactions between the offices and the public. The principal aim of the model, therefore, is to enable these offices to carry out daily operations speedily, transparently and effectively, thereby making the transition towards achieving good governance constructs.

The envisaged overall e-government functional model for the *kebeles* of the city government of Addis Ababa is represented in the six-layer functional model shown in Figure 4.1.

FIGURE 4.1   Proposed e-government functional model for the *kebeles* of the CGAA

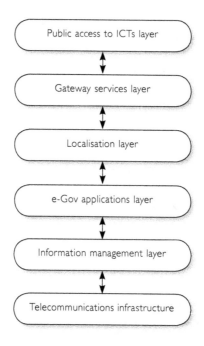

- The 'Public access to ICTs' layer represents the various means through which citizens or *kebele* residents can gain access to information technologies to obtain services online. To streamline the use of ICTs for citizen-oriented services, additional mechanisms to increase access to ICT need to be in place. This could be done by creating ICT access points in selected areas of the *kebeles*.
- The 'Gateway services' layer is the layer through which access to e-government applications is made possible. This is facilitated

through various ICTs tools that open access to citizen-oriented services from their respective *kebele*.

- The 'Localisation' layer is the model's answer to the requirement that e-government systems need to provide local language interfaces.
- ICTs can help *kebele* offices to streamline internal processes. Such functions would be in the domain of the 'E-government applications' layer.
- The 'Information management' layer deals with the management of information on residents. In addition, it would also deal with data recovery, backup and security (ranging from the obvious password protection to data encryption mechanisms).
- The 'Telecommunications infrastructure' layer has a critical function. This study revealed that currently *kebeles* only have LAN connectivity that is being used by those in the revenue section. However, to offer online services to citizens, a better telecommunications infrastructure, with wider geographical area coverage, is required. The infrastructure layer of the proposed e-government functional model can meet this need, since it is capable of establishing Internet, Extranet and Intranet connectivity. The Intranet connectivity is intended to improve the internal processes of the *kebele* offices, while the Extranet connectivity would handle the communication that takes place between the offices and other public bodies. Lastly, the Internet connectivity would target citizen-oriented service delivery.

In summary, these layers form the basic ingredients of an e-government functional model for the *kebeles* of the CGAA. However, the model does require changes in the institutional structures of the *kebeles*. These would be substantive and create an environment for good governance practices. In essence, therefore, the use of the proposed e-government functional model needs to be pegged to the availability of good governance constructs as prerequisites. In recent years there has been an ongoing effort to reform the operations of the *kebeles* (Government of Ethiopia, 2006b), which is a positive development for the proposed model.

The Kebele Life-Event Services System (KLESS)

This study contributed to the researchers' development of the Kebele Life-Event Services System, KLESS. The process of developing this prototype system covered three phases and had iterations in each. This factor ensured there was adequate user participation during its development. The prototype is a showcase for kebele employees, the kebele administration, and city government officials to see how e-local governance can be facilitated by deploying ICT-based solutions. This could motivate them to adopt ICT-based systems. There were indications that due to KLESS, the researchers had been able to persuade *kebele* officials of the importance of applying ICTs to improve the internal processes of their offices. The development of the prototype involved a number of initiatives.

One initiative was the use of several modelling techniques to capture the requirements for life-event service delivery. In addition, the researchers made use of certain modelling artefacts. This focus was supported by the effective use of subsystem decomposition, design interface specifications, persistence layer modelling and the subsequent mapping of the design specifications into a code through open-source development tools such as PHP and MySQL. The prototype system uses the open-source product Apache to run. Figures 4.2 and 4.3 are sample screenshots of what could be done through KLESS.

The researchers demonstrated the versatility of KLESS to *kebele* officials and employees. The demonstration was attended by more than 93 people, drawn from 50 of the 99 Kebeles in the CGAA. On this occasion, KLESS was warmly received. The demonstration convinced the government of the city of Addis Ababa that computerisation is important. Subsequently, after the demonstration, the city government launched a programme entitled 'ICT for Community'. The programme organised and sponsored the training of employees drawn from 55 *kebeles* in basic computer applications.

The research team had conducted three major awareness campaigns targeting both decision-makers and *kebele* officials, and

FIGURE 4.2   Screenshot for registering a *kebele* resident

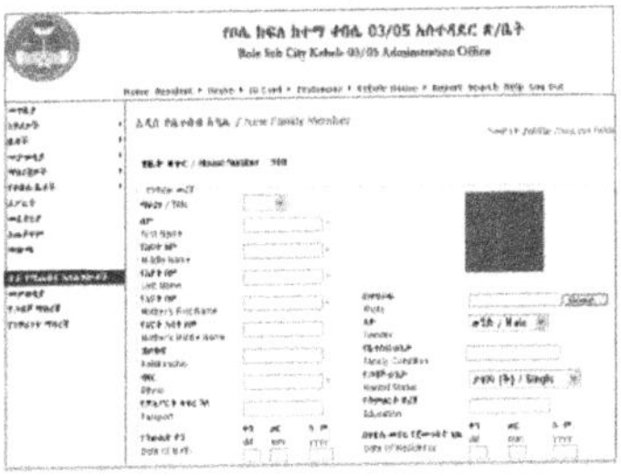

FIGURE 4.3   Screenshot for editing or updating information on residents

convinced them that the computerisation of life-events services needed to be preceded by training on ICTs. In addition, the city government requested that the researchers provide the source code and manuals so that they could start implementing the system. They also asked the research team to upgrade the prototype into an operational system ready for implementation. The team obliged. By the end of the research, the system had been installed in one of the *kebeles*. This is evidence that the research team had been successful in raising awareness that computerisation is important, that effects on governance after computerisation of life events were a worthwhile justification for automation, and that ICT training needed to precede computerisation.

Conclusions

The principal objective of the work reported in this chapter was to explore the *kebeles* of the CGAA in order to identify the relevant factors for a successful transformation to e-local governance in relation to life-event service delivery. The study identified the key factors for successful e-local governance implementation at the *kebele* administration level as well as at the residents' level. These need to be addressed by CGAA in the immediate future in the drive towards e-local governance.

The study has also demonstrated the potential of using ICTs for local governance purposes in the *kebeles* of the city government of Addis Ababa. In particular, the demonstration of the prototype KLESS system, along with the awareness created by the researchers that ICT training was critical, convinced the city government to carry out training and computerise life-events services. This shows the power of prototypes in convincing decision-makers to adopt e-governance systems.

Finally, the researchers developed an e-local governance functional model that is suitable for the *kebeles*. The study's KLESS prototype represents one way of localising a system for local needs. This model needs to be tested and its relevance established.

5

ICTs and financial management in Mavoko and Nyeri municipal councils, Kenya

Winnie Mitullah and Timothy Mwololo Waema

The local authorities (LAs) play a central role in local economic development in Kenya, although they face a number of challenges, one of which is the collection, storage and dissemination of information. Most of these authorities, like others in Africa, rely on manual, file-based information storage systems, with hardly any feedback and dissemination taking place. This study focused on information communications technology (ICT) in relation to financial management in local authorities, with the overall objective of assessing the influence of computerised financial management systems. Two LAs were used as case studies.

The LAs have a high demand for information services, which include: ICT training, Internet and email access, desktop publishing, word processing, printing and photocopying. However, the availability of these services is limited at the LA level. File-based information storage, which most LAs are using, is cumbersome and often not up to date. In isolated cases, where LAs have begun embracing ICT, it is limited to financial management and to secretarial word-processing services. Based on these facts, the study operated on the assumption that the adoption of full-fledged ICT services had the potential to promote and support routine business service needs. Its potential can also cover the promotion of trade and investment and be an avenue for joint planning and development cooperation in identified areas of interest. It is for these reasons that the study set out to interrogate the status of ICTs and local governance and identify the research priorities in this area.

Analysis in this research is based on data collected through case studies of two urban councils, Nyeri and Mavoko, which were in the first phase of the implementation of computerised Integrated Financial Management Information Systems (IFMIS). The study focused on how ICTs were being used to realise effective local governance at three main levels: that of the internal organisational processes; that of the provision of information and service delivery; and that of public interactions. It also looked at the constraining or enabling influence of other factors in the context of the study. These include the influence of the policy, legal and regulatory frameworks on local e-governance.

To ensure the presence of a seamless interface between its focus on these aspects and the pan-African conceptual framework detailed in Chapter 2, the study examined the linkages between e-administration, e-services and e-society in relation to the two municipal councils. This orientation was crucial in determining the overall objective of the study, which was to assess the influence of computerised financial management systems on local governance, based on the following constructs of good governance: participation, responsiveness, transparency, accountability, and efficiency and effectiveness. Of particular interest to the study was the investigation of:

- the scope, usage, successes and challenges of the automation of the financial management function in the LAs;
- the influence of the automated financial management systems on internal organisational processes, from the perspective of how the influence could result in improvement of accountability and transparency, reduction in the cost of financial transaction, and enhancement of overall institutional efficiency;
- the effects of an automated financial management system on access to information and service delivery, resulting in the following: ease of customer access to information; openness and

clarity in processes and procedures; equity in service delivery across income groups and other social variables; increase in the number of customers; effectiveness in service delivery; improvements in quality of service delivery; customer satisfaction;

• the effect of the automated financial management system on councils' interaction with stakeholders, especially from the angle of the information flow between the LAs and the following: residents; the business community; central government; civil society; and development partners.

The motivation for the study was the awareness that LAs face a number of governance problems, one of which is in their management of finances. In fact, financial management challenges affect virtually all the mandated services provided by local authorities. The poor financial management in LAs is largely due to their failure to document and track revenue collection and expenditure. This shortcoming has resulted in unpaid land rates and bills, and has been exploited by LA officials to deny essential services to consumers. It has in addition attracted corrupt practices as officers and consumers collude to distort bills and meter readings, as is the case with water supply. In most cases, the records are never readily available; and when they are available, they are often either difficult to access or incorrect. Honest consumers, who are in the minority, take months and even years to have their billing queries investigated and resolved.

In general, the least satisfactory area is the billing of services. To date, the use of electronic billing for certain services has led to some improvement in revenue generation and collection, as well as contributing to transparency and accountability. Although ICT programmes are in their infancy in a few local authorities in Kenya, it is assumed that the efficient use of ICT has the potential to reverse the trend of ineffective governance. This would bring about greater participation, transparency, accountability, responsiveness, effectiveness and efficiency. The study examines the validity of this assumption, with the ultimate goal of informing policy and practice not only in Kenya but also in the region.

Kenya has an e-government strategy that has been conceptualised largely at the central government level. Thus it is appropriate to assess the strategy's potential and applicability at the local level. It is also the case that LAs face serious local economic development and governance challenges which the use of ICT may resolve. Previous attempts to integrate ICT in local governance have worked in Kenya, with the introduction of IFMIS leading to better management and governance of public funds. This study was therefore expected to provide lessons relevant for the adoption of IFMIS across LAs.

The next section gives an overview of the ICT and local governance context in Kenya. This is followed by an account of the conceptual foundation of the work and its methodology. There is then a brief description of the study sites and a detailed presentation of the study's research findings and conclusions.

ICT and local governance context

National ICT context

The Government of Kenya recognised the importance of ICT in 2004, when it launched an ambitious three-year (2004–07) e-government strategy (Government of Kenya, 2004). The e-government strategy was designed to achieve a set of goals and objectives, namely: to deliver efficiently government information and services to the citizens; to promote productivity among public servants; to encourage participation of citizens in government; and to empower all Kenyans in line with the development priorities outlined in the *Economic Recovery Strategy for Wealth and Employment Creation 2003–07* (Government of Kenya, 2003).

The e-government priorities include: instituting structural and operational reforms; reviewing the regulatory and legal framework; developing a reliable and secure infrastructure. The priority activities and implementation framework over the immediate, medium and long terms have considered the following settings: government to government (G2G), government to business (G2B), and government to citizen (G2C). In the G2G setting, the strategy aims to expand the information infrastructure, initiate the integration of internal government processes, and increase the efficiency and effectiveness of internal operations in the short term. In the medium term (by 2007), the plans envisaged the completion of the information infrastructure within the government up to the district level, the development and implementation of web-enabled databases, and the operationalisation of other information systems that are currently being developed.

The e-government strategy also aims to establish electronic forums for discussion and feedback on issues in the G2B setting and ensure increased involvement of citizens in decision-making and in public activities in the G2C setting by 2007. Regrettably, the e-government strategy does not mention local authorities. According to the e-government permanent secretary, LAs were to be addressed through their parent ministry, the Ministry of Local Government. Unfortunately, the e-government strategy ended in 2007. Its achievements have since been evaluated and a draft strategy prepared to cover the next five years. By the time of completing this study, the next e-government strategy had not been officially sanctioned.

The Kenya government has been working on an ICT policy for several years (Waema, 2005). The past years have witnessed significant policy activity, marked by the finalisation of an e-government strategy, the issuance of a universal access report, the development of two ICT policy drafts, and, most importantly, the government's acceptance of the need for multi-stakeholder participation in the drafting process. The policy was discussed and approved by the Cabinet in January 2006 and an ICT policy document published in March 2006.

The national ICT policy (Government of Kenya, 2006) highlights the overall goal of e-government, which is to make the government more result-oriented, efficient and citizen-centred. The e-government strategy, in comparison, aims to redefine the relationship between the government and the citizens, with the objective of empowering them through increased and better access to government services. The broad objectives of e-government, according to the policy, are to:

- improve collaboration between government agencies and enhance efficiency and effectiveness of resource utilisation;
- improve Kenya's competitiveness by providing timely information and delivery of government services;
- reduce transaction costs for the government, citizens and the private sector through the provision of products and services electronically;
- provide a forum for citizens' participation in government activities.

It is hoped that the new e-government strategy to be launched will be consistent with the national ICT policy. The current strategy had been developed before the national policy, which was a demonstration of the failure to harmonise strategy and policy. It is also hoped that the new e-government strategy will highlight the role of LAs in delivering services to citizens and in effecting local social and economic development. Implementation of the Integrated Financial Management Information System (IFMIS) could be a key factor in improving service delivery.

The system is part of public-sector reforms aimed at improving not only the public sector but also local governance in Kenya. This factor is the reason for regarding the Kenya Local Government Reform Programme (KLGRP) as another face of public-sector reforms. One of this programme's notable components is the IFMIS, which is intended to improve financial management and revenue mobilisation in local authorities. The two case studies in this research, Mavoko and Nyeri Municipal Councils, were the first to benefit from IFMIS in 1999.

Since 1999, the implementation of IFMIS has been extended to six other LAs: Karatina, Embu and Eldoret Municipal Councils; Kiambu, Wareng and Kirinyaga County Councils. In these councils, IFMIS is used for all financial management activities. These include: billing and collection of all local revenues; preparation of payrolls; enabling of all expenditure controls; issuance of vouchers;

procurement; payment of statutory debts; project expenditure management. The financial administrative activities are linked through the budget monitoring system and generate a series of operational and management reports to assist in controlling, monitoring and managing all financial activities within the LAs. The IFMIS began as a national programme and was later broadened to include LAs, resulting in the Local Authority Integrated Financial Operations Management System (LAIFOMS).[1] The effect of this system on good governance occupies the major part of this study.

Local governance context

The Kenyan local governance system is composed of the Ministry of Local Government and the four tiers of LAs, namely: city, municipality, town and county councils. These councils are corporate entities that were established under the Local Government Act Chapter 265, which is currently under review. In addition to the Act, the LAs draw their legal powers from the constitution of Kenya, other Acts of Parliament, ministerial orders and by-laws.

While the legal foundation of local government in Kenya can be traced to statutory provisions, the reach of local governance in the country extends to provinces, districts, locations and sub-locations. These administrative units have technical staff drawn from various ministries. Apart from the ties between local government and the local governance system, there is in addition the overlay of various public and private institutions and the civil society organisations. Kenya has no decentralisation policy that rationalises power sharing, responsibilities and resources between the central government ministries, parastatals, District Development Committees, LAs and the civil society organisations. This factor has affected operations at the local level, and created a lack of synergy in institutional and organisational initiatives.

Few LAs are able to realise their mandate, because of the daunting nature of the challenges facing them. These include: expectations associated with service delivery and the management of infrastructural and financial resources; inadequate human resource capacity; inability to manage rapid growth; demands related to their institutional and legal framework. These challenges have resulted in poor service provision and poor management practices, with many analysts criticising the LAs and questioning their role in local development. It is such criticisms that provided the rationale for a re-examination of their role and subsequent launching of the LGRP. Not surprisingly, the pressure forced the LAs to embrace new forms of management, including adoption of computerised financial management systems.

Since the beginning of 1990, when the Government of Kenya began implementing structural adjustment programmes (SAPs), followed by civil service sector reforms in 1993, a number of reforms have been considered. In particular, there has been a deliberate attempt to decentralise governance by moving away from a centralised political system, where citizens hardly make any contribution in the management of resources, to a decentralised political system where input from citizens is viewed as critical to development (Rockcliffe-King and Mitullah, 2003). This shift has been reflected in attempts to review the constitution and the Local Government Act Chapter 265. While the country's constitution was passed in a 2010 referendum, the review of the Local Government Act has been on hold pending completion of the constitutional review process. On other fronts, refreshing signals for the reform agenda have been apparent in the review of various Acts of Parliament, the preparation of strategic plans by government ministries and parastatals, and the adoption of results-based management (RBM) by public institutions.

In 1996, a decentralisation initiative under the Local Government Reform Programme (LGRP) was launched. Its aim was to strengthen LAs. The programme was meant to achieve the following: rationalise central–local financial relations; improve financial management in LAs and assist in revenue mobilisation; strengthen citizen participation in planning and ownership of programmes. The programme recognised the importance of LAs in enhancing economic governance, in improving public service delivery, and in increasing economic efficiency, accountability and transparency (Government of Kenya, 1999). Recent reforms have led to the adoption of the following: Fuel Levy Fund; contribution in lieu of rates (CILOR); Rationalisation of User Charges; Single Business Permits (SBP); and IFMIS. The reforms are intended to help restructure the local public sector and, more importantly, strengthen local-level accountability mechanisms.

The KLGRP began with financial reforms aimed at enhancing intergovernmental fiscal transfers and improving financial management. The programme also targeted debt resolution and the streamlining of budgeting systems. Its other areas of focus included service provision and capacity building for LAs. A key instrument for the programme was the enactment of the Local Authority Transfer Fund (LATF) in 1998. The LAs began accessing LATF during the financial year 1999/2000. The Act provides 5 per cent of national income tax to LAs, based on the criteria of population density, resource base and financial performance.

In order to access LATF, LAs are administratively required to develop a Local Authority Service Delivery Action Plan (LASDAP) through a participatory approach. Disbursement of LATF funds depends on strict conditions, which if adhered to would not only improve financial management but also enhance accountability and the participation of citizens in the affairs of the councils. The LATF complements local authority revenue, which mainly comes from two sources: grants from central government and revenue from local sources. Local revenue includes user charges and taxes from local sources such as property rates, single business permits (SBP), plot rent, market and bus park fees. Water and agricultural cess, national reserve and park fees also serve as revenue sources.

Municipalities rely more on water and sewerage fees, property rates and Single Business Permits; while county councils and town councils rely on Single Business Permits, market fees, bus parks and cess revenue. Prior to the setting up of the LATF, there was limited sharing of resources with the central government. Apart from the LATF, grants from the central government to LAs also come from the Road Maintenance Levy Fund (RMLF) and the contribution in lieu of rates.

Conceptual framework, methodology and study sites

Conceptual framework

This study was carried out using the pan-African LOG-IN e-governance assessment framework, which uses various constructs of good governance, as detailed in Chapter 2. The Kenya study isolated six constructs of good governance: participation, transparency, responsiveness, effectiveness, efficiency and accountability. After that, the researchers developed outcome and output indicators for each of these variables to evaluate the implementation of the financial management system from the perspective of the following dimensions of e-government: computerised financial processes (e-administration); access to information/knowledge and service delivery (e-services); society interactions (e-society). Participation was the only good governance construct that the study assessed in the dimension of e-society.

Methodology

Secondary and primary data were used for the study. The secondary sources included relevant literature such as government and academic publications and reports. The primary information was drawn from surveys, key informant interviews and focus group discussions (FGDs). The survey data came from a sample of staff members of the two councils and consumers of their services. The key informants were drawn from both councils and the central government.

The study's quantitative data on LAIFOMS was collected through a standard information gathering template. A pilot survey was carried out between 26 February and 3 March 2007. This was followed by the main survey, which took place between March and May 2007. In total, 36 council staff questionnaires and 104 consumer questionnaires were administered. The information that was gathered through these methods was then triangulated by using outputs from key informant interviews and from FGDs with senior officers of the councils, councillors and consumers, as separate groups. The results obtained were used to draft a preliminary report that was presented at a stakeholder forum to corroborate the findings.

Questionnaires were analysed using Epidata 3.2, which generated basic frequencies for analysing the data. In addition, information from key informant interviews and the FGDs was thematically grouped and content analysis applied to synthesise the information.

Study sites

Nyeri Municipal Council (NMC) is a medium-size council with a population of about 110,000. It has a staff capacity of 323 members on permanent terms of service and room for 57 employees on casual terms. There are ten wards in the council. In comparison, Mavoko Municipal Council (MMC) is a comparatively young municipality, divided into five wards and located 30 km from Nairobi City Council. The council is large, covering 693 sq km, but with a population of only 48,936. The sources of revenue in these municipalities include: single business permit; bus park fees; market fees; house rents; land and plot rates; markets; development approval fees; transfers from central government in the form of LATF, Fuel Levy and CILOR. The major sources of the council's revenue are SBP and bus parks, although in terms of income flow they are the most fluctuating and unpredictable sources of revenue.

The Nyeri Council had full-time Internet access and LAN, which had been used to run its LAIFOMS. However, the network did not cover the entire town hall but only specific offices, including those of departmental heads. In Mavoko, the LAIFOMS operated through a 100 megabit per second (Mbps) LAN, which was able to serve all the offices at the town hall. Both councils began implementing LAIFOMS in 2000. The system handles budget monitoring, revenue collection and expenditure management, through system-based accounting codes. The application of LAIFOMS in the two councils had increased revenue collection and performance in both councils, according to the findings of the study.

General findings

Respondent characteristics

Background information on informants is important in analysing responses from any sample of respondents. Such information includes the gender, marital status, age and education levels of respondents. The study was conceptualised with gender as one of the social variables and covered almost equal numbers of women (54 per cent) and men (45.5 per cent). In Mavoko, equal numbers of female and male staff members were interviewed, while in Nyeri more women (58.3 per cent) than men (41.7 per cent) were interviewed.

Services in LAs are consumed by the entire population, and in order to get good information on consumers one needs to gather information from both genders. Since gender is an important variable in planning and in managing services, the application of ICT in communication and in service provision has the potential of lessening the time women take to seek information. For instance, if LAs can relay information electronically through mobile phones, residents – and in particular, women with multiple roles – can save on the time used to look for information.

The study found that the educational level of respondents was comparatively high. A majority of employees, 53 per cent, had a secondary-level qualification, while 34.8 per cent had tertiary (but non-degree) qualifications. Those with university-level education constituted 10.6 per cent of the sample. Only 1.5 per cent of the sample had primary education. There was nobody without some formal education. The case was slightly different for consumers, where 40.9 per cent had tertiary (but non-degree), 38.9 per cent secondary, 13.3 per cent university, and 5.9 primary qualifications; 1 per cent lacked any formal educational qualifications. The respondents' levels of education were higher in Mavoko, except for the case of those with tertiary non-degree education.

Women had comparatively lower levels of education. In fact, the 1 per cent that is indicative of respondents without any formal education from Nyeri represents responses from women. The same case applies to those with primary-level education, who with the exception of one male respondent were all women. Overall, the data indicate that respondents had high levels of education and thus implementing ICT programmes should not be a problem. The high level of education is a reflection of literacy levels in Kenya, where almost every adult citizen has received primary education, with a significant percentage having a secondary education qualification. Others have had some additional training in tertiary institutions of learning. However, the gender dimension of education raises certain concerns that require solutions.

Marital status also proved to be an important variable in examining the characteristics of respondents, and in determining the type of services individuals may require. In many cases, married people have more responsibilities and require more services in comparison with those who are single. In the sample, a majority of both staff members and consumers were married. In the combined sample of staff members in both Nyeri and Mavoko, 74.2 per cent were married, 18.8 were single and 7.6 per cent were separated. Most of the single respondents were women.

Use of ICT in local authorities

Although the history of ICT in Kenya dates back to the early 1990s, all those interviewed had good knowledge of almost all types of ICT. This was the same for both women and men. Among the nine listed ICTs, the mobile phone was known by all and used by over 90 per cent of respondents. CAD/CAM (computer-aided design/computer-aided manufacturing) was least known and least used. However, considering the specialised nature of this type of ICT, the 27.7 per cent who knew about it and the 15.3 per cent who stated they had used it demonstrate the central role of ICT in the country. In another study conducted in Kenya on micro- and small enterprises (MSEs), only 7.8 per cent of the study's sample of 105 entrepreneurs was familiar with CAD (Mitullah and Odek, 2002).

A further probe in the LA study asking the respondents whether they used ICT for communicating with their councils had a high percentage of positive responses from staff members (93.9 per cent) and a high percentage of negative responses from consumers (75.5 per cent). It also emerged that fewer women than men were using ICTs to communicate with their councils. Overall, the use of ICTs to communicate with councils was higher in Nyeri (34.6 per cent) than in Mavoko (26.3 per cent).

Another question on whether the staff of councils had access to a computer in their offices showed a high percentage of staff members did not (78.8 per cent). In the case of consumers, 75.4 per cent had no computers in their households. Computers are still out of reach for many Kenyans, including those in middle-class households. This implies that programmes aiming to use ICTs have to reflect on the cost of computers, including the availability of computer infrastructure.

Having access to computers in the office and at the household level is a requirement for ICT compliance. It enables workers and consumers to interact effectively with the councils and to provide inputs and feedback. Unfortunately, the findings show that most consumers do not have computers in their households and have to rely on cybercafés, which are expensive for ordinary Kenyans.

Participation and responsiveness

Participation in the activities of LAs is crucial for provision and management of services. The study shows that a high percentage, 81.8 per cent, of staff members and an average of 58.6 per cent of consumers were satisfied with the services provided by the two councils. From these figures, it would be expected there would be complaints from those who were dissatisfied with the services and compliments for the councils from those who were satisfied. The study revealed, however, that only 32.5 per cent of those dissatisfied had complained, while only 14.8 per cent had complimented the councils.

The study's assessment of whether respondents participate in council activities, and of the nature and effectiveness of such participation, was based on the following parameters: participation in LASDAP; participation in meetings called by social workers;

participation in meetings by the mayor/councillors, chief officers, residents; participation in clean-up activities. Findings reveal
that, in general, there was low participation in council affairs. A
significant percentage (47.8 per cent) limited their participation to
clean-up activities and to meetings called by residents (45.7 per
cent). Meetings called by social workers attracted the participation
of 37 per cent of those assessed, while those called by the mayor
and councillors had a 21.7 per cent participation rate. The other
figures were as follows: 19.6 per cent, 17.4 per cent and 15.2 per
cent of respondents participated in meetings called by departments,
LASDAP and chief officers respectively. This implies that there
is minimal interaction between councils and residents. Most of
the consumers appear to be disengaged and only participated in
clean-up activities and meetings called by residents. These meetings dealt with sanitation and security concerns.

The finding is a challenge to the ongoing LA reform programme, which has put in place a participatory framework, the
LASDAP, to encourage residents to participate in council affairs.
Its weakness may be inferable from its tendency to use representative stakeholders, who may not be providing feedback to those
they represent (Mitullah, 2004). This could explain the minimal
participation of residents in council affairs.

Participatory governance is inclusive and involves all stakeholders. Kenya is slowly emerging from the era of an autocratic
regime which did not encourage the participation of citizens. In the
past, participation was largely restricted to the election of leaders
every five years without any open dialogue and active civic engagement. This denied the residents of LAs a voice in the provision and
management of services. Currently, the LGRP tool of LASDAP
provides an avenue for involving residents in council affairs, since
its application is a precondition for accessing the LATF from
central government. To a great extent, the LASDAP process had
opened up opportunities for participation that are necessary for a
transparent and consultative approach to development.

When asked whether the participation of consumers made a
difference in the nature of service provision and management,

58.8 per cent said that it did. The findings further reveal that fewer women than men thought their participation had made a difference. A majority of these respondents were from Mavoko. In general, participation without inputs and feedback is not conducive to efficient management. Thus inputs and feedback from stakeholders are crucial for the effective engagement of residents in council affairs. As indicated earlier, the use of a representative stakeholders approach may be a contributory factor to ineffective participation, since they have no capacity to trigger an input feedback process.

On being asked whether they knew how councils obtained inputs and feedback from stakeholders, a majority indicated that they did. The positive response was higher, at 93.9 per cent, in the sample of staff members, as compared to 60.6 per cent in the sample of consumers. This outcome was not exceptional, since staff are privy to council affairs, in addition to being the implementers of council policies. Consequently, they are likely to give a positive answer, even in cases where they are not conversant with the method of securing inputs and feedback.

LAIFOMS implementation

In both councils, LAIFOMS modules to handle business permits, rates, miscellaneous billing, payroll management and expenditure management had been successfully rolled out, except for two modules needed for abstracts of accounts and final accounts. These were expected to be incorporated in the module on financial management. The inputs of this final module will be automatically generated from the other modules of LAIFOMS, and could not therefore be rolled out before all the other modules had been successfully implemented. In both councils, training had been done. Thus the users of specific operations were proficient in all modules.

In Mavoko Municipal Council, the One Stop Shop and the cash office were the major users. The council had not experienced any problems with the system and most staff and consumers were aware of the system. Awareness was higher in the sample of staff than was the case in the sample of consumers, with less than 50 per cent of consumers indicating awareness. The effect of LAIFOMS in both municipal councils was best captured by key informants, who noted that LAIFOMS had enhanced financial management, streamlined revenue collection and improved expenditure monitoring. It had also made the councils more transparent and accountable, thereby building trust between them and the residents. This has improved the participation of residents in council affairs. Overall, 98.2 per cent of staff and 94 per cent of consumers thought computerisation had improved the provision and management of services.

General effects of computerisation

Computerisation had significantly improved services to the customers and ensured the flow of information to departments. Staff in both councils indicated that services were efficient and that records were available in all departments. They also indicated that financial management had improved and that it was now easier to process and pay bills. In addition, they pointed out that staff could now achieve more in less time. Consumers were equally appreciative. They noted that the pace of service delivery had quickened, as reflected in timely billing and in enhanced financial transparency and accountability.

Computerisation was also found to have been effective and efficient in mobilising resources, as well as in planning, management, budgeting, billing and record-keeping. In all these areas, over 90 per cent of staff affirmed that computerisation had either been 'effective and efficient' or 'very effective and efficient', while the corresponding figure for consumers was much lower, at about 70 per cent. It is significant that neither staff nor consumers gave a high rating to the role of computerisation in improving communication with residents. This may be due partly to the lack of a website to provide information to consumers, or to the absence of public facilities for accessing information and services.

TABLE 5.1   Effects of LAIFOMS on participation

Indicators	Assessment of changes
Extent of internal participation in decision-making	*Mavoko* Decision-making on financial matters involved only the town clerk and the treasurer before computerisation. The rest of the staff in finance participated only in implementation. After computerisation, the process proved to be very consultative. The accountant and the audit clerk not only served as advisers, but actually participated in decision-making, especially on budgetary matters.
	Nyeri Like in many other councils, decision-making had been left to the town clerk, treasurer and the senior accountant before LAIFOMS. Departmental heads only had to submit budgets, which could be trimmed without consultation. They were involved in the whole process, and in cases where budgets have to be revised they are the ones requested to prioritise the needs of their specific departments.
Stakeholders involved in key council activities	*Mavoko* Before the introduction of LATF in 1999 there was hardly any participation of residents in the affairs of the council. Its introduction as a requirement for LATF opened up citizen participation in many ways. Most council activities that involved meeting residents were due to the LASDAP concept, which had enhanced participation. There were 'neighbourhood meetings' between council officers, councillors and stakeholders within close proximity of the council. These included large businesses operated by individuals, export processing zone (EPZ) authorities, and cement manufacturers. The companies supported council projects that assisted in alleviating poverty; for example, the opening up of roads leading to slum areas. One of the cement factories funded the town hall gate and also tarmacked the road that led to its manufacturing plant.
	Nyeri Unlike many other councils, Nyeri has always involved stakeholders in its development programmes, though in a very limited way. For example, in 1995 *Soko Mjinga* (market) was set up as a direct

Indicators	Assessment of changes
	consequence of discussions with stakeholders who raised funds for the project. The introduction of LASDAP as a requirement for LATF had enhanced citizen participation in council affairs. The LASDAP Committee visited every ward on set dates to discuss development matters with residents and their councillor. The composition of the meetings included individuals, business persons, organised groups and, at a later stage, development partners like GTZ and Constituency Development Fund (CDF) committee representatives. This was done to avoid duplication of development projects.
Disaggregation of individuals involved in key activities e.g. LASDAP	*Mavoko* There was very limited involvement by residents in council affairs before 1999 (i.e. before LATF). LASDAP topped the list of council activities that involved residents. There were meetings involving community development assistants (CDAs), and between education department officers and parents and others, organised when the need arose. The composition of these meetings depended on the issues to be addressed; e.g. for LASDAP, organised groups (women's, youth, church, etc.) were asked to send representatives. Actors such as community-based organisations (CBOs) were also represented, and a few individuals were selected to represent residents in various forums. One officer indicated that women were especially well represented, since they formed the bulk of most organised groups.
	Nyeri There was very limited involvement of residents in council affairs before 1999 (i.e. before LATF). LASDAP topped the list of council activities that involved residents. Stakeholders had become aware of the additional funding available to the council through LATF and demanded to know how the funds were spent. Lobby groups had been formed to represent the interests of residents. In 2007, a business lobby group demanded that the council streamline parking areas in the town, and a parking fee was introduced in February 2007, though suspended because the parking slots were not adequately marked. CBOs including women's groups, faith-based organisations, non-governmental organisations, individuals, youth groups and even sports groups were all involved in the activities of the council.

Indicators	Assessment of changes
Disaggregation of individuals with access to key financial services	*Mavoko* All stakeholders in the council had access to all financial services and information, which were available to any interested parties. With increased involvement of citizens in council affairs, there was a marked growth in interest in the council's financial performance.
	Nyeri Prior to LAIFOMS, fewer businesses were paying for their licences. Before computerisation, it was hard to send bills because information was not readily available. But at the time of the research the identity of consumers was known and their bills were being sent directly to them. Since LAIFOMS, accessing services has been made very easy. The key financial services were SBP and land rates.
Timelines for sending of specific reports to the Ministry of Local Government	*Mavoko* The major documents that are prepared by the council for submission to the ministry are the budget and quarterly financial reports. Before computerisation in 1998 it took five to seven months to prepare the budget, while the quarterly reports were never done on time. After LAIFOMS, even though budgeting was not done wholly using the system, it took less than two months. Budget preparation starts in mid-March. Discussion at provincial level must be completed by 15 May. The minister in charge must approve the budget by June. Initially, the budget would be approved after the beginning of the financial year in July. Whereas quarterly financial reports would always be late, with LAIFOMS they were always on time, since it only took only a few hours to run the data. This was because accounts could be adjusted automatically and cross-checked easily to reveal any errors. Preparation of monthly payroll used to take the whole month. Now, it took only a few hours, thus enabling staff to assume other responsibilities.
	Nyeri Quarterly reports used to be up to three months late. This meant that reports were always behind schedule by one quarter. Budget preparation used to take up to eight months. With LAIFOMS, it took two weeks to do the quarterly financial reports and about three months to prepare the budget.

Indicators	Assessment of changes
Turnaround time for sending bills to customers	*Mavoko* Before computerisation, no bills were mailed to customers. An advertisement was usually placed in the newspapers in October reminding residents to start paying bills for the following year. It took about four months to process the bills. With LAIFOMS, processing of bills was done in November and mailing began in December. By the beginning of January, most consumers had received their bills. The whole process took two months. *Nyeri* As in the case of Mavoko, before computerisation bills were sent to very few customers, since there was no up-to-date customer list. It took up to six months to process and deliver bills to the consumer. Subsequently, processing of bills was done in November and dispatching of bills in December. By the beginning of January, most consumers would have their bills. The whole process took just two months.

Effects of LAIFOMS on e-governance

Participation

The study revealed a number of changes in specific participation indicators brought about by the implementation of LAIFOMS, as reflected in Table 5.1.

A closer examination of different indicators of participation before and after implementation of LAIFOMS shows a significant change, as summarised in Table 5.2. It is evident that there was minimal participation before LAIFOMS was implemented in the two municipal councils.

Participation seems to have increased tremendously after implementation of LAIFOMS, in particular from the staff perspective. Among all the benefits of LAIFOMS, timeliness of processing and mailing bills to customers stands out. This was acknowledged and appreciated almost equally by staff (96.2 per cent) and consumers (88.4 per cent).

TABLE 5.2   Rating of different indicators of participation before and after implementation of LAIFOMS

		Communication with residents (%)	Participation of residents in municipality activities (%)	Interactions between council and residents (%)
Before	staff	8.0	4.0	6.1
	consumers	4.3	3.2	1.1
After	staff	81.1	80.7	75.0
	consumers	53.8	43.0	48.4

As reflected in the narrative in the previous section, most of the changes relating to participation of residents had been due to LATF and LASDAPs. However, the study found, through focus group discusssions, that the influence of LAIFOMS modules in relation to participation in the areas of business permits, rates, miscellaneous billing, payroll and expenditure had enhanced participation in both municipal councils. In both, LAIFOMS had made it possible to send bills to consumers on time. Consumers also paid their bills on time due to the penalty imposed for late payment. The same case applied to payment of rates. The residents now trusted the councils because all payments were receipted, and records properly kept. In addition, the preparation of payroll expenditure and the processing and issuance of cheques took a very short time, compared to the period prior to the implementation of LAIFOMS.

Responsiveness

The findings revealed that the implementation of LAIFOMS had increased the responsiveness of the councils to consumers. According to 85 per cent of staff and 70 per cent of consumers

TABLE 5.3   Rating of different indicators of responsiveness before and after LAIFOMS implementation

		Quality of service (%)	Customer satisfaction (%)	Timely receipt of bills (%)	Payment of bills (%)
Before	staff	4.0	4.1	6.1	4.0
	consumers	2.2	1.1	4.3	5.4
After	staff	80.8	76.9	78.0	82.4
	consumers	62.4	60.0	75.2	77.4

who had been interviewed, the following areas showed marked improvement: quality of service delivery; customer satisfaction with service delivery; timely payment of bills for services. A rating of staff and consumers based on different indicators of responsiveness, before and after implementation of LAIFOMS is illustrated in Table 5.3.

It is evident from the perspective of both staff and consumers that the criterion of responsiveness was poor before LAIFOMS was implemented in the two municipal councils. This criterion, especially when applied to the processing and payment of bills, had a higher rating after the implementation of LAIFOMS.

In both councils, the study revealed there were more users of LAIFOMS, specifically ten direct users and four trainees in Mavoko, and fourteen direct users and four trainees in Nyeri. The study estimated in addition that over 40,000 and 30,000 users in Mavoko and Nyeri respectively accessed computerized financial services. The number of complaints per month on financial services had also reduced due to proper record keeping, categorisation of businesses and proper billing. In Mavoko, the number of complaints had reduced from about 100 per month to 10 per month, while in Nyeri complaints had reduced from about 45 to

20 per month. Both councils had begun to get compliments from the public on the quality of their service delivery.

In both Mavoko and Nyeri, it used to take between 180 (Nyeri) to 270 (Mavoko) days before some bills could be serviced, with some even remaining without service altogether because it was almost impossible to keep track of all payments. That was no longer the case. In both councils, bills that had been sent out in December had 31 March as the deadline for payments, with a penalty thereafter on any late payment, resulting in prompt payment. On the whole, the degree of satisfaction with services provided through LAIFOMS was very high, with consumers observing that LAIFOMS had tremendously improved financial management.

The respondents also indicated that the issuance of business permits hardly faced any delays, unlike previously, when it used to be a major source of complaints. In addition, the study observed tremendous improvement in revenue collection, especially those requiring miscellaneous billing. This was not a surprise, since instances of revenue collectors' failure to remit all collected revenue had reduced remarkably. More residents were also making payments for rates, against a backdrop of improvements in payroll management, due largely to LAIFOMS, as it had enabled all expenses to be monitored in real time, making it possible to reduce unauthorized payments.

Transparency

Transparency is not an easy variable to assess. In doing so, the study used the following indicators: documentation of financial policies and procedures; feedback from residents; information accessibility, including accessibility of budgetary, supply and tender information; instances of corruption cases in procurement; openness in the tendering process. Both staff (95 per cent) and consumers (80 per cent) indicated that computerisation had had a positive effect on transparency. Members of both councils felt that the councils had become more transparent and accountable to residents because of

TABLE 5.4   Changes in transparency following implementation of LAIFOMS

Indicators	Assessment of changes
Financial policies and procedures documented	*Mavoko and Nyeri* There were no financial processes documented and shared locally at the councils as a result of LAIFOMS implementation.
Feedback from residents	*Mavoko* Before computerisation in 1998, there was hardly any feedback from residents. Residents did not know what to expect from the council (e.g. when street lights were not working, they complained to Kenya Power and Lighting Company, yet they were supposed to raise the matter with the council). With computerisation and improvement in communication (Mavoko had telephone extensions installed in every office, including the boardroom and the office at the gate); there were many channels for feedback. A customer-care desk had been set up at the entrance of the town hall and was a major source of feedback. Most complaints were reported at the gate in person or by telephone. Another major source of feedback (about 80 per cent) was at council counters as residents made payments.

Nyeri   Before computerisation, the level of feedback was very low at around 20 per cent. This was mostly from organised lobby groups that understood the operations of the council. Due to activities like LASDAP, feedback had improved at an estimated rate of 50 per cent. Most feedback was through complaints, which the council, in collaboration with councillors, responded to at ward meetings. |
| Access to information (budget, supply, tender, etc.) | *Mavoko and Nyeri*   Before 1997, the only way residents could access information about the budget and tenders was through the newspapers. This meant that access was very limited, as very few residents read newspapers. During the study, information on the budget was published in the newspapers and posted on notice boards around the municipality. Any interested persons |

Indicators	Assessment of changes
	could obtain the complete document from the council for a minimal fee. Tender documents and any other related information were also posted on all public notice boards. Residents' involvement in council affairs through the LASDAP process had improved their understanding of the budget. However, full engagement of residents in council affairs was still wanting.
Corruption cases in procurement	*Mavokoi* There had been only one reported case of corruption (1998). This involved a member of staff who had purchased pipes worth Ksh 30,000 and was given a bicycle in appreciation of the purchase. This may be viewed as corruption, although in the view of the respondent it was not. According to staff interviewed, there had been no other corruption case reported in the whole council.
	Nyeri According to staff interviewed, there had been no reported case of corruption in procurement. The process was well organised and managed. Any complaints arising could be from disgruntled suppliers, but the process was very open.
Openness in the tendering process	*Mavoko* According to staff interviewed, the tendering process of the council was very transparent and clear. Though previously it may have been corrupt, under current directives from the Ministry of Local Government all major tenders had to be advertised in the leading newspapers. There were always complaints, however, since most of the time whoever misses out on a tender suspects foul play. The process was currently 100 per cent open.
	Nyeri According to staff interviewed, the tendering process was very open. There had been no cases of corruption. One respondent noted: 'Let's say it is 99 per cent open, while it might have been 90 per cent open before computerisation.'

TABLE 5.5   Rating of different indicators before and after
LAIFOMS implementation

		Transparency in council operations (%)	Financial transparency of the council (%)	Access to budgets and other financial information (%)	Clarity of financial processes (%)
Before	staff	8.0	8.0	8.1	4.1
	consumers	3.2	0.0	3.2	1.3
After	staff	77.4	88.7	86.8	76.5
	consumers	64.5	64.0	51.6	60.3

the use of computers. Table 5.4 summarises the information on changes following the implementation of LAIFOMS.

Staff of both councils, were overwhelmingly (100 per cent) in agreement that computerisation had improved financial transparency. However, consumers were not as confident as staff; 75 per cent and 53 per cent in Mavoko and Nyeri Municipal Councils, respectively, acknowledged that computerisation had had a positive effect on transparency.

As an illustration of the effects of the implementation of LAIFOMS on transparency, Table 5.5 shows staff and consumer ratings of different indicators of transparency before and after the implementation of LAIFOMS.

It is evident that there was hardly any transparency before the introduction of LAIFOMS, as highlighted by the zero indicator of consumers. The assessment shows a dramatic change with the implementation of LAIFOMS. It is also remarkable that the rating of consumers is lower than that of staff, with only about 50 per cent sharing the view that there had been improvement in access to budgets and other financial information.

The study's assessment reveals that transparency had been enhanced and that the issuance of business permits was consistent and based on straightforward procedures in both councils. The same conclusion applied to rates. These had a unique property number, which had made their calculation consistent and easy, while billing was tightly controlled, because all payments had to be receipted. Overall, it was almost impossible to incur expenditure without approval and reports were easily generated, thereby blocking any underhand dealings, which previously were common.

Accountability

Accountability was measured mainly by using indicators of the number of reports generated per year and of the number of people accessing such reports. While the number of reports generated per year had increased, the number of persons accessing such reports remained the same. However, the study shows that reports of both councils, including budgets, were more readily available, not only to council staff but also to proactive residents. The improvements can be attributed to the Revenue Enhancement Plan, and to the LASDAP process, which had stakeholder forums for exchanging information on council affairs.

Some 90 per cent of staff thought that LAIFOMS had improved council accountability to residents, with Mavoko Municipal Council having a higher (96 per cent) proportion of staff holding this view. The corresponding overall figure for consumers dropped to 71.6 per cent, with Mavoko having a higher (74.4 per cent) proportion supporting the view that LAIFOMS had improved accountability to residents. The overall effect of computerisation on accountability is shown in Figure 5.1.

Improvement in accountability in the two councils reflects a trend that is similar to the improvement in financial transparency. The data on the period before the implementation of LAIFOMS shows that only 8 per cent of staff and zero per cent of consumers

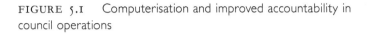

FIGURE 5.1   Computerisation and improved accountability in council operations

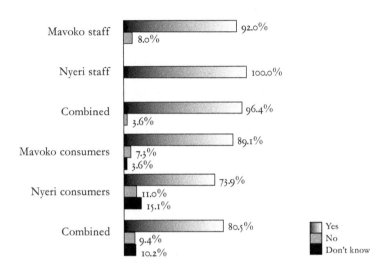

rated accountability in council operations as 'excellent' or 'good'. After the implementation of LAIFOMS, the figures for staff jumped to 92 per cent, in the combined rating for 'excellent' and 'good', while for consumers the corresponding rating stood at 64.5 per cent. It is therefore evident that the implementation of LAIFOMS had a tremendous effect on accountability in the operations of the two councils.

Efficiency and effectiveness

LAIFOMS had contributed remarkably to efficiency and effectiveness in both councils. All financial information was captured in the system and the budget was closely monitored. The turnaround time from lodging payment requests to actual payment – which used to be long and cumbersome, taking between 30 and 60 days – had reduced due to the use of an efficient payment management system. In addition, standard financial reports, such as budgets, balance sheets and reconciliation of accounts, were now generated by the system.

Key informants revealed that revenue collection in Mavoko had increased significantly, with the proportion of outstanding debt collection jumping from 30 to 85 per cent, as the council could easily track debtors. The council's revenue had also increased from Ksh 38,813,000 during the 1998/99 financial year to Ksh 134,334,036 during the 2004/05 financial year. This growth was due to increased efficiency in revenue collection, brought about by the implementation of LAIFOMS. In this regard, as an example, the streamlining of revenue collection through LAIFOMS had ensured the inclusion of small income streams, which were monitored, unlike in the past, when such income remained uncollected and/or poorly documented.

Although Mavoko Council had experienced an increase in efficiency and effectiveness, not all improvements could be attributed to the implementation of the financial management system. The indicators that can be attributed directly to LAIFOMS include increased revenue collection, increased outstanding debt collection, reduced turnaround time from lodging payment request to receiving payment and increased payroll accuracy.

Overall, most of the staff (96 per cent) in both councils thought computerisation had improved the efficiency and effectiveness of the councils' operations. Consumers were less positive (82 per cent) than staff (96.4 per cent) on this issue. Furthermore, the staff of both municipal councils agreed (100 per cent) that LAIFOMS had enhanced the financial management of the councils. A high percentage (90 per cent) of consumers also agreed that this was the case.

In its assessment of staff and consumer perception of the level of enhancement, the study found that 96 per cent and 89.3 per cent of the staff in Mavoko and Nyeri municipalities, respectively, thought the level ranged from 'enhanced' to 'very enhanced'. The corresponding figures for consumers were 56 per cent and 51 per cent respectively for Nyeri and Mavoko.

TABLE 5.6   Effect of different indicators of efficiency and effectiveness

	Staff			Consumers		
	Mavoko (%)	Nyeri (%)	Comb. (%)	Mavoko (%)	Nyeri (%)	Comb. (%)
Paying bills at council counters	100	89	94	86	92	88
Effective and efficient delivery of services	96	86	91	79	84	81
Increased productivity of finance staff	96	82	89	63	76	70
Reduced cost and time of accessing services	100	89	94	88	86	87
Overall financial management	88	86	87	70	72	72

Table 5.6 summarises the responses of staff and consumers, who acknowledged that the implementation of LAIFOMS had positively affected different indicators of efficiency and effectiveness. From these responses, staff and consumers in both municipal councils overwhelmingly agreed that the implementation of the financial management system had positively affected different indicators of efficiency and effectiveness.

The effects of the implementation of LAIFOMS on efficiency and effectiveness, using different indicators of efficiency and effectiveness before and after LAIFOMS was implemented, are summarised in Table 5.7.

TABLE 5.7 Rating of efficiency and effectiveness indicators before and after LAIFOMS implementation

	Before		After	
	staff (%)	consumers (%)	staff (%)	consumers (%)
Mobilisation of resources	8	2	84	66
Planning	12	1	81	57
Management	12	1	84	55
Budgeting	4	1	79	48
Processing of bills	4	3	87	83
Billing	6	4	87	80
Record-keeping	4	3	81	73
Efficiency and effectiveness	8	2	85	61

From the table, it is clear that staff and consumers held the view that the efficiency and effectiveness of the councils were very low before LAIFOMS was introduced. In addition, staff overwhelmingly acknowledged that there was a tremendous change in efficiency and effectiveness after the implementation of LAIFOMS. Consumer rating of the more internal aspects of efficiency and effectiveness was 50 per cent. They were very specific that billing processes and record-keeping had significantly improved.

Overall, LAIFOMS had enhanced effectiveness and efficiency in managing business permits, rates, miscellaneous billing, expenditure, as well as the payroll, in both councils. In addition, more businesses and properties had been registered and more clients looped into the councils' databases. This had resulted in a marked increase in revenue collection, with staff being able to concentrate on other council affairs, instead of dealing with the tedious work of payroll preparation. Both councils had also reduced unauthorised expenditure and corrupt practices.

Challenges of LAIFOMS

The implementation of LAIFOMS had not been without challenges, a number of which had been experienced in each of the good governance areas. In the area of participation, a major challenge remained the educating of residents on the mandate of the councils. This has the potential of exposing residents to council requirements on business permits, on payment of rates and on miscellaneous billing. With regard to the module on expenditure management and payroll, there was an initial scare that non-computer-literate staff would be dismissed or redeployed, but this did not happen.

In the case of transparency, the misconception by consumers that councils were always corrupt had been problematic. This view was slowly weakening, as the councils opened up and shared information with consumers. Consumers still held the perception, however, with reference to accountability, that councils misappropriated funds, while the feedback given on responsiveness suggested there was room for improvement. Delays were reported to occur due to data entry mistakes, rather than because of system failure. As for efficiency and effectiveness, the failure to implement all modules, especially that on Abstracts of Accounts, had reduced the level of efficiency. Once implemented, it would serve to increase efficiency in financial management.

Conclusions and recommendations

Conclusions

LAIFOMS implementation   Five of the seven LAIFOMS modules had been successfully implemented in both municipal councils, although neither had an ICT department or ICT staff. Nyeri

Municipal Council had employed a new programmer/system analyst to assist in implementing the new computerised system. In both councils, finance department staff acted as system administrators for the computerised financial management system. Awareness of LAIFOMS in the two municipalities was very high in the case of staff and relatively low with regard to consumers. Overall, staff from both councils felt strongly that LAIFOMS had improved financial management and enhanced service provision to residents.

General effects of computerisation　　Most staff and consumers agreed that computerisation had improved the provision and management of services. The key areas where computerisation had the greatest effect were in making information available to departments, possibly to support decision-making, and in improving services to customers. Neither staff nor consumers rated the role of computerisation in improving communication to residents as highly as the other service areas. This may be partly due to the lack of a website to provide information to consumers, as well as the lack of public facilities for accessing services and information.

Effect of LAIFOMS on participation　　Internal participation by staff as well as participation by residents increased in the period following the introduction of LAIFOMS in both municipal councils. However, the tremendous increase was largely attributed to the introduction of LASDAP, as a requirement for LATF, rather than to the implementation of LAIFOMS.

Effect of LAIFOMS on responsiveness　　On the whole, the implementation of LAIFOMS had increased the responsiveness of both councils. For example, the system had hastened the issuance of business licences. The study also found there were fewer errors in payroll processing and that expenses were being monitored in real time. In Mavoko, about 61 per cent of consumers had access to finance information generated by LAIFOMS, compared to 32 per cent in Nyeri. In addition, the number of complaints went down by a factor of ten in Mavoko, while in Nyeri the number dropped by around 50 per cent. Most complaints were associated with errors in billing and with delays in the issuance of business permits, which LAIFOMS reduced drastically. After LAIFOMS, customer satisfaction levels were relatively high, as inferable from the low number of complaints. Finally, implementation of LAIFOMS had improved the timeliness for preparing documents required by the Ministry of Local Government and the councils. For example, the time to prepare budgets had been reduced from between five to eight months to between two to three months, while the preparation time for quarterly reports had been reduced from months to a few days or even hours. The turnaround in the processing and mailing of bills to customers had been reduced from six to two months, following the roll-out of LAIFOMS. In addition, the number of customers receiving bills rose steeply, because the system has an up-to-date list of consumers. This had in turn increased council revenue collection.

Effect of LAIFOMS on transparency   Overall, staff and consumers in both councils agreed that the implementation of the financial management system had led to increased transparency. For example, the system had facilitated all payments to be receipted and the issuance of business permits to be transparent, consistent and straightforward. It had also rendered unapproved staff overspending difficult and reduced corrupt practices. Although the staff in both councils were unanimous that computerisation had improved financial transparency, consumers were not so confident. Whereas 75 per cent and 53 per cent of the staff in Mavoko and Nyeri municipalities, respectively, agreed that computerisation had a positive effect on transparency, in contrast only about 50 per cent of consumers held the view that there had been improvement in access to budget and other financial information. This suggests there is work to be done to improve perceptions on the transparency of the councils.

Both councils had in the last few years experienced increased feedback from residents, but this could not be associated with the implementation of the financial management system. As was the case with participation, the increase in feedback could only be associated with the implementation of LASDAP. Openness in the tendering process had increased in both councils in the recent past, but this can be associated with the implementation of public procurement guidelines, under the direct supervision of the Ministry of Local Government, rather than with the computerisation of financial functions.

Effect of LAIFOMS on accountability   In general, staff and consumers in both councils agreed that the implementation of LAIFOMS had enhanced accountability. In this connection, the system had enabled all business permit licences to be tracked very easily. The councils were also able to keep a record of all properties they possessed, since each property possessed a unique identification number. Furthermore, revenue collection was monitored and employee payrolls tracked to ensure there were no ghost workers. Moreover, there was tracking of all payments made by the councils from the time they were authorised to the time they were received. The study also observed an increase in the number of reports on the effectiveness of internal control systems in Mavoko Municipal Council. However, this increase was attributed to the introduction of the Revenue Enhancement Plan and LASDAP, rather than to the introduction of LAIFOMS.

Effect of LAIFOMS on efficiency and effectiveness   Staff and consumers in both councils acknowledged that the implementation of LAIFOMS had enhanced financial management and the efficiency and effectiveness of the councils' operations. For example, the system had enabled a marked increase in revenue collection and more business registrations, given the ease of issuing business permits. This had resulted in increased revenue from rates and an expanded customer base. There had also been an increase in staff productivity. Consumer rating of the internal aspects of efficiency and effectiveness indicated that about 50 per cent felt these aspects were 'excellent' or 'good'. They strongly maintained that billing processes and record-keeping had improved significantly. Mavoko had experienced an increase in efficiency and effectiveness, although most of it could not be attributed to the implementation of the financial management system alone. The indicators to be directly associated with LAIFOMS include increased revenue collection, increased outstanding debt collection, reduced turnaround time from lodging payment request to receiving payment, and increased payroll accuracy.

Recommendations

Given the tremendous effect of the implementation of LAIFOMS on good governance in the two municipal councils in Kenya, it is makes sense to roll out LAIFOMS in other local authorities in Kenya and share its benefits across the region. The Ministry of Local Government is best placed to take charge of the roll-out, due to the limits on resources in local authorities. In addition, completion of the roll-out of unimplemented modules should be done to enable local governments to carry out all the financial functions electronically. Some functions are still carried out manually, leading to non-optimal realisation of the benefits of automation.

In addition, service provision and availability of access to information through a website should be used by municipalities to enhance the quality of their services to customers and other stakeholders. The roll-out of an Integrated Financial Management Information System in central government has met many challenges and has generally failed to meet its objectives. Thus the central government should study the implementation of the same system in some of the more successful local authorities and draw relevant lessons. In essence, this suggests that the more complex e-government applications could initially be tried in local government before being rolled out in central government, taking account of lessons learned.

Note

1. LAIFOMS is a computer-based system that integrates financial and operational activities involving business transactions in a local authority. The system has three main components: revenue, budgeting and financial management, and expenditure. Each component is integrated with the others to create a comprehensive system to monitor all operational activities (Government of Kenya, 2007).

6

Revenue management systems in municipal and district councils in Mauritius

Taruna Shalini Ramessur
and Hemant Birandranath Chittoo

Research context

Government system and policy

Mauritius has developed from a low-income economy to a middle-income economy in a relatively short time. The economic growth enjoyed by the country over the past two decades was sustained by four main pillars: agriculture, manufacturing, tourism and financial services. Recently, the government has been giving high priority to the development of the information and communications technology sector to transform the country into a cyber-island. The ICT sector is set to give way to a knowledge economy (ADB, 2004). ICT sub-divisions such as information technology enabled services (ITES) and call centres have now become main employment- and investment-generating sectors.

Good governance is a critical concern om the island. Given that one of the principles of good governance is to safeguard the fundamental rights of the citizen, the government has placed emphasis on customer-oriented activities and service delivery. In this regard, the Ministry of Civil Service Affairs and Administrative Reforms has taken several initiatives (ADB, 2004). These include the introduction of a Customers'/Citizens' Charter as a written commitment to provide services according to set standards, and also to inform customers of their rights to good service. There is also a 'Code of Ethics' to promote ethical conduct and to sensi-tise public officers on their roles, responsibilities and obligations in interacting with customers. Moreover, there is ongoing training for customer care in several ministries/departments to improve the skills of the front, middle and back office staff. This will help to reduce queuing and response time and also provide a congenial environment for the public.

Civil society and the private sector have also played and con-tinue to play a critical role in sustaining the progress of gov-ernance in Mauritius. For instance, in the implementation of e-government projects, the private sector, professional associations and non-governmental organisations (NGOs) play an important role. Examples of this partnership can be seen in projects such as the Servihoo Portal, which is intended to be the portal for the Republic of Mauritius. It is essentially a Telecom Plus initiative that provides personal email hosting, interactive chat, electronic greeting cards, e-commerce sales, forums, polls and a guest book. Another initiative is Virtual Mauritius, an e-commerce platform to sell services, including online shipping, real estate, insurance and entertainment. Finally there is the Virtual Appeal Clip, managed by an NGO, which focuses on skills training, using ICT to create a new generation of a creative and productive workforce from marginalised and illiterate children.

According to the World Audit Organization, Mauritius is the third highest ranked developing nation in terms of democracy, and the country also ranks high on the World Bank's governance indicators with values higher than for sub-Saharan Africa. This rapid economic growth can be attributed to several factors, namely sound and responsible macro-economic management, backed by a stable political system and a dynamic private sector. The island also enjoys cordial public–private-sector relations, a functioning legal system, a well-developed transport and communications infrastructure, reliable air and sea links, an attractive fiscal regime and a cohesive multi-ethnic society.

Local governance system

Local Government in Mauritius dates back to 1790, but is still subject to tutelage. According to the Local Government Act 1989 (Act No. 48), amended by the Local Government Act 1992 (Act No. 30), the local authorities fall under the responsibility of the Ministry of Local Government and Solid Waste Management.

Local government institutions comprise five municipal councils in the urban areas, and four district councils with a lower tier of 124 village councils in the rural areas. Local elections in urban areas have been conducted on the basis of full adult suffrage since 1956. That of 1962 was to elect village councils. All municipal and village councillors are directly elected. Village councils are organised under district councils. They have the mandate to select district councillors. However, it is disappointing to note that the level of democratic participation in elections is always very low in terms of voter turnout for local elections. This suggests there is lack of democratic interest among the public, despite the fact that local authorities are close to citizens. They are also well placed to provide basic sanitation services, as well as social and welfare services.

The Local Government Act 2003 was meant to give local authorities greater autonomy and responsibility in development matters. Additionally, it was expected to empower the local population by giving them a voice in the management of the affairs of their respective regions. The Act provides a basis for restructuring procedures to enhance efficiency in service delivery and for ensuring accountability and transparency in the day-to-day running of local authorities. This objective requires local authorities to 'play a more proactive role in combating poverty, improving the quality of life, and developing appropriate structures for the promotion of sports, cultural and welfare activities' in their areas. Unfortunately, the Act has not been fully implemented, though steps are being taken to introduce a new Local Government Act to replace that of 2003. This initiative follows the will of the government to transfer more autonomy to local authorities and allow community participation in the affairs of local councils.

National ICT policy and e-government strategy

The Mauritian government has long recognised the importance of ICT in public administration. That is why a data-processing division was created in the Ministry of Finance as far back as 1970. Five institutions were subsequently established in the late 1980s to promote the use of ICT in government. These were:

- the National Computer Board (NCB, http://ncb.intnet.mu);
- the Central Informatics Bureau (CIB, http://ncb.intnet.mu/cib.htm);
- the Central Information Systems Division (CSD, http://ncb.intnet.mu/cisd.htm);
- State Informatics Limited (SIL; http://sil.intnet.mu);
- State Informatics Training Centre Limited (SITRAC).

Institutionally, the ICT sector is guided by the Ministry of Information Technology and Telecommunications (MITT) and umbrella statutory bodies such as the National Computer Board (NCB) and the Information and Communication Technology Authority (ICTA). The synergies created by these institutions over the years have resulted in the formulation and implementation of various projects, the major one being the Civil Service Computerization Programme (CSCP). Initiated in 1989, the CSCP continues to computerise ministries and government departments.

The government has been paving the way to e-government through numerous projects. These include the Government on the Internet project, a portal to all ministries/department websites, initiated in 1996. There is also the Tradenet project, which has been operational since 1994 under the Ministry of Finance. It allows the Customs Department to authorise electronically the delivery of goods. Through the project, it is also possible for shipping agents to submit electronically sea manifests and process bills of entry. In addition, it has proved efficient in the transfer of containers. Other initiatives include the Government Email Services project, launched in 2001, which has provided 2,620 senior officers with email accounts. About 20,000 civil servants (out of 55,502) have been trained in office automation applications related to specific activities. Government employees can in addition obtain loans, made possible by the government, to facilitate the purchase of PCs for home use (eUser, 2004). To complement these efforts, the Government Online Centre (GOC) was initiated in the same year by the National Computer Board (NCB) to create a 'connected government' through which ministries and departments will communicate and work together for better delivery of governmental services.

The government has also taken certain measures to address the regulatory and legal framework for ICTs. In this regard, several bills have been drafted, and with the passing of the Copyright Bill at the National Assembly in July 1997 the legal challenges posed by the use of ICTs are bound to be reduced significantly. This can be deduced from an assessment of the Information and Communication Technologies Act 2001, which lays out the institutional and procedural guidelines for the regulation and democratisation of information and communications technologies and related matters (National Computer Board, 2003).

On 5 February 2001, a high-powered ministerial committee on ICT, chaired by the prime minister, was set up. The three task forces set up under the aegis of this committee were: the Cyber cities and Business Parks Taskforce, headed by the deputy prime minister and minister of finance; the E-Education Taskforce, headed by the minister of education and scientific research; and the e-Government Taskforce, headed by the minister of information technology and telecommunications.

In 2002, the government adopted the ISO/IEC 17799 information security standards for implementation throughout the civil service in order to address threats posed by viruses, hackers, fraud, natural disasters and other dangers. These standards have been successfully implemented in four pilot sites and will be rolled out throughout the civil service. In the meantime, the Government Intranet System (GINS) project is serving as an important component of e-government infrastructure for the interconnection of governmental bodies. Under this project, all ministries and departments have been wired and all buildings interconnected into an integrated and secure network to facilitate collaboration, information sharing and coordination of activities within the civil service.

Perhaps the most visible government initiative is the Cyber City project. It was envisaged that when fully completed (with a target date of 2007) the Cyber City would employ some 20,000 people, including 5,000 to 7,000 computer professionals. It was expected that the project would have a spillover effect and spread ICT throughout Mauritius, from the Cyber Tower to the Cyber City and finally to the Cyber Island. Apart from this major undertaking, a number of initiatives have been started by the government for human resource development in ICT. These include the setting up of the e-Education and Training Task Force, the establishment of the Human Resource Development Council (HRDC) in 2004 and the introduction of pre-operational training grants.

It is the policy of the government to ensure widespread access to affordable info-communication services. A Universal Service Fund is being set up to provide ICT services in every corner of the country, especially in remote areas where operators are reluctant to offer services. The Universal Service Fund has been structured to take into account the parameters of affordability, accessibility, availability, quality of service and sustainability. Today, all ministries and most governmental bodies have websites. Furthermore, connection to the Internet is via dedicated leased lines for agencies that can afford it and dial-up for others. Large e-government projects, like Government Online, an e-government intranet and a crucial step towards electronic service delivery, are being planned. To support these developments, there is a strong emphasis on training and education to sensitise the population and to try to meet the projected shortfall in ICT professionals. The E-government Master Plan, which charts out strategies and action plans for the short-, medium and long-term phases for e-government, was prepared in 2003. Its objective is to establish a roadmap towards a coherent and integrated approach to the implementation of e-government.

Moreover, the island's National ICT Strategic Plan (2007–11) sets out the government's vision to make ICT the fifth pillar of the economy by increasing ICT contribution to GDP and by building collaborative ventures in the field of ICT with countries of the region. This new plan also includes programme monitoring indicators and milestones that will ensure the right track is followed in achieving ICT targets. To realise this vision, the Plan targets four strategic areas: providing support to the legal, institutional and infrastructural framework related to ICT; promoting e-business adoption; accelerating ICT adoption in society; transforming the island into an ICT expertise hub in the region, able to take up leadership roles and become an investment nucleus for ICT. This achievement would make the island a global point of reference for offshore services in the fields of ITS and ITES (Information and Communication Technologies Authority, n.d.).

Local authority context

Good governance has raised the profile of the island. Against this backdrop, the government is giving a high priority to the development of the ICT sector to transform Mauritius into a cyber-island. Consequently, local authorities have become conscious of the need to adopt ICT in order to enhance their efficiency and productivity in administrative tasks and contribute to good governance. This is reflected in the nature of various initiatives. For instance, all five municipalities and four district councils have websites which provide general information on services provided, activities undertaken and information on organisational structure. At the Pamplemousses and Rivière du Rempart District Councils, citizens can make complaints online through an embedded feature in the websites.

In the case of the municipality of Quatre Bornes, the annual budget is accessible online. The websites of Quatre Bornes Municipality and Pamplemousses District Council make it possible for citizens to post 'upcoming events' or social programmes they are organising, with date, time, venue and event descriptions. They can also create their own email accounts. In addition, they can use the websites to give online feedback on the web portal and cast their votes online in opinion polls. Between October 2004 and May 2008, the Quatre Bornes website registered 15,592 visitors. Between March 2005 and October 2007, the district council of Pamplemousses had registered 49,410 web page views.

Almost every local authority on the island has an IT section, headed by an information technology officer and assisted by a database supervisor (Board of Investment Mauritius, n.d.). Their main responsibility is to ensure the smooth running of the computer systems of the councils, the proper management of hardware and software equipment and the maintenance of security aspects. This investigation found, however, that certain councils did not update their websites.

Despite such shortcomings, in 2002 the municipality of Beau Bassin/Rose Hill set up an 'e-town' committee with the aim of directing the council towards becoming an 'e-town'. Presently, the council has a cyber-centre with 64 personal computers, intended to empower the less privileged children of the township with IT skills.

Another notable project is the E-Business Plan for Local Authorities, which is intended to provide online services to citizens and the business community 24 hours a day, 7 days a week. Implementation of the project in four pilot sites (Port Louis, Black River, Pamplemousses/Rivière du Rempart, Vacoas/Phoenix) was expected to be completed by February 2009 and replicated in other local authorities by August 2009. The prime objective of this project is to improve operational efficiency and service delivery by local authorities through the optimisation of ICT.

The E-Governance Portal for Local Authorities, which forms part of the E-Business Plan, is expected to enhance interaction with local authorities, in cases requiring clearance permits and licences. It will allow online payment of fees and rates through the payment gateway of the e-governance portal. The treasury module will also be integrated with the trade fee module to ensure the availability of online updated information on the fee. In order to enhance transparency, this portal will provide a secure login area for businessmen and citizens. This will enable customers to check the status of payments made and of any arrears. The proposed portal will also allow electronic data exchange with external entities such as the Registrar of Business and the Valuation Office.

These developments do not mark the end of traditional payment modes. Local Authorities will continue to provide the existing traditional payment facility through cash counters at Treasury Department and at Citizen Facilitation Centres. They can also give direct debit instructions through banks. Running parallel systems may imply higher costs, but initially this may be important to allow the gradual elimination of resistance to change. Once people get used to the online system, the traditional one can be phased out.

Research methodology

Research problem and objectives

Following a preliminary assessment of the websites of the local authorities that was undertaken as part of this study, it was noted that despite an increasing rate of personal computer and Internet penetration at national level and the presence of legal frameworks to protect privacy and ensure security over electronic transactions, the use of online transactions was still at its infancy stage in local authorities.

The levels of IT adoption in the various local authorities show that out of the five municipal councils, only Port Louis is equipped with an IT section, headed by an information technology officer and assisted by a database supervisor responsible mainly for the proper management, physical/logical security aspects, and smooth running of the computer systems of the municipal council. The study also found that most websites are informational rather than interactive, and mainly transactional in orientation. In addition, updated information is rarely available on council decisions and on organized activities. In general, local authority website information tended to relate only to rules and regulations, government notices and the legal framework of local government. In fact, the websites placed more emphasis on organisational structure, composition of committees, duties of departments and services provided. Only a few gave the names of senior public officers and their responsibilities and powers.

It seems to be the case, based on hindsight, that the problem is not associated with lack of computer and Internet literacy or even to lack of access, but rather to a lack of trust, the small geographical size (jurisdiction) of municipal and district councils, and the fact that local inhabitants can easily access council premises physically. Inhabitants are also used to the existing tax payment modes and the culture of standing 'in line' rather than going 'online'. These problems also reflect the vulnerability of a small island developing state like Mauritius in taking full advantage of inland e-commerce and e-government for the benefit of citizens. Given these factors, there is a need to gauge the nature of the barriers that are likely to impede the success of e-local governance in Mauritius.

The main aim of this research work was to assess the application of e-local governance in the country, focusing on specific projects in specific local authorities. To achieve this aim, the study had a set of objectives. The first was to gather information on the current implementation of ICT in municipal councils. Research and published information on local governance in Mauritius is scant, which was a key hurdle for the study. Literature on the state of e-local governance is even more difficult to find.

The next objective was to identify an e-local government project which had been operational for more than a year in a majority of the municipal councils. Once the councils and the projects had been identified, the study's next objective was to assess the chosen projects based on two categories of the application of e-local government, namely e-administration and e-services. This meant in essence that the success and/or failure of a given project was to be determined from two perspectives: that of the back office/technical staff (e-administration) and that of front-office staff and citizens (e-services) served by the councils. The perspectives of other stakeholders had also to be taken into account to gain more insights.

FIGURE 6.1 Front- and back-office features of RMS

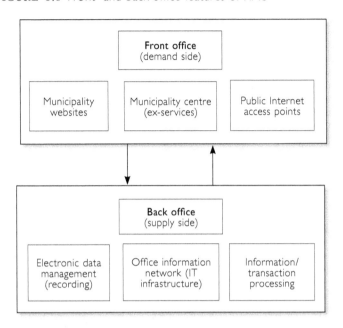

Since the final goal of implementing any LOG-IN Africa project is moving towards good governance, the selected projects were assessed in relation to the four constructs of good governance, as discussed in the pan-Africa LOG-IN Framework in Chapter 2. These constructs were transparency, responsiveness, effectiveness and efficiency, and equity.

Choice of e-local governance project and study sites

In order to choose the e-local government project which had been operational for more than a year in the majority of municipalities, and which at the same time met the requirements of e-administration and e-services, the following steps were taken: first, site visits were made to all the municipalities and their respective IT officers were interviewed; second, the functions of

TABLE 6.1   Matrix on computerised systems in municipalities

	Port Louis	Beau Bassin/ Rose Hill	Quatre Bornes	Vacoas/Phoenix	Curepipe
Billing	No	No	No	No	No
Payroll	Yes	Yes	Yes	Yes (Unix, Oracle)	Yes (Cobol)
Personnel/HR	Yes (partly)	Yes (partly) employee leave record	Yes	No	Subsystem of payroll
Revenue management	Yes	Yes	Subsystem	Subsystem	Yes
Library	Yes	Yes (ALISE)	No	Yes	No
Purchase	Yes	No subsystem of expenditure	Subsystem	Subsystem	No subsystem of expenditure
Stock/inventory	No	Yes	Subsystem	Subsystem	Yes
Registry	No	Yes (Cobol)	No		No
Property management system (PMS)	No	No	Yes		No
Expenditure management	Subsystem of purchase	Yes	Yes		Yes
Publicity/advertising	Subsystem of revenue	No	Yes		Subsystem of revenue

all the systems in operation were studied and their characteristics listed; a matrix was then constructed showing all computerised systems that had been implemented in all the municipalities, as illustrated in Table 6.1.

From Table 6.1, it can be noted that the systems which have been operational for more than a year in all the five municipalities include the payroll, revenue management, and expenditure management systems. However, since only the revenue management system (RMS) had both front-office and back-office features, it is the e-government project that was the focus of this study. Figure 6.1 illustrates the front- and back-office features of RMS from an e-model perspective.

The municipalities that were selected to serve as case studies in the implementation of RMS were Port Louis, Beau Bassin/Rose Hill and Curepipe. These municipalities had fully implemented the system.

Data collection methods

Given the lack of data and access to information on e-local governance in Mauritius, the first part of the project was devoted to gathering primary data and to collecting secondary data to better conceptualise e-local governance in the context of the island. For this exercise, there were site visits to the local authorities, municipalities and district councils, as well as to relevant ministries. These site visits helped in the choice of RMS as the e-local governance

TABLE 6.2   Data collection sample for each questionnaire

Questionnaires	Sample (all three municipalities)	Response	
		(no.)	(%)
Front-line staff	30	24	80
Technical/back-office operators	30	21	70
Consumers	1,500	1,166	78

TABLE 6.3 Local e-governance conceptual framework for RMS

E-government Good governance constructs	E-administration		E-services	
	Outcome indicators	Output indicators	Outcome indicators	Output indicators
Transparency	Staff awareness of changes in rates, policies, policy for writing off bad debt Less discretionary waiving of taxes Increased transparency in revenue collection	Number of staff with access to processes and procedures on revenue collection Number of staff aware of changes in rates, policies, etc. Number of times in a month pertinent revenue information is communicated to staff Reduction in discretionary waiving of taxes Online payments as % of total payments	Access to information and public services Public awareness on changes in policies, procedures and rates	Number of stakeholders accessing revenue/billing information % of public aware of changes in policies, procedures and rates Number of times in a month changes in policies, procedures and rates relating to revenue are communicated to staff
Responsiveness	Extent of feedback from staff Extent of staff satisfaction with computerised system/service	Number of responses and feedback from staff Frequency of the circulation of data and information between staff % reduction in complaints from staff	Online revenue collection system developed (Transaction Phase) Fewer bad debts Improved revenue collection (better cashflow for local authorities) Fewer fines due to late payment Increased customer	Number of complaints registered Number of bad debtors registered Reduction in court litigation Fines paid due to late payments as % of all payments Increase in revenue

			Less cost mitigation	
Effectiveness and efficiency	Reduction in administrative costs, ROI downsizing staff, Increase in staff productivity Improved cash inflow for local authority More efficient revenue collection More people using the computerised revenue system on their day-to-day activities	Access efficiency of processes Management institutional efficiency Increase in staff productivity Change in number of staff working in revenue/billing Admin cost as % of total expenditure Adequacy of cashflow of LA Average waiting time for customers Number of simultaneous users of revenue system Reduction in operational costs	Decreased cost to citizen due to payment made on time Due to ICT SMS More efficient and effective delivery of public services Better quality of services	Fine paid as % of total payments Decrease in cost due to early payment Number of complaints registered Increase in no of public accessing services
Equity	Extent of equity in computerised revenue service; access by staff without discrimination	Number of staff at all levels accessing computerised system	Extent of equity in computerised revenue service; access by local government residents and other stakeholders	Number of males/females accessing revenue information Number of rich/poor accessing revenue information Number of urban/rural accessing revenue information

project and the three case study municipalities as outlined above. Once the municipalities and RMS had been selected, the Treasury departments of the three municipalities were contacted to gather secondary information on their respective RMS implementation.

A participatory approach was used for the study, which involved roundtable discussions in May 2007 involving the Ministry of Local Government, all municipalities and district councils and various ICT stakeholders. At a later stage, policymakers and developers of e-government/governance initiatives were interviewed to gain their insights on the ICT projects of the government of Mauritius. To further consolidate the qualitative data, steps were taken to gather quantitative data. This was done by administering two question-naires. One was for the front-line staff and technical/back-office operators, and the other was for the citizens who received services from the three municipalities. Table 6.3 provides information on sample sizes for each questionnaire and the response rates.

E-local governance evaluation framework

The e-local governance assessment framework discussed in Chapter 2 was used to guide this research project. Table 6.3 highlights the outcome and output indicators from the e-administration and e-services perspectives that were used to assess the current RMS and the barriers to its effective implementation, based on the five constructs of good governance in the three municipalities.

Findings of the study

General findings

For the roundtable discussion, participants were mainly from the Ministry of Local Government, the Ministry of Information Tech-nology and Telecommunications, municipal and district councils, private organisations and non-governmental organisations. The participants revealed that computerisation started in the municipal councils in the early 1990s. Prior to that period, there was no IT section or IT personnel in local authorities. Cash books, documents and ledgers were sent to the Central Information System Division for data entry and processing. All records were done manually and filed in alphabetical order. As part of computerising the various processes in local authorities, IT sections were created; although their structure was standardised across municipalities, each municipal council used a different system.

The main objectives of RMS included:

- saving time in information and data processing;
- better control of accounts and monitoring of debtors;
- easier forecasting;
- reducing fraud and errors;
- faster retrieval and communication of information to citizens;
- improved and faster delivery of services;
- provision of updated management information system reports to the Finance Committee.

Interviews targeting policymakers and developers of e-government/governance initiatives, but more specifically the financial controllers of municipal Councils of Port Louis, Curepipe and the accountant of the municipal council of Beau Bassin/Rose Hill, revealed that the rationale for computerising revenue management could be traced to both internal (the need for a better recording and reporting system for internal audit) and external pressure (citizens' demand for quicker services).

From the surveys used in the study, 29 per cent of the front-office staff worked as cashiers and only 16 per cent as revenue collectors or as heads of the Income Section. In addition, the majority of respondents (54 per cent) were female. As for the technical officers, only 33 per cent had a university degree, although 76 per cent of all the technical staff worked as supervisors, middle-level managers or heads of department.

Most of the citizens who were interviewed (72 per cent) had computer facilities at home. In addition, 8 per cent of those who did not have a computer at home indicated they did not get access to such facilities at all. The study also shows that 94 per cent of respondents had ICT knowledge and were aware of many

ICT devices, partly due to the basic ICT training programme undertaken by the NCB. Of the 66 per cent of respondents who had Internet connection at home, 42 per cent stated they had never accessed the websites of local authorities.

The focus group discussions, involving people from the Ministry of Local Government, the Ministry of Information Technology and Telecommunications and the staff of the municipal councils, mainly validated the results obtained from the surveys, in addition to providing updates on e-local governance policies in the pipeline.

Effects of revenue management systems on good local governance

In response to the issue of how the RMS helps to promote the participation of stakeholders in council affairs, interviewees stated that although only the staff of the Treasury department had access to the system, councillors could request reports, while other stakeholders had the leeway to give ideas on how to upgrade the system. Respondents also stated that other staff, such as those in the nonfinance departments, could channel suggestions through their respective heads of section. The issue of how queries from citizens were handled elicited the response that in a majority of cases citizens wanted further explanation of how their taxes were determined. The Customer Information Centre handled such matters.

On the whole, the responses suggested that the RMS enhanced the control mechanism, named Audit Trail, by making it possible for reports and information to be accessible to the administration and planning department. It also made it possible to trace any amendments that might have been made in relevant documents.

The following is an assessment of the study's findings in relation to the constructs of good governance.

Transparency

Transparency promotes effective governance by opening up decision-making processes to public scrutiny and by enhancing the degree to which constituents can hold governance institutions accountable. 70.8 per cent of front-office respondents stated that customers were aware of how the sum paid was calculated because they were given detailed information on their claims and reminders. The claims sent to them showed the percentage of rate applicable and the proposal made by the Valuation Office. However, 29 per cent mentioned that customers were not aware how the sum payable was calculated because they still asked for information related to calculation of tax and how the valuation office decided on the amount to be levied. This could be indicative of the fact that many people could not read and understand the information provided on invoices sent to them.

The majority of back-office respondents indicated that the websites did not show procedures for paying tax and rates and were not regularly updated. 57 per cent stated that revenue information was communicated on a weekly basis to staff concerned with finance and other senior managers. However, the most common means of communication on changes in tax policies and rates was still paper circulars. This could be indicative of continued resistance to change and sticking to paper through cultural inertia.

Consumers generally agreed that computerisation of the revenue system had increased public access to information on revenue collection procedures and on specific rates. However, respondents were indifferent concerning whether the system was disseminating information about the internal processes and changes in revenue policies. Only 37 per cent of consumer respondents agreed that there had been increased transparency in council operations. The Local Government Act 2003 clearly stipulated that residents with the authorisation of the minister could inspect any documents, books, accounts, vouchers, deeds, contracts, receipts and any other document of a local authority. It seemed that the public were not aware of this legal provision

Effectiveness and efficiency

This construct of good governance is emphatic that governance institutions should demonstrate good stewardship of resources by achieving concrete results with a minimum of waste, while following agreed-upon standards and procedures. The responses of front-office respondents reveal that the number of customers served barely increased after computerisation. In addition, the number of customers served during peak and off-peak times after computerisation had remained the same. Paradoxically, the time taken to serve a customer had decreased from 10 to 20 minutes before RMS implementation to less than 10 minutes afterwards. For back-office staff, RMS implementation had increased productivity, for example by reducing the time needed to drill down and obtain information. Respondents, however, complained that the gains in efficiency and effectiveness were negated by lack of rules, guidelines and regulations to ensure efficient use of human and material resources in the revenue system. Further, the hardware and database platform on which RMS ran had become outdated/ obsolete and as a result the system response time was slow. For example, when many users accessed the system simultaneously, the technical performance of the system was poor. A further technical problem that compromised efficiency and effectiveness was the fact that RMS was not integrated with the other systems in the local authorities. Finally, there still existed pockets of resistance to RMS.

To enhance effectiveness and efficiency, respondents drew attention to the importance of ensuring that local and international standards be used in gauging the quality of security, financial reporting and auditing in the implementation of IT. At the same time they indicated that there was need for more investment in updated IT software, hardware and infrastructure, given that outdated RMS software and hardware impeded effectiveness and efficiency.

From the consumer perspective, RMS had cut average waiting time, reduced files complaints, increased innovative service provision and made transaction simpler and easier. However, 45 per cent of respondents disagreed that the system had improved the overall quality of service. To increase effectiveness and efficiency, citizens have proposed the following steps be taken: simplification of the procedures for undertaking transactions; conducting frequent evaluation of procedures; putting in place mechanisms for detecting fraud.

Responsiveness

Achieving efficiency requires effective and responsive policies for building and maintaining efficient institutions to deliver quality services. The main recommendations in this context concern providing training for all staff. This is to enhance their knowledge of system functions, components and the organisational and legal requirements related to IT and finance. 44 per cent of the citizens who were interviewed agreed that, compared to the initial system, the computerised RMS had improved service provision (in processing and billing time) and created a willingness in staff to help. Front-office respondents further claimed that reminders were easily generated and the detailed amount due was provided on claims. However, 25 per cent of front-office respondents claimed that key information was still not being provided on claims and there were many enquiries from customers. This could be partly because the level of education of many customers may not be sufficient for them to understand what was written on documents given to them.

Back-office respondents agreed that RMS had had the following benefits for consumers: reduced application processing time; improved response time to events; and improved interactive communication, particularly between government and remote communities. Internally, however, only 33 per cent of back-office respondents mentioned that system users had a fair knowledge about system functions, components, organisation and legal requirements related to IT and finance. The major complaints the system users had were the paperwork load, inadequate system reliability and hardware/software operation faults. This pointed to the need for investing in better hardware and software, as stated by those participating in the roundtable discussion.

The citizens interviewed agreed that, compared to the initial system, the computerised RMS had improved service delivery (reduced processing and billing time and shorter queues), enhanced convenience in terms of wider choice of payment method, improved personalised attention, and brought a willingness among staff to help. However, 38 per cent stated that computerisation of RMS had not led to a reduction in late payment and fines.

To improve responsiveness, the study deduced from the citizens' responses that the system should be redesigned to allow:

- ratepayers to access their accounts and claims through secured login, which would enable them to keep track of any arrears and enjoy the benefits of personalised service;
- citizens to effect online payments through the payment gateway and hence reduce cases of delayed payments;
- tracking of any complaints made and sending of feedback on the service to improve it.

The following initiatives may further improve responsiveness: setting up of hotlines to encourage more dissemination of information; creating a virtual information desk, where citizens can send queries through email; setting up public relations offices to provide personalised services; and providing Internet public kiosks in the municipalities to serve citizens.

Equity

Equity is a prerequisite for putting in place participation and consultation mechanisms that can be used to identify and establish the will of constituents. Front-office staff indicated that on-the-job training was provided to all staff in the finance department to use the computerised system, indicating that no discrimination existed, at the level of gender, age or ethnic background. In addition, between 11 and 20 (out of 35) of the back-office staff were using and getting access to the system and on-the job training was offered to all staff irrespective of their organisational position.

A majority of citizens believed that the system had not created any disparity with regard to access to information, be it on a regional or a gender basis. At the same time, a significant proportion of citizens believed that other forms of disparity had been created as the system discriminated between educated and less educated citizens, low and high income earners, and young and old citizens. Citizens thought that equity could be further enhanced through the use of the Creole language on websites. They also felt that there should be standardised service and that training should be given to residents, especially the old and less educated citizens, as well as housewives, to make them able to use the online features of the system on the Internet.

Barriers to e-local governance

The roundtable discussion and the survey results drawn from the responses of municipality staff and citizens show that the major barriers to e-local governance are as follows:

- obsolete technology and outdated hardware;
- budgetary constraints;
- lengthy procedures, which sometimes entailed dependence on inputs from external bodies such as the Government Valuation Office for review of property values;
- absence of standardised accounts;
- resistance to organisational change (e.g. at the levels of management, staff or even trade unions);
- difficulty in designing customer-focused services (to satisfy customer demands and be able to respond to user feedback);
- privacy and security concerns;
- management of technology (from the perspective of technical implementation or procurement of new technology);
- external barriers (e.g. legislative/regulatory, digital divide);
- lack of clarity in institutional responsibilities.

Conclusions and recommendations

The results of the research project reveal that RMS had improved both transparency and responsiveness. However, these gains in governance were negated by the lack of adequate and most up-to-date information on local authority websites, the limited educational level of some of the citizens and the obsoleteness of the software and the platform on which the system was running. The effect of the system on efficiency and effectiveness was mixed. The more positive effects were also negated by a number of system and institutional factors, including lack of regulations governing resource allocation and use, outdated/obsolete software and platform, lack of integration of RMS with other systems, and users' resistance to change.

With respect to equity, the implementation of the revenue management system was done impartially. However, a significant proportion of citizens believed that other forms of disparity had been created with system usage on grounds of education, age and language. Citizens felt that equity could be further enhanced through training to make all able to use the Internet.

The main recommendations that emerge from this study are: closing technology gaps and negating the drawbacks of the present system; eliminating semi-manual work to prevent the running of parallel systems; and ensuring that local and international standards are respected in dealing with security, financial reporting and auditing.

The guidelines for a roadmap for the successful implementation of e-local governance must involve the following major steps: baseline assessment, master plan and implementation. In the Mauritian context, the first two steps have already been taken, as exemplified by the E-Business Plan for Local Authorities. The next major step remains implementation. Given that one of the major barriers pointed out by respondents is resistance to change, special attention should be paid to managing change in order to prevent resistance. This means that the actions for implementing the E-Business Plan should be treated as a change management process. The shift in focus implies the importance of creating a Change Management System, involving process enablement, people enablement, infrastructure enablement and system enablement.

For Mauritius, the two crucial areas are people enablement and system enablement. People enablement would ensure that the right human resources are in place for managing and driving change. Change takes time; for people enablement this implies channelling efforts towards changing practices, knowledge and skills, behaviour, beliefs and values. System enablement would entail the procuring of ICT equipment to run on the established infrastructure, as presented in the business requirements of the e-local governance vision. Once the implementation phase is over, steps must be taken to ensure the sustainability of e-local governance by nurturing a trusted environment, protected by a suitable legal framework. These conditions would facilitate the progressive transition of humanity towards working, living and learning in a wired world.

As for the RMS, the study observed that, currently, municipalities have large-scale debtors who have not made general rate payments. These require a great deal of administrative work to generate claims and reminders, which inflate costs. Given this factor, the RMS must be redesigned as an integrated system, with a database that has all the procedures related to taxable properties. The main advantage of the high integration level would be its ability to manage all taxes that are interrelated, such as real estate, property and refuse collection charges, by using the same administrative procedure. Moreover, it would be possible to handle all the taxes levied on the same taxpayer as they would be grouped together to reduce administrative costs.

Another important area for consideration is the office network. Given that the staff complained that one of the major problems they faced was system breakdown, there is a need for a centralised database which would make it possible to solve the problems of taxpayers from any point in the jurisdiction of a municipality. The network would be required to have a redundancy system to be operative in case of a breakdown at any access point. The RMS would also incorporate integrated digital cartography visualisation options, with alphanumerical information to enable the visualisation of aerial photographs, pictures of the facade of a building or plan, digital cartography, scanner maps and any other features linked to the geography of property. Such information is very useful in inspections against fraud.

To conclude, the Internet is a great tool that local authorities can use to give citizens and taxpayers information and added value. Consequently, the RMS must be redesigned in such a way that more services can be offered via web services. Examples of such services include those dealing with municipal regulations, office locations, tax payment periods and downloadable formats. The redesigning of the system must also emphasise applications that can reduce the time between the date when a property or a service becomes taxable and the time representing the actual payment of the tax.

7

Roadmap to 'e-government for good governance' in a developing country context: Morocco

Driss Kettani and Asmae El Mahdi

National governance context

Morocco is a constitutional monarchy. It gained its independence on 2 March 1956 and embraced a multiparty system. Morocco adopted its first constitution on 10 March 1962. Since then, the constitution has been amended five times. It outlines the institutional framework of governance with its underpinnings of legislative, executive and judicial powers.

Legislative power is derived from two institutions, parliament and the government. The constitution of 1996 introduced structural reforms in the legislative body of parliament which transformed it into a bicameral legislature. Through this change, the country now had a House of Representatives, with 325 members directly elected for a five-year period, and a House of Advisors, with 270 members indirectly elected for a nine-year period. Members of the House of Advisors include representatives of sub-government institutions as well as representatives of trade unions and associations (PNUD, 2003). The constitutional reform of 1996 is viewed as a strategy to empower parliament, since it was intended to enhance government accountability to parliament (UNDP, 2004). In the current arrangement, both parliament and the government, especially the prime minister, can propose laws.

Executive power is vested in the government and the administration. The government is composed of the prime minister and ministers. They are accountable to the King and parliament. A minister fulfils his/her executive tasks via divisions located at central, regional and provincial levels (PNUD, 2003). The state administration encompasses central and local administrative entities. The central entities include general directorates that exercise a degree of executive power. The local administrative entities are of two types: the first consists of the external divisions that are expected to execute decisions made at the central level. The second consists of agents who are essentially state representatives in different sub-government entities. These entities are as follows, in ascending hierarchical order (PNUD, 2003): urban communes (led by a *pacha*); rural communes (led by a *caid*); district units (led by a super-*caid*); provincial units (led a governor); and *wilaya* (led by a *wali*[1]).

Judicial power is independent from the legislative and executive powers, according to the constitution of 1996. There are various courts in Morocco with specific jurisdiction. Starting from 1997, the judiciary underwent some changes that included the creation of commercial courts as well as the development of human resources through the provision of appropriate training programmes (UNDP, 2004).

Local governance context

Decentralisation is a common term in governance literature. As a concept, it refers to how responsibility is transferred for planning, management and resource mobilisation and allocation from the central government to the lower levels of government (Work, 2002). The concept of decentralisation dates back to the 1950s when the British and French colonial powers started to cede tasks, functions and responsibilities to the local authorities of their respective colonies in order to pave the way for their eventual independence. Subsequently, the decentralisation concept evolved worldwide as a tool for a country's development.

Morocco opted for the decentralisation policy in the 1960s as a step towards the democratisation of state institutions and as an initiative intended to involve the population in achieving sound governance at the local level (Ziani, 2003). Decentralisation has since emerged as the face of major institutional reforms in Morocco (PNUD, 2003). The decentralisation experience in Morocco has gone through three main phases. The first phase, which lasted from 1960 to 1975, set up the legal framework to regulate the institutions of local government. Its effect was to assign a legal status to these institutions. The second phase ran from 1976 to 2003. This gave the decentralised entities financial and administrative autonomy; and granted them a wide range of competencies to deal with local socio-economic issues. The third phase started in October 2002. It aimed to develop further the legal structure underlying local government entities (Ziani, 2003).

The constitution of 1996 defines the institutions of local government. They include communes led by mayors, provinces led by governors, and regions led by *walis*. These sub-government entities elect their respective councils, which are in charge of managing affairs democratically (PNUD, 2003; UNDP, 2004).

The three entities of local government reflect three levels of decentralisation. There are 1,552 communes, of which 252 are urban communes or municipalities and 1,300 rural communes. The communal councils represent the first level of decentralisation. They provide public services that include the distribution of drinking water and electricity. They are also responsible for sewage management, garbage collection, maintenance of streetlights and urban public transportation. Communal councils are also responsible for protecting the environment, managing sports and socio-cultural centres, as well as signing conventions of cooperation intended to foster local development (PNUD, 2003; UNDP, 2004).

After independence, Morocco adopted a new administrative division that resulted in the creation of provinces as intermediary entities between central government and communes. In essence, the 71 provinces represent the second level of decentralisation. Provincial councils study and then take a vote to approve provincial development action plans.

The constitution of 1996 also created regions as the third level of decentralisation. There are 16 regions in Morocco. The regional councils manage regional affairs and work towards promoting regional development. They are considered to be major actors in fostering local development. Consequently, they are essential partners in enabling socio-economic progress.

The decentralised entities are not fully autonomous. Rather, the functioning and actions of the local government institutions are shaped by various ministries. For instance, the Ministry of Finance controls the financial affairs of the municipalities. Similarly, the Ministry of Interior has power over the administrative matters of the decentralised entities. Furthermore, the provision of many of the services of the municipalities is determined by the ministries of health, water and education (UNDP, 2004).

To a large extent, the government decentralised entities have underperformed. It has been observed, for example, that the delivery channels of public administration have failed to improve the low coverage and efficiency of its community-oriented services. In addition, the public administration has problems of overstaffing that have had a negative impact on budget planning and on project implementation. Such projects target the social sectors of education and health. The public administration also suffers from paralysis brought about by its bureaucratic management approach, whose end product is a high wage bill that accounts for 12 per cent of GDP (UNDP, 2004). It is significant that in the last 23 years, the number of public-sector personnel increased from 26,500 in 1977 to 145,117 in 2001. To compound the problem, most public-sector employees have low educational qualifications (PNUD, 2003). Moreover, the sector is not citizen-friendly, resulting in a situation in which citizens are often not able to obtain information on basic administrative procedures. Faced with this reality, they endure unprofessional treatment and travel long distances to seek assistance from unwilling officials. Furthermore, the public administration sector is not investor-friendly. A study found that 50 per cent of surveyed firms have full-time employees to handle administrative bureaucracy (UNDP, 2004)

To reverse the challenges posed by this situation, administrative reforms are needed. The central government is still thinking about effective ways of introducing these. One option is to come up with comprehensive reforms that will positively benefit the administrative environment. The starting point for the central government was to put in place an institutional infrastructure that will facilitate the successful introduction of administrative reforms. To achieve this objective, the country created the Strategic Committee for Administrative Reform, headed by the prime minister, as well as the Ministry for Public Function and Administrative Reform (MPFA). The country also established a Higher Council for Public Office (UNDP, 2004).

The steps that were taken had some effect. For instance, procedures were developed to minimise unnecessarily high public expenditure. There have also been large-scale reforms that include the preparation of a legal framework to enhance training programmes for public-sector employees. In addition, there have been reforms to control the high wage bill. Other areas that have been targeted concern making the public administration more citizen-friendly by combating unethical behaviour and by making classical Arabic the language of public service delivery.

ICTs and e-government/governance context

Morocco's interest in ICTs is reflected in the report *Strategie e-Maroc 2010: Realizations, Orientations & Plans d'action, Reussir* (Government of Morocco, 2007), published in September 2007. It contains important information on the country's ICT policy. It also outlines the nature of Morocco's interest in ICTs for the period 1995–2007. The interest became pronounced in the 1990s with the 1993–97 programme that modernised and extended telecommunications networks. Internet connectivity was first introduced in Morocco in 1995 at Al Akhawayn University. The following year, Morocco completed its initiative on 'Competitive Morocco' (*Maroc Competitif*), which made it possible for the country to present its competitive development strategy, resting on, among other pillars, electronics and ICTs. In 1997, Morocco launched a telecommunications liberalisation programme, and parliament adopted the 24-96 Law on Posts and Telecommunications. Through this statute, the country managed to set up the required liberal legal framework (Lengrand, 2004) to encourage the growth of the ICT sector.

There were more structural transformations in 1998. One of these enabled the former National Post Office and Telecommunication Agency to be divided into two different institutions: Maroc Telecom for telecommunications services, and Postes Maroc for postal services. In addition, the National Telecommunications Regulatory Agency (NTRA) (ITU, 2001) was created. The main objective of the NTRA is to facilitate the rapid growth of ICTs in Morocco via regulation and by fostering competition in the market environment (Ibahrine, 2004). It is also significant that there is a clear indication of what Morocco's ICT policy must target in using ICT as a development model that can contribute to the country's sustainable socio-economic development (Government of Morocco, 2007). In this context, the use of ICTs is viewed as a 'national aspiration'. This interpretation was first officially articulated in a speech of King Mohamed IV, which was delivered in 2001 during the symposium on Morocco in the 'Global Society of Information and Knowledge' ('Le Maroc dans la societé globale de l'information et du savoir').

The *Strategie e-Maroc 2010: Realizations, Orientations & Plans d'action, Reussir* (Government of Morocco, 2007) also indicates how 2002–04 marked an important period for ICT initiatives. It was in 2003, for instance, that the prime minister created the 'e-Government Committee' to implement the e-government national programme (l'Administration en ligne). The period is also significant in marking the implementation of the first web-based services, such as eDouane (eCustoms), DAMANCOM (social security) and eJustice (for the judiciary). Morocco's central government conceded that the country's (2002–04) e-government phase was unsatisfactory since many ICT initiatives did not progress as expected or were abandoned altogether. This can be deduced from the country's low ICT penetration, as well as from an assessment of diffusion and usage patterns in specific sectors such as education, commerce and public administration. In response, the country launched the second phase of ICT reforms and initiatives, driven by a national comprehensive cyber-strategy that was developed after consultation with different stakeholders (*une cyber-strategie nationale globale concertée*). The country's focus on the role of ICT received an added boost in 2005, with the launch of a national strategy, eMaroc 2010, to become an information society and a knowledge economy. Evidently, it took Morocco at least 13 years to develop a national ICT strategy (1993–2005).

eMaroc 2010 strategy

The eMaroc 2010 Strategy has two strategic objectives (Government of Morocco, 2007):

1. Reducing the digital divide towards 'eInclusion' via four strategic areas of intervention, which are:
   - developing useful Moroccan content;
   - making available affordable, functioning ICT infrastructure;
   - enabling access to information for all Moroccans;
   - providing relevant training in ICT for different categories of Moroccans.
2. Developing a productive, competitive, and export-oriented ICT industry to reposition Morocco at the international level via the following four strategic areas of intervention:
   - developing a productive, competitive ICT industry;
   - developing an export-oriented ICT industry (*télé-services*);
   - enabling access to information for all Moroccans, for their benefit and for that of enterprises and companies specialising in ICT;
   - providing training in ICT for different categories of Moroccans and in particular for those working in the HR departments of enterprises and companies specialising in ICT.

To ensure an accurate evaluation of the effectiveness of the eMaroc 2010 Strategy and its related achievements, its deployment is being conducted by linking each of the strategic areas to specific 'measurable, acceptable, realistic and temporal' action plans with identified performance indicators and desired results. This indicates that ICT is viewed as able to provide a real opportunity for Morocco to develop. This would be done by overcoming the barriers of time and distance, through the technology's transversal structural transformative capabilities. In addition to this perspective, ICT is also viewed as a path towards achieving a 'historical leap' (*saut historique*) via the development of an ICT industry of national merit.

This vision is adequately covered in the phrase *le rattrapage technologiue et economique*, which highlights the country's quest for a technological and economic leap. The quest has had to consider developments in the international arena. These include the influence of globalisation, spurred on in part by the expansion and diffusion of ICT. Another consideration lies in the emerging new comparative advantages that are largely intangible in nature. These include knowledge, technological innovation and R&D.

The conceptual foundations of the notion of an 'information society' were advanced mainly through two complementary events of the Global Summit on Information Society, which was held first in Geneva in 2003 and then in Tunis in 2005. In this evolving international context, Morocco expressed its wish to fit in. However, there had been concerns that Morocco's official ICT expectations would not be put into practice.

Morocco's recent report on the implementation status of the eMaroc 2010 strategy (Government of Morocco, 2007) indicates clearly that there have been numerous ICT initiatives and projects. The report draws attention to the challenges of completing these ICT initiatives and projects. One of them at the time the report was prepared was the complete absence of e-local (back office and front office) ICT projects.

The report highlights government attempts to limit the negative impact of the digital divide by enabling Moroccan citizens and enterprises to gain Internet access through a number of initiatives, one of which would make access packages affordable. Between 2004 and 2006, Morocco had the fastest growth rate in the world in the Digital Opportunity Index (DOI) ranking. It was also arguably the first country in Africa to have improved Internet access via ADSL. Some comparative statistics from the report provide a continental picture of the country's position in ICT-related matters (Government of Morocco, 2007):

- Morocco has 6.2 million Internet users, compared to 5 million in Egypt and 3.6 millions in South Africa.
- In addition 444,633 Moroccans have access to ADSL, compared to 111,358 people in Egypt and 100,000 people in South Africa.

The eLarache project

The eLarache action-oriented project is a contribution to the LOG-IN Africa research initiative. It builds on the successfully accomplished IDRC-funded Fez e-government project (eFes). Action research simultaneously assists in practical problem-solving and expands scientific knowledge. This type of research also enhances the competencies of participating actors as if carried out collaboratively in a situation that uses data feedback through a cyclical process. The aim of such research is to increase our understanding of a given social situation. Most action research targets change processes in social systems (Hult and Lenning, 1980).

Specifically, the eLarache research project was intended to replicate the experiences of eFes by functioning as a learning platform through which there would be adjustments and further enhancements of the e-government-related outcome assessment framework that was used in eFes. Ultimately, it was hoped eLarache would result in a roadmap to serve as a guiding implementation reference tool for e-local governance. The research project also aimed at generating ICT-related outputs in a real-world environment, through the full involvement and active participation of project stakeholders, including citizens, decision-makers and politicians. Given this perspective, the objectives that underpinned the eLarache project consisted of two main categories:

- The first concerned 'Software Development Objectives'. The scope of these objectives included the design, conceptualisation, development, implementation and deployment of an e-government platform that would enable the automated/online delivery of citizen-oriented services. This technology development part of the eLarache project was conducted using action research.
- The second category of objectives was in relation to investigating ways of generalising ICT4D projects in Morocco by developing an outcome assessment framework to generate knowledge of the successes and failures of e-local governance initiatives. The results obtained could then be used to prepare a practical roadmap to assist in setting up e-local governance projects, based on lessons from the eFes and eLarache projects.

Research methodology

The eLarache project is an example of an ICT project that was implemented using action research and in which the ICT4D researchers (in academia) collaborated with Larache stakeholders (in public administration) to design and build a real-life e-government system. Apart from the system's participatory iterative implementation, the eLarache project extensively investigated changes produced as result of e-government deployment. Consequently, data gathering and analysis were a key element in gaining insights on the requirements of project implementation. There was intensive fieldwork, which included formal and informal in-depth interviews. Focus group discussions (FGDs) and regular workshops also provided essential data. Field notes and journal entries were used as data collection instruments.

The rationale for a design method based on the eLarache experience was the recognition that ICT projects should not be implemented without considering their socio-organisational context. Instead, socio-organisational realities and desired values in the context of the project (which in this case was good govern- ance considerations) should be an integral part of an ICT project design/implementation cycle. This perspective has its theoretical foundations in the fact that technology can only be meaningful with social theory which plays a major role in helping to under- stand and interact with the societal, organisational and personal contexts (Rose, 2001).

The British sociologist Anthony Giddens made an influential contribution to social theory. In 1984 he developed structura- tion theory (ST), which is considered a 'meta-theoretical social framework'. Compared to the two conflicting sociological streams of the structuralist/functionalist school that advances the view that structure determines individual actions and the competing hermeneutics/phenomenology school that advances the position that individuals must have control over structures in social life, Giddens's ST is different. His focus is on how individuals' knowl- edgeable actions interact with structures in a dual manner, result- ing in the production and reproduction of structures. The theory states in addition that the bi-directional influence of an individual's knowledgeable actions and structures in the context of social life may result in social practices that evolve as 'routines' through a 'routinisation process' over time and space. This can lead to the rise of 'established' practices and eventually to the presence of 'institutionalized features' in a given social context (Rose, 2001).

Structuration theory, according to Pozzebon and Pinsonneault (2001) suggests that human actions simultaneously condition and are conditioned by institutional properties in social contexts. In addition, they argue that organisational change is the joint effect of the actions of individuals interacting with institutional structures like business strategies and information systems. These structures enable and constrain the daily actions and thought processes of people, but do not determine them.

Over the last decade, ST has appealed to researchers in informa- tion systems (IS). The underpinning motivation is the recognition that ST provides conceptual tools that can be used to gain insight

FIGURE 7.1   Orlikiwski's structurational model of technology

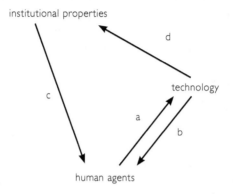

a   Technology as a product of human agency
b   Technology as a medium of human interaction
c   Institutional conditions of interaction with technology
d   Institutional consequences of interaction with technology

Source: Rose, 2001.

into the context for developing ICT artefacts. Therefore there have been several efforts to adapt ST and use it in the IS field. A major contribution in this regard is the work of Wanda Orlikiwski, who used ST to conceptualise and explain how technology relates to organisations. In fact she used Giddens's idea of the 'duality of structures' to advance the idea of a 'duality of technology', through which technology is perceived as a product of human actions and as a medium intended to serve the needs of individuals. Orlikiwski used the idea to develop the 'structurational model of technology' through which technology can trigger change in organisations. Orlikiwski's model of technology is represented graphically in Figure 7.1.

This model influenced the roadmap that is recommended in this work, since it includes the interaction dimensions of technology in an organisational setting. Such interaction is evident in

Kettani et al. (2007), where there is a graphical overview of the contribution of this model in an e-government context. In the context being discussed, the researchers were able to produce the Good Governance egov Development and Deployment Method (GGegovDD Method). It has four main phases, as follows:

- *Phase 1*   Used to sustain favourable conditions during the project.
- *Phase 2*   The inception phase.
- *Phase 3*   Reserved for developing and deploying ICT/egov system.
- *Phase 4*   Necessary for the systematic assessment of project outcomes.

The first phase has to be kept active in the life of a given project in an organisation. It demands creating and maintaining conditions that will favour the progress of the project. In general, it mainly involves various stakeholders, among whom are the project's e-champions to promote and support the project at all the critical levels of an organisation's power structure. The project's management team must also be aware that certain stakeholders and e-champions may change from one phase of the project to another and consequently must be prepared to take appropriate action to maintain favourable conditions for the project, given the fact that changes would be taking place in the organisation.

Figure 7.2 gives a graphical representation of the GGegovDD Method. The thin dashed arrows in the figure illustrate how favourable conditions influence every phase of the project.

Phase 1, which focuses on *sustaining favourable conditions*, was in the form of various actions related to the eLarache project. As an example, the Larache/ICT4D team was actively engaged in establishing partnerships with Larache decision-makers. One method was to showcase existing ICT solutions (such as the eFes system) and how their deployment had transformative effects. Seeing concrete examples on the ground was very effective and laid the foundation for the right conditions to gain support for

FIGURE 7.2   Graphical representation of the GGegovDD method

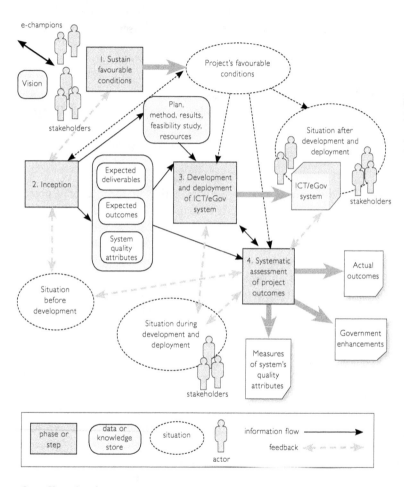

e-champions

Vision

stakeholders

1. Sustain favourable conditions

Project's favourable conditions

Plan, method, results, feasibility study, resources

Situation after development and deployment

2. Inception

Expected deliverables

Expected outcomes

System quality attributes

3. Development and deployment of ICT/eGov system

ICT/eGov system

stakeholders

4. Systematic assessment of project outcomes

Actual outcomes

Situation before development

Situation during development and deployment

Government enhancements

Measures of system's quality attributes

stakeholders

phase or step

data or knowledge store

situation

actor

information flow

feedback

Source: Kettani et al., 2007.

eLarache implementation. This phase has been and is still active through various actions at the central government level, where the Larache/ICT4D team succeeded in initiating contacts.

Phase 2, the *inception* phase, is also critical for an ICT/eGov project that can only start when a minimal set of favourable conditions have been met. Among these is the strong will and influence of high-ranking e-champions to support the project. The favourable conditions should be built up in Phase 1, at which time the e-champions must have a clear and structured vision of the outcomes of the project for the organisation and its clients. The phase is also important in helping e-champions to shape and refine their expectations of project outputs or deliverables, as well as their expectations of project outcomes or results. The latter are often different from and more global in scope than deliverables. It is also during this important phase that the most critical stakeholders are led to share the project's vision and reach consensus on its main targets (outputs and outcomes). This increases the favourable conditions for the project, as represented by the large dashed arrow linking rectangle 2 to rectangle 1 in Figure 7.2.

With regard to the eLarache project, there was intensive fieldwork to further refine the project vision and negotiations with stakeholders to meet the demands of their expectations. The interactions were also useful in helping to identify needed ICT outputs.

The third phase, the *development and deployment* phase, starts whenever the GO decision has been made by relevant authorities, after completion of the inception phase. A critical success factor during this phase is the assurance that favourable conditions will be maintained throughout. In addition, all the outputs of the inception phase should be available during the development of the ICT/eGov system. This phase also requires those technical norms and goals based on quality criteria that had been set up in the first phase to be refined, in readiness for the development and deployment of the ICT/eGov system.

When eLarache moved to the third phase, project stakeholders played an active role in a number of ways. In this connection, the software team and stakeholders received explanations on good governance considerations; and on how they should be integrated in technology work. Furthermore, once a module had been prepared, the researchers made it available for stakeholder evaluation. They were able to the receive feedback on how it could be improved. This phase also took into account organisational issues such as people's readiness gap. For this reason, the researchers developed a tailored training package to teach personnel how to operate the system. The training included sessions on good governance considerations that focused on the need to integrate in this sector not only technology use in public administration but also good governance practices.

The systematic assessment of project outcomes marks the last phase. Its goal is to systematically assess and monitor the evolving situation during the course of the project with respect to the goal of achieving expected project outcomes. eLarache conducted systematic assessment to obtain feedback and generate knowledge. Assessment for feedback is for internal use. This entails using feedback to readjust activities and improve the system in an iterative way. In comparison, an assessment to generate knowledge is for external use.

Developments in the project

Although the project followed the required method phases, the unexpected happened. The governor who had supported eFes replication in Larache was moved to a higher position. This change coincided with the end of the funding provision for the project in 2008. Subsequently, the project stalled.

Over the three years 2007–10, the eFes experience had been used to scale up the application of the system in Fez. The task involved extending the connectivity infrastructure, improving the functionalities of the ICT-based governance platform, and building city-wide capacity. A number of people have benefited from training opportunities brought about by the project. The efes platform benefited from improvements in features and functionalities following its replication in six pilot counties in Fez. After the successful completion of eFes replication in the six pilot government offices in Fez, the researchers did the same for the remaining 24 government offices.

In 2009, the Larache vice president participated in a training workshop for the eFes replication activities cited above. During the workshop, he saw the capabilities of the eFes platform. He arranged a meeting with the Larache mayor and convinced him to take a set of quick actions: assign eight computers to Larache Bureau État Civil (BEC) register office and reallocate personnel by assigning 16 municipality employees to work in the BEC office in two shifts. The former BEC officer (currently head of personnel) appointed the employee who had attended April 2009 training as a trainer. This junior administrator trained the 16 newly assigned employees and coached, monitored and supervised their data conversion operations, while the IT technician made daily trips to the BEC office for the purposes of maintaining the IT infrastructure to ensure no technical problems arose that could delay the employees' work. This marked the revival of the eLarache project. Between January and March 2010, the BEC had been able to use the eFes platform to populate its database with 17,000 records of citizens' life events. This was a prerequisite for automated service delivery. Thereafter, the Larache BEC launched its electronic system for the issuance of life-event certificates. For the last two months, Larache BEC was able to launch its electronic issuance of life events certificates.

Thus one training beneficiary of eLarache research funding was able to change the attitudes of the municipal leadership and to influence their policy choices in favour of rescuing eLarache from abandonment, and was able to build the needed in-house capacity prerequisite for implementing the eLarache system. The overall objective of the Larache head of personnel was to use this pilot BEC as a demonstrator site to facilitate the municipal allocation of the needed budgets for eFes generalisation within the four remaining BEC offices of Larache. One result of these behavioural changes was the moving of the eLarache system from the Larache provincial level to the municipal level. Accordingly, eLarache implementation was completed two years after the termination of eLarache research funding, and electronic issuance of citizens' live-event certificate became a reality.

In Larache there has been demand for the immediate allocation of material resources (eight PCs) and human resources (16 employees, a supervisor and an IT technician) to finish work on the database.

The eLarache case surprised the researchers. The Larache experience did not follow the exact path of Fez. Events did not progress in a linear way; movement was instead cyclical with events triggering a regressive trend leading to the complete abandonment of the eLarache project. But, again, certain dynamics emerged and evolved, creating a momentum that revived interest in eLarache implementation (even after the termination of research funding). An interesting aspect of the project was that automation operations for BEC data conversion were accomplished exclusively by municipal employees. Fez, for its part, contracted out data conversion operations. Larache employees did not ask for monetary incentives to complete such tedious operations; rather, their only incentive was to enable the shift from BEC manual certificate issuance to automated certificate issuance as soon as possible.

Clearly, ICT-mediated organisational change cannot be determined on the basis of other ICT projects' experiences. However, these can serve as test-bed environments to inform researchers and practitioners on how to bring about desired organisational change aimed at fostering good governance practices. The bottom line is that no organisational change can take place in ICT projects unless the public mindset changes correspondingly. This was discussed in one of the UN's latest eGovernment Readiness surveys (United Nations, 2008).

FIGURE 7.3   Total aggregates of automated issuance of BEC
certificates

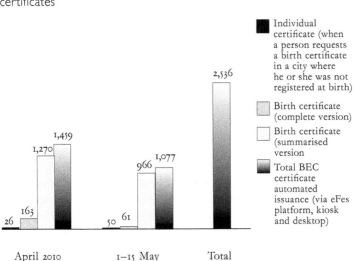

April 2010   1–15 May   Total

Emerging results

Figure 7.3 shows the issuance rate of the system that was launched in 2010.

The eFes and eLarache projects did not follow the same path in the shift from manual service delivery to automated service delivery. As the automated issuance of certificates became a reality in Larache, the researchers resumed fieldwork to identify and observe governance changes. Specifically, they used indicators that had been refined through the eFes project. They also linked the project to features of good governance as defined by the UNDP. Based on the UNDP definitions of these attributes, researchers generated related working definitions adapted for the purposes of the project's area of intervention. They were subsequently able to track specific attributes. Before the implementation of eLarache, the manual service delivery system had been observed and analysed in order to collect baseline data (UNDP, 2002). With the launch of

185

TABLE 7.1 Emerging results from eLarache

Governance attributes	Measured indicator	Value before automated system deployment	Value after automated system deployment
Transparency	Visibility of workflows for citizens via automated service delivery	No. Since the BEC back office is completely manual, sub-processes of requesting birth certificate, processing the request, and filling out the needed copies are carried out as separate tasks (sometimes by different employees). The citizen cannot monitor the progress of this process (e.g. the nature of/reasons for a delay in processing are neither accessible nor visible).	Yes. Like eFes, the principle of first come, first served is respected as certificate issuance sub-processes were merged into one process.
Effectiveness and efficiency (as a citizen user)	Efficiency: optimal use of resources for citizens to request and obtain birth certificate	No. Requesting and obtaining a birth certificate is costly for citizens: extended waiting time; several trips to BEC; need to tip (or use social connections)	Yes. Like eFes, Citizens started making time/money/effort savings in requesting and obtaining a birth certificate: no waiting time; one trip to BEC; no trip.
Effectiveness and efficiency (as taxpayer)	Efficiency and effectiveness of using scarce public resources	No. When demand is low, to deliver a birth certificate BEC needed to full-time employees. When demand is high (summer and early fall: from June to September), all BEC employees (20) stop their respective tasks in order to process birth certificate requests	Still under investigation. (The Larache office is still in a transitional phase.)

Equity	Citizens served in equitable manner	No. Usually queuing/waiting creates motives and conditions for bribery. Citizens find themselves obliged to tip the employee in charge in order to be served, especially when they are in a hurry to meet tight deadlines for submitting paperwork.	Yes. Citizens started to be served in a timely/real-time manner. ICT noticeably eliminated the need for citizens to tip or beg to be served.
Rule of law	Laws are applied impartially	No. Equity is violated; and violations are perceived as normal: many violations of law as people have paid for special privileges (queue jumping).	Yes. Rule of law is being reinforced: as citizens started being served on a timely/real-time manner and motives to tip or beg to be served disappear.
Responsiveness (process of disintermediation: elimination of middle person in service delivery)	Services are responsive to citizens' requirements	No. Citizens were not able to control the process of service delivery as it affected them (with possible negative consequences on service delivery arising from issues occurring in the workflow).	Yes. Automated issuance of certificates has enabled the serving of citizens in a timely/real-time manner.
	Dependency on bureaucracy: dependence of citizens on employees' goodwill	Yes. Citizens were at the mercy of employees to get served.	No. Automated issuance of certificates seems to liberate citizens from employees' abusive treatment, as employees no longer control the workflow (still under study).
Accountability	Existence of standards to hold individuals accountable	No. No standards because of the opaque and inconsistent system.	Yes. The issuance system is no longer opaque; rather, it is becoming more predictable (still under study).
Participation	n/a		
Consensus orientation	n/a		
Strategic vision	n/a		

the automated system for issuance of certificates, the researchers began to identify changes that were taking place in the offices. Table 7.1 gives a picture of the emerging results.

Table 7.1 reveals one major empirical insight. Although eLarache did not follow the Fez path in making the shift from manual to automated service delivery, emerging preliminary results tend to confirm the Fez outcomes. This underscores the need to complete the eLarache fieldwork to see whether the outcomes of the two projects completely converge or whether they diverge in some aspects.

Concluding remarks

Using the development deployment methodology (GGegovDD) was useful and an eye-opener for the researchers. It provided a framework for systematically extending the eFes platform to a new geographic–institutional environment, namely Larache City.

The researchers also noted that the stalling of implementation generated a rise in demand within Larache municipal governance structures for a platform that could improve service delivery. This rise in demand was a positive turning point for the eLarache project. This comes as no surprise to ICT4D theorists. For instance, Unwin (2009: 57) notes that 'most studies of information in poor countries have concentrated much more on the supply-side than they have on the demand that poor people have for information.' Consequently, Unwin (2009: 310) strongly recommends efforts to 'ensure that ICT applications are development- and demand-driven, not technology- or supply-driven, thus ensuring cost-effective investment in ICT for maximum development impact.'

The eLarache project illustrates the critical importance of championship in the successful deployment of e-local governance projects. The replication of eFes in Larache came to a standstill when the leadership that supported this project was appointed to a different position outside the local government. This underscores the importance of a sustained e-local governance leadership throughout the life of a project.

The eLarache project also illustrates some of the challenges that need addressing in scaling up information systems. In this regard, Sahay and Walsham (2006: 187) offer a fitting conclusion: that the 'problem of scaling has not received the attention required by IS researchers'. Scaling should not be viewed 'merely as a technical problem, but as a socio-technical one involving a heterogeneous network constituted of technology, people, processes, and the institutional context'.

Note

1. Morocco is a constitutional monarchy. The supreme head of the country is the king. As part of the decentralisation process, Morocco has been divided into several administrative regions. The representative of the king in a specific region is called the *wali*.

8

Influence of the e-government implementation process on outcomes: case study of the Land Management Information System in Mozambique

Gertrudes Macueve

Context of the study

Mozambique is a developing country ranked 168 out of the 177 countries in UNDP's 2006 *Human Development Report* (UNDP, 2006a). Since almost 80 per cent of the population live in rural areas, with agriculture the activity on which 90 per cent of the population depends, land management is a crucial component of the development agenda of the government. Agriculture and rural development constitute the first priority, and land is an important asset for promoting social welfare and economic development. It remains an indispensable resource for the production of agro-cattle breeding; forestry and fauna exploitation; the conservation and maintenance of biodiversity and for ensuring ecological equity.

The current Land Law in Mozambique was issued in 1997. This law states that the government owns the land, but grants usage rights to individuals, communities and companies in the form of 100-year lease agreements, which can be transferred but not sold or mortgaged. Usage rights emerge either through occupancy or by a specific grant through the state. The government can issue use right title documents (land tenures) to land holders, although those who occupy the land for more than 10 years acquire permanent use rights without the need for title documents.

The institutional context of land management in Mozambique is complex, with at least 22 ministries, ordinary people and local authorities involved in the granting of land concessions. Land occupies a major segment of customary laws, especially in the allocation of land use rights, resolution of conflicts, and the management of resources. The current Land Law encourages the adoption of participatory approaches by involving communities in the provision of land tenures and recognises customary laws. This focus does not mean, however, that the government is overlooking the role to be played by ICTs in streamlining issues relating to the management of land, by considering what can be achieved through e-government.

Many developing countries are engaged in the implementation of e-government. This engagement is motivated by the need to improve the quality of governance in line with the Millennium Development Goals (UNDP, 2006a). It is also motivated by the need to reduce bureaucracy (Kaboolian, 1998), re-engineer processes, modernise service delivery (Navarra and Cornford, 2003) and meet the challenges of globalisation (Polidano, 1999; Jeger, 2000). Others argue that the interest in e-government lies in its potential to bring about social and economic development (Ciborra and Navarra, 2005). According to Bhatnagar (2004), expected benefits of e-government include: improvements in government administrative service, as well as in information provision; improvements in transparency, due to ease of access to government information, rules and procedures, resulting in openness and accountability; public-sector reforms that are needed for efficiency and responsiveness to citizens.

E-government is no longer seen as an option but as a necessity for all countries aiming at having better and efficient governance (Gupta and Jana, 2003). Meanwhile, each country follows its own models and processes and determines its own stages of e-government implementation. While developed countries followed a process which was accompanied by the evolution of ICTs and was sequential in nature, developing countries are pressured into putting aside the stages involving external forces (Ciborra and

Navarra 2005). This mode of implementation has adverse consequences on the final results.

Many scholars have proposed various stages of e-government development (Layne and Lee, 2001; Bhatnagar, 2004; Siau and Long, 2005). These stages consist of four phases: web presence, interaction, transaction and transformation. The transformational phase of e-government implementation is the main level of maturity for e-government initiatives and the target. Thus it is also the most challenging phase to reach (Layne and Lee, 2001). Generally, it is assumed that e-government in each country grows sequentially through these stages, regardless of the specific context and of the available resources.

Studies on the impact of following the sequential growth of e-government or on the impact of using a different method are scarce. Therefore, it was the aim of this case study to investigate the relationship between these stages of e-government and the impact of their sequence on the expected outcomes of a project.

The study was conducted in Mozambique, which is a less developed country engaged in the implementation of e-government for development. Among various ongoing initiatives in the country, the implementation of a Land Management Information System (LMIS) is one project which started in 2004, aimed at helping the government to manage natural resources and improve the quality of decision-making processes on land allocations.

The study represents a useful contribution to the debate on 'why e-government in developing countries fails or succeeds'. It has used Bhatnagar's (2004) implementation process, which proposes four stages of implementation.

The subsection that follows is a description of Mozambique's ICT Policy and e-Local Governance Strategy. This is followed by an overview of the study's analytical framework. The next section has key information on the design of the study. The following two sections give an account of the findings of the study with analytical discussions. The conclusions and recommendations of the study are covered in the final section.

Mozambique's ICT policy and e-local governance strategy

There is a great willingness in the top leadership of the government of Mozambique to implement the use of ICTs in poverty alleviation and development initiatives. Such willingness can be observed in the government's engagement in ICT-related decision-making and in its interest in relevant projects.

Mozambique has been a reference country among developing nations in the way it has conducted the process of issuing ICT regulations and laws (Marcelle, 2000; Rowan, 2003). The Mozambican ICT policy was approved in 2000, setting education, human resource development, health, universal access, infrastructure and governance as priorities. According to Rowan (2003), many developing countries put emphasis on infrastructure policy development, and neglect the dimensions of human resource development and information content. The Government of Mozambique was aware that ICT policy would support its poverty reduction activities. Hence, this would increase its efforts to support capacity building and create an enabling environment underpinned by policy development.

In 2001, the policy was transformed into an action plan and respective efforts turned to drafting an implementation strategy approved by the Council of Ministers in 2002. The strategy is a reference point for people and organisations that are interested in the use of ICTs to foster development in Mozambique. In 2004, the e-government strategy was approved by the Council of Ministers.

In addition to the formulation of regulations, visions and strategies, there are a number of ICT projects and e-government initiatives that are ongoing. For instance, there is a project on community multimedia centers (CMCs), which in essence are combinations of community radio and traditional telecentres. Currently, there are more than 20 CMCs distributed across the country. Such projects aim to expand connectivity and provide opportunities for using ICTs in remote areas.

Expansion of ICTs to benefit remote areas contributes to the ongoing reforms in the country through which the government has been attempting to modify and upgrade social and economic infrastructure. In this respect, the government has transferred power to the local communities and traditional authorities and built a legal framework that allows these bodies to exercise power. Such efforts have a complementary role in supporting decentralisation initiatives and in nurturing democracy.

The use of ICTs can also enhance the participation of local authorities in governance and in the decentralisation process. Although traditional local communities and traditional authorities have been involved in the decision-making process, ICTs are expected to modernise the participation process and make it more effective. Therefore ICTs and e-government applications are gradually being implemented at the local level. For example, through the reforms in the public sector that are supported by the implementation of an e-government application (the e-SISTAFE), all provincial level administrative offices and some districts currently benefit from computer-related resources.

The local governance development strategy lies in its commitment to include people from all walks of life in community decision-making. The hope is that as the government comes closer to the people, more people will participate in the politics of the country. All sorts of constituencies, which include women, minorities, small businesses, subsistence farmers, rural and urban inhabitants, will then get equal participation in decision-making. This will give them representative status, which is a key element in empowerment, and a significant voice in public decisions. Policy decisions at the local level will be the impetus for providing more appropriate infrastructure, better living conditions, and enhanced economic growth. It is hoped these improvements will reduce poverty and enhance equity in all groups.

The agenda in the current process of social and economic transformation in Mozambique includes the implementation of a decentralisation policy that can stimulate democracy, policy equity and the active participation of people at the local level through autonomous and democratically elected local government. These, in turn, will enhance accountability, transparency and good governance. It is also expected that decentralisation will increase management efficiency, as well as efficiency in financial performance through increased revenue generation and rational expenditure decisions, apart from providing a better environment for public–private partnership.

Another ICT project is SchoolNet, which aims at strengthening computer literacy at the secondary school level and enhancing learning opportunities for students, teachers and the surrounding community via the Internet. By 2006, computer labs had been established in 75 schools, 25 of which were connected to the Internet. There are also One Stop Shops, which are community centres that use ICTs to provide integrated services that enable people to pay their water, electricity and telephone bills. The shops can also be used to make requests for certificates, identity cards, driving licences, passports and visas. Through them it is possible to fill out forms to pay taxes and other fiscal fees, and to identify business and investment opportunities, all in the same physical office. E-SISTAFE, GovNet, LMIS, provincial digital resource centres and mobile ICT units are the other e-government initiatives that are significant (CPInfo, 2002).

These projects are aligned with the National Poverty Reduction Strategy Paper (PRSP), which focused on contribution to poverty reduction in the country by promoting ICT as an enabler for development in all areas (CPInfo, 2002). Table 8.1 shows the priorities (fundamental areas of action) of the National Poverty Reduction Paper and the ICT Implementation Strategy. Priorities of both institutions overlap in most cases, which illustrate their common interests.

Analytical framework

The analytical framework used in this study has two parts: the first part is drawn from the UNDP (1997) concepts of good governance and provides the conceptual foundation for assessing the outcomes of the implementation of the LMIS. The second part, which is based on the evolutionary stages of e-government implementation,

TABLE 8.1   PRSP and ICT implementation action areas

	Priorities
PRSP	Education, health, infrastructure, agriculture and rural development, good governance, legality and justice, macroeconomic and financial policies
ICT implementation strategy	Education, human resource development, health, universal access, infrastructure, governance
Example of projects from the ICT implementation strategy	SchoolNet, Science and Technology Network, Institute for Communication Technology for Mozambique, Information System for HIV/AIDS, VSAT communication network, digital agencies, telecentres, GovNet, State Personnel Information System, LMIS

was the instrument for assessing whether they had influenced the implementation of the LMIS and how this factor could affect final outcomes.

Good governance principles

Good governance constitutes one of the motivations for e-government implementation. This study draws upon the nine characteristics of good governance as outlined in the UNDP framework (UNDP, 1997). The framework was adopted because of its stronger focus on people and its more holistic inclusion of aspects of good governance and development. At a fundamental level, it is grounded in the definition of good governance as the exercise of political, economic and administrative authority in the management of a country's affairs, including land. In addition, it is underpinned by the principles of participation, strategic vision, rule of law, transparency, responsiveness, consensus orientation, equity building, effectiveness and efficiency and accountability. These principles have been defined in Chapter 2. In this study, a subset of the relevant principles of good governance were selected and adapted to assess the LMIS. They included:

TABLE 8.2   Adapted UNDP principles for LMIS

Good governance principles	UNDP definition	Definition applied to LMIS
Participation	All men and women should have a voice in decision-making.	A process through which individuals, groups and organisations are consulted on land issues or have the opportunity to become actively involved in activities or decisions concerning the land question and the related development of tools for land management. Participation can take place through electronic or non-electronic means.
Responsiveness	Institutions and processes try to serve all stakeholders.	Taking into account the expectations of civil society, government, civil servants and citizens, responsiveness is the capacity and flexibility of the land management system to respond rapidly to these institutions.
Effectiveness and efficiency	Processes and institutions produce results that meet their needs while making the best use of resources.	Effectiveness: the land system, when used under ordinary circumstances, does what it is intended to do. Efficiency: adequacy of the system in accomplishing a particular result; the degree to which the system produces outputs and outcomes by avoiding waste of resources.

- *Participation*, because of the study's empirical focus on land and on issues of land concession, which have in the past been the subject of administrative and management challenges, often requiring the involvement through participation, of different constituencies and stakeholders.
- *Responsiveness*, to cater for the awareness that the genesis of the land conflicts in many countries is the inordinate amount of time taken to solve them within existing legal frameworks,

which indicates that the time frame for this process should be reasonable.

• *Effectiveness and efficiency*, because of the scarcity of land resources and the severe pressures on it that make these qualities important criteria to consider in assessing the LMIS.

Table 8.2 illustrates how these principles were adapted to make them context sensitive for the study.

E-government evolutionary stages

The proposed stages of e-government implementation vary from scholar to scholar. These stages revolve around four phases: web presence, interaction, transaction and transformation (Baum and Di Maio, 2001; Layne and Lee, 2001; Bhatnagar, 2004). Some scholars extend the stages to five or six. For example, the United Nations and American Society for Public Administration (2002), Hiller and Bélanger (2001) and Moon (2002) propose five stages, while Deloitte and Touche (2001) propose six stages. This study opted for the four-stage model proposed by Bhatnagar and other scholars. The model has been widely used in the literature on e-government compared to the models with more than four stages.

In the four-stage model, the first stage is *web presence*. It represents the simplest and least expensive entrance into e-government, but it also offers the fewest options for citizens. At this stage, an agency can provide a website for posting agency-specific basic information to the public. In such contexts, the website has no interactive capabilities.

The second stage is that of *limited interaction*. It allows online interactivity, and clients can download applications for receiving services. Although interactive web-based initiatives offer enhanced capabilities, efforts in this group are still limited in their ability to streamline and automate government functions. Interactions tend to be relatively simple and generally revolve around information provision. These types of initiatives are designed to help the customer to avoid a trip to an office or to make a phone call by providing commonly requested information and forms throughout

TABLE 8.3   Four-stage model of e-government

Stage	Capabilities
Web presence	Agencies provide a website to post basic information to the public.
Interaction	Users are able to contact agencies through websites (e.g. email) or perform self-service (e.g. download document).
Transaction	Users (including customers and businesses) can complete entire transactions (e.g. license application and procurement) online.
Transformation	Governments transform the current operational processes to provide more efficient, integrated, unified and personalised service.

the day. These resources may include instructions for obtaining services, downloadable forms to be printed and mailed back to an agency, or perhaps email contacts to respond to simple questions.

The third stage is the *transaction*. It handles the electronic delivery of services with some or all the stages automated. Its applications include the issuance of certificates and the renewal of licences.

The last stage, *transformation*, represents the image of a 'joined up' government in which all stages of transactions, including payments, are done electronically. The relevant applications for the stage include government portals. It is also the stage for the electronic delivery of services and the stage where more than one department may be involved in processing a request or services.

In general, the higher a stage is in ranking, the greater is its ability to offer more value to citizens. Given this factor, this stage offers the greatest challenges at the level of implementation and technology requirements. Table 8.3 summarises the four stage model of e-government maturity.

Design of the study

Rationale

The focus of this study was the analysis of the implementation of the electronic Land Management Information System that the Government of Mozambique started rolling out in 2004.

Land management in Mozambique had been done manually using paper since colonial times. This required the flow of documents and tacit information to involve different levels of administration (localities, districts, provinces and national-level offices). During the period 1975–90, the government tried to continue using the system left by the colonial government and at the same time customise it for local needs with very limited resources (qualified human resources and capital).

Attempts to build a computerised Geographic Information System (GIS) using Arcview software started in 1991, with little impact due to problems in redefining the paper-based flows, both in content and with regard to who was involved. Despite such problems, it was deployed in all the country's ten provinces. The system was not complete, but was a stand-alone, which required the manual movement of data from the different provinces to the central database in Maputo, where the national cadastre was updated. With the end of the contract of the system developer and the Y2K problems in 2000, the development of the system was stopped. A new development initiative started in 2004.

Apart from the historical lack of an organised and complete computerised system, land management remained a social and political issue that had long been a source of conflicts and discontentment for the Mozambicans. For instance, in the colonial regime, the Portuguese government granted concession of land in fertile areas to larger commercial interests and moved the local people to less fertile areas (Hanchinamani, 2000).

With the shift to the new government after independence in 1975, departments within the government granted land use rights to foreign interests and other influential individuals at the expense of small landholders and private interests. Principles of equity and rule of law in good governance were violated. In addition, tensions heightened because of numerous overlapping land requests and the provision of land use concession during this period (Hanchinamani, 2000; PASS, 2003). The land concession process began to proceed over time, without direction, transparency or equitable competition for resources. With the government's recognition of land conflicts as one impediment to the country's development, it decided to strengthen land management through modern means to establish good governance.

The implementation of the electronic Land Management Information System (LMIS) running on the Internet was one of the available solutions for taking advantage of the potential for data sharing among the different stakeholders, who would also enjoy the following benefits: higher capacity for data storage; enhanced ability to integrate different institutional databases; availability of speedy and more accurate responses to requests. This initiative was in line with the broader processes of public-sector reforms that were ongoing in Mozambique; hence the importance of assessing how its implementation influenced its outcomes.

The electronic LMIS in the national context

The LMIS was conceived as an integrated system that was supposed to offer the capability to register electronically land plots and tenures, and in the future potentially to provide citizens with the capacity to access the system via the web to apply for land tenures and follow up applications for land registration and tenures. From an institutional perspective, the LMIS was expected to provide cross-sectoral information to decision-makers by relating, for instance, the use of land for business investments and its use for mining and for the building of new roads. The LMIS was also designed to establish a land inventory to aid the better management and administration of natural resources.

The LMIS was installed in all provinces; data about land concessions and tenures were recorded in the system. The project was implemented by the National Directorate of Geography and Cadastre (DINAGECA, the acronym in Portuguese) under the aegis of the Ministry of Agriculture. DINAGECA is responsible for national mapping activities (topographic and thematic), land administration and land management.

Research methodology

Epistemologically, this research falls under the category of an interpretive study which assumes that similar situations can be interpreted differently by researchers. According to Orlikowski and Boroudi (2001), the aim of interpretive studies is not the construction of an 'objective' account; rather, it is the description of social and shared understandings around the phenomenon under study. Furthermore, interpretive studies do not seek to generalise from a setting to a population, but to develop an understanding of the deeper structure of a phenomenon (Walsham, 1993).

This study took place in the provinces of Maputo, Sofala and Cabo Delgado in Mozambique where the LMIS was being implemented. Specifically, the respective Ministry of Agriculture and DINAGECA offices were visited during 2006–07. Studying the same system in the three provinces helped to provide different insights on the research problem, given the heterogeneity of each province compared to the others.

Data collection procedures

The data collection methods used in the study included semi-structured interviews, document analysis, direct and participatory observation. Respondents included managers of the systems and decision-makers from different departments in the Ministry of Agriculture. In addition, technicians, system users, local authorities and some ordinary citizens were also interviewed. Table 8.4 gives a summary of the relevant information from the interviews.

A number of issues were explored in the study, with special emphasis on the users of the system and land technicians (surveyors), who could provide information on their perceptions of the system's achievements so far and on the challenges they experienced in working with it. With reference to system managers, apart from getting feedback from them on the potential of the system,

TABLE 8.4   Interviewee characteristics

Province	Number of interviews	People interviewed
Maputo	4	2 managers of LMIS
	12	4 LMIS users + 1 central
	2	2 local authorities
	12	12 normal citizens
Sofala	2	2 managers
	4	4 users of LMIS
	6	6 local authorities
Cabo-Delgado	2	2 managers
	5	5 users of LMIS
	7	7 local authorities
Total	56	47

the study also tried to gather information on the ongoing process of developing the system and on the main problems facing the exercise. The interviews typically lasted from about 30 minutes to two hours and took place at the informants' offices. For ordinary citizens and local authorities, interviews took place either in their homes or out in the streets.

Observations were carried out in the field visits as part of the aim of viewing the system on site, the equipment in use, and the interaction of people with the system in their everyday work. The documents that were analysed included Mozambican land law, government development policies, brochures about the profiles of the provinces, procedures of land concession and documentation on the development of the system. These documents helped the researcher understand the different perspectives of the implementation of the LMIS and the processes involved.

Data analysis

During fieldwork, short notes were made on observations and interviews that had been conducted, from which daily summaries were developed, expanded, organised, and made ready for analysis. Analysis of the empirical data was done through a 'manual' process (Glasser and Strauss, 1967) of reading the field notes several times and reflecting on the readings by linking them to observations, document analysis, interview notes and context before, finally, constructing themes.

The UNDP-based principles helped to provide a guiding frame for describing the themes, and for comparing and contrasting different data types. In addition, the four-stage model of e-government implementation helped the study to cross-check what was being done in terms of the implementation processes, in order to meet the e-government goals, and whether the outcomes obtained under the experience of e-government implementation were related to following a sequence based on the four-stage model.

Findings

In this section, there is a discussion on the expectations around the LMIS as governed by the principles of good governance defined in Chapter 2. Next, the LMIS is evaluated with reference to these principles, namely participation, responsiveness, and effectiveness and efficiency. A summary table is then presented that compares and contrasts the LMIS expectations with the findings of the study.

LMIS expectations

The strategic vision of the government was to implement a modern, efficient, reliable cross-sectoral and transparent LMIS capable of improving efficiency in the management of land-related issues within the cadastral services, the national directorate, its provincial services, and the relevant municipal directorates. The aim was to support cross-checking and validation of all legal requirements for the registration of land rights as well as for land administration and management. In addition, the LMIS was expected to facilitate the administration and management of land and other natural resources within the government institutions. These aims were to be met by the LMIS through a comprehensive and integrated database.

By implementing the LMIS, the government intended to improve its accountability by delivering high-quality national geo-referenced data and land information in a cost-effective manner involving modern and state-of-the-art ICTs. Using a cross-sectoral database, the government aimed to reach consensus on matters concerning land administration by involving relevant stakeholders. This process of sharing and consensus-building was expected to help improve visibility and enforce the rule of law and impartiality. The new approach was different from the 'black boxed' and informal approach of the past. In the new approach, transparency would be enhanced through the use of the web, which would enable the public and other constituencies to follow up on their applications.

Good governance principles and the LMIS

This study found that although the LMIS had not been completely deployed, all the provincial directorates had received an order from the central offices of DINAGECA to digitise the existing data and land tenures in the LMIS for the purposes of creating a land inventory to show what land was occupied and what land was available.

Since the land concession process should involve the participation of many different institutions, the researcher wanted to find out how this had been carried out in the LMIS, with regard to the system users and land surveyors. In this respect, it was important to find out, for instance, whether the users had participated in discussion meetings on the system specifications and its underlying requirements. Unfortunately, all the system users and land surveyors who were interviewed answered in the negative. This meant that only the top-level managers had been involved. The users said they had played a very passive role and only got in touch with the top-level managers when something in the released modules was not working properly.

Responsiveness was assessed at both internal and external levels. While the internal level concerned the activities within the government agencies (land surveyors, geographers and decision-makers), the external level concerned the interface with customers, both public and business in general. Improvements in the internal processes were meant to strengthen the external interface. Internal interviewees reported that the LMIS had helped to organise land information better and simplified the process of carrying out information searches.

However, at the external level customers did not experience a reduction in response time, although they were expected to do so in the future. A number of factors could affect response time. It was noted in this respect that the process of digitising land tenures at the provincial level was complex and compartment-linked. Attribute data related to land tenure had to be entered in the LMIS at the provincial level. With that task completed, the corresponding spatial information was entered at the central offices of DINAGECA in Maputo. Coordinating these processes simultaneously was institutionally complex, resulting in special demands. It was not surprising, therefore, to find that due to the incomplete nature of the LMIS land surveyors had to deal with both electronic and manual systems simultaneously. It also came to the attention of the study that a majority of the procedures on land registration were performed manually, while the LMIS was used to digitise the paper-based land tenures.

Evaluating efficiency and effectiveness involved understand-ing the capability of the LMIS to improve operations without the need for additional resources (software). This study found various types of software – for example, Excel spreadsheets to control payment of land taxes; mapping systems for building maps; ArcGIS and Arcview software of different versions – still being used without any effort to integrate them. The LMIS in this context was an added-on resource, without visible impacts on operations. According to the managers, the LMIS was still at the

TABLE 8.5   Summary of the LMIS expectations and identified themes

Good governance principles	Expectations of the LMIS	Themes identified	Examples of findings
Participation	Transfer the participation inscribed in the manual system to the electronic system of land administration and management	Participation in the development of e-government systems	Users did not provide alternative solutions for the current status of LMIS
	Provide the same opportunities to all citizens to access land information	Use of local knowledge and participation of local communities in e-government	Local communities provided useful information on land for the land surveyors to build the land cadastre and inventory
		e-participation comprised direct and indirect use of the application	Workers operating the LMIS and citizens did not enjoy the benefits of LMIS
Responsiveness	To be proactive in land conflicts	Internal response time	Reduced time for searching specific data
	Improve the response time to customers	External response time	Time to process a land application did not change
	Automate the land administration and management processes		
Effectiveness and efficiency	To integrate different databases and software in use by the different institutions	Parallel systems	Use of alternative software to accomplish the aims of LMIS
	Delivering high-quality national geo-referenced data and land information in the most cost-effective manner		LMIS not yet integrated
	Build a cross-sectional database using the same source of information		

development stage due to lack of internal technical capacity in GIS, which was a national problem. This problem was to be expected. The development of LMIS was initiated in 2004 through foreign human resources, and after their departure development came to a standstill, leaving only limited modules partially deployed in the provinces. The released modules were used to enter text data into the database, while maps of land processes were sent via email from the provinces to the national level, where the land cadastre was updated.

Table 8.5 gives a summary of the LMIS expectations and themes as identified in the study.

Analysis and discussion

The evolutionary model of e-government implementation based on the four stages of maturity presupposes its introduction in parts that are functional and that are delivered gradually. These parts can be considered as modules that at each stage provide services to citizens and that are electronically more advanced than the ones in the previous stages.

This model of e-government implementation allows implementers to test the physical infrastructure, showing the potential for delivering electronic services to many people at once, as well as demonstrating the ability to handle different and numerous customer requests and enabling the gradual implementation of system functionalities. It also has provisions for training and for organising skilled human resources gradually as preparation for the final stage of e-government – the transformation stage. There is scope in the model therefore for citizens to familiarise themselves with the technology gradually.

While this is the philosophy behind the evolutionary model based on the stages of maturity, according to the findings of this study the implementation of the LMIS was based on a different philosophy. When the implementers did kick off the implementation of the LMIS, the aim was to create a web-based system that had to follow the sequence of the four stages. Unfortunately, efforts and resources were applied to develop a fully functional web-based application without considering all the aspects related to web interaction, such as the testing of infrastructure and ensuring that the citizens were comfortable with the new technology. This happened because there was pressure to solve land problems with the support of an electronic system, but limited funding forced the managers to concentrate on ideal solutions and not on the feasible solution. In addition, there were contextual factors surrounding e-government solutions at the time that influenced the nature of the decisions that were taken.

In this respect, in the period from 2003/04 to 2006 the country was initiating several of the e-government applications that were running, which made it important to show the core functionalities of the applications being used. Most of these functionalities are in the transaction and transformation phases of the e-government maturity model. According to this study, the applications in the LMIS were delivering limited functionalities and restricted good governance outcomes. As an example, participation was still based on customary processes and not on electronic channels. In addition, external responsiveness, effectiveness and efficiency had not been verified at all. Furthermore, a web page which was supposed to be the instrument for testing the maturity of the LMIS had not been developed based on the requirements of the four-stage model.

It was also significant that the LMIS implementation was focusing on improving internal processes related to land management and overlooking the importance of improving external processes that link the system to general customers. The internal processes are systems capabilities that incorporate features that enable, as an example, the registration of land information and the sharing of this with other institutions involved in the land management process. The information-sharing capability in the LMIS project was made possible by using an integrated database and Internet communication facilities. In comparison, external processes refer to the ability of citizens to get information on land-related matters and be able, if they so wish, to register land electronically and monitor the progress of the transaction through Internet-based follow-up activities. Improvements in internal processes could be attributed to the digitalisation of land tenures.

If the four-stage model of e-government implementation is viewed as an analytic parameter, it is noticeable that the first three stages of the model do not mention anything about the internal aspects of e-government. Instead, everything in the model focuses on the external relations or on the front end of the system. This is a drawback, because in order to provide a good front end, transformations should also take place at the back end. Back-end transformations attract some attention in the fourth stage, when the issue of departmental integration and improvement of service delivery is mentioned.

The e-government maturity model assumes that e-government in each country grows sequentially through the four stages, regardless of the specific context and of the available resources. In the case of the LMIS, the study found that this model of development of e-government applies only to some aspects, but not necessarily in a sequential progression. Furthermore, the four-stage model does not reveal in an explicit way the human and inherent organisational implications concerning, for instance, the capabilities that should be created to enable the successful realisation of each stage. It is also important to notice that the basic principles of this model of e-government development were not shaped by considering the unique characteristics of developing countries such as Mozambique. Despite this oversight, the researcher recommends its application as a tool for monitoring progress in relation to criteria that can benefit citizens. It is also recommended for purposes of monitoring e-readiness status.

Conclusions

After considering the current status of the implementation of the LMIS, the study concluded that this technology is still very far from meeting the expectations that can contribute to good governance and consequently to social and economic development. This indicates the need for more pragmatic solutions from decision-makers to bring about changes in the development of the system. Such changes will include hiring skilled people to develop the system, as well as improvements in infrastructure.

As for the implementation process, there was more emphasis on improving internal processes and less on external ones. In addition, the preliminary stages that were essential for reaching the transaction and transformation stages were not followed. In view of this, a parallel and gradual emphasis on both external and internal processes is recommended. This will help each stage to identify the necessary prerequisites such as infrastructure improvements and institutional reforms.

Finally, the four-stage model of e-government maturity should be extended to include indicators that measure how the model behaves in the context of e-government initiatives in adverse social and economic conditions.

9

E-governance for social and local economic development: a case study of Gauteng province, South Africa

Lucienne Abrahams and Lutske Newton-Reid

A purpose for e-governance

ICT innovations in general and electronic governance in particular have continued to draw significant attention. Many cities style themselves as 'digital cities' or as cities where communication and transactions are conducted using electronic devices and networks. These cities have an outward focus, presenting themselves to the world as global hubs of connectivity for business and culture. They also have an inward focus, towards ensuring that citizens have access to advanced communications and convenient access to services, often using electronic resources. In countries where poverty rates are high and ICT access is low, municipal governments can play a critical role in ensuring access to basic voice and data connectivity, viewing ICT infrastructure as bulk infrastructure like water, refuse removal and environmental services. From an ICT-for-development perspective, municipalities can adopt effective e-governance to encourage social development and facilitate local economic development.

South Africa has a comprehensive local government system consisting of 231 local, 47 district and 6 metropolitan municipalities (Government of South Africa, 2004), the majority being peri-urban or rural. The South African constitution and relevant legislation set local government objectives to include the promotion of social and economic development. Government policy, as outlined in the Information Society and Development Plan, sets out the vision 'To establish South Africa as an advanced Information Society in which Information and Information and Communications Technology tools are key drivers of economic and societal development.' Digital inclusion is one of the four pillars of this policy and a four-phase approach was adopted for e-government, with the first phase focusing on the Batho Pele information portal. The policy envisages a final phase of personalising citizen profiles and of tracking life events (Government of South Africa, n.d.). The first electronic government document, *Electronic Government: The Digital Future*, was written as an IT policy to support service delivery, rather than as an e-government policy (Government of South Africa, 2001).

This case study on e-governance for social and local economic development explored the purpose of e-governance in a local government context. The study focused on the Province of Gauteng, the economic hub of South Africa, and its 14 municipalities that constitute the system of local government. The research was undertaken in the period between February 2007 and August 2008. The choice of Gauteng as a study area was informed by the vision to re-create the province as a globally competitive city region. Achieving the objective of being a 'global city region' is dependent on, among other things, having productive social and economic capabilities relative to other global cities. Notable among these is the e-governance experience, enabling citizens, business and SMEs to interact with government, using the full range of electronic media and providing ease of access to health, educational, cultural and economic services. While municipalities are introducing ICT and broadband infrastructure, it is often asked whether this investment focus has a social and economic development purpose. Other questions concern the nature of the challenges faced in fostering ICT-enabled development.

In responding to these questions, a review of the relevant literature and a conceptual framework on e-governance are presented in this study, against a South African background. Perspectives from interviews and consultative workshops that were conducted with metropolitan, district and local municipalities were then used as data sources. These sources, including a survey of the Emergency Medical Services and of the South Africa Police Services Call Centre for Gauteng, as well as content from a review of municipal websites, were then analysed and conclusions drawn. These provided the necessary suggestions on strategy and some advice for policymakers.

It can be said, therefore, that the study has an overview of the state of e-governance in a selection of municipalities and applications in provincial government from which ideas for local level e-governance strategy can be drawn. The problem under discussion concerned the strengths and weaknesses in the current state of e-governance in relation to social and local economic development and in relation to the good governance characteristics of strategic vision, responsiveness and transparency (UNDP, 2006b). The research incorporated interviews with key informants, case studies on e-governance operations and workshop-format focus groups.

Framing e-governance for South Africa

South Africa is classified as an upper-middle-income country, yet the society suffers high levels of poverty and of inequality. In Gauteng, poverty affects up to 15 per cent of households in the metropolitan areas and up to 50 per cent of households in the local municipalities, with a number of poverty pockets of greater than 50 per cent of households (Human Sciences Research Council, 2005). South Africans experience many forms of poverty, including infrastructure, services and information poverty. Information poverty refers to lack of access to ICTs and the services that they facilitate, including electronic transactions and Internet banking, government services online, access to online educational content or entertainment. The South African digital divide shows major differences in ICT access between and within provinces. Gauteng is no exception to this divide. For the majority of the population,

TABLE 9.1   ICT access by type

ICT access	Yes (%)	No (%)
Mobile phone	81	19
Landline telephone	25	75
Internet facilities at home	12	88
Radio	80	20
Television	75	25

communications choices are either a call from a public phone or a short call or SMS from a mobile phone.

A feature of South Africa's ICT landscape is the rapid growth of the mobile telephony market. In the period 2000–08, mobile telephony grew significantly, with the market offering affordable contact via SMS, easily available second-hand handsets and prepaid call packages. However, mobile communications are less often used by low-income households or by small businesses for data communications, either for accessing social services or for conducting economic activities. Thus, mobile growth masks the 'development of the "data divide" between those with access to the Internet and the benefits it provides and those without access' (Gillwald et al., 2005: 130).

Table 9.1, extracted from Statistics South Africa's Community Survey 2007 (Statistics South Africa, 2007) confirms the view that the evolution of e-governance in South Africa will hinge to a large extent on households having access to a mobile phone, since households are three times more likely to have a mobile phone than a landline and Internet access remains low.

The statistics in the table, while providing limited insight into the community level of ICT penetration, do suggest that the successful introduction of e-services would need to be based on the realities of low levels of Internet access and high levels of mobile voice and data (SMS) access. SMS or short message service is extensively used in the commercial environment, with its applications varying from financial services such as credit card debits and account payment notification to advertising. Similarly, municipal (and provincial) governments could create a menu of e-services that citizens will value. This becomes a double proposition with advances in mobile Internet technology.

Public-sector reform, good governance and ICT for development

E-governance requires an institutional context within which it can flourish. Key components of such an enabling context include non-technological interventions such as the following: public-sector reform to improve service delivery; good governance to ensure that investments are generally beneficial; and applying ICT for development purposes.

Public-sector reform was a major theme in the 1990s' literature on managing public institutions and ranged from the 'reinventing government' concept in the United States (Osborne and Gaebler, 1992) to the 'computerisation of the public service' approach in Malaysia (Government of Malaysia, 1995). These concepts had an influence in the study as well as the interpretation of the multiple changes that took place in public services around the world during the early period of 'globalisation through technology'. The importance of public-sector reform remains valid in South Africa today, which still operates under the weight of a rule-driven bureaucracy, instead of being driven by a flexible bureaucracy, energised by management excellence.

Good governance addresses the responsibilities of the state, private sector and civil society to create an environment within which human endeavour can benefit society. It focuses on political, economic and administrative components of governance. 'Good governance ensures that political, social and economic priorities are based on broad consensus in society and that the voices of the poorest and the most vulnerable are heard in decision-making over the allocation of development resources' (UNDP, 2006b).

ICTs, including telephony, computing and broadcasting, can contribute to sustainable human development and poverty eradication (United Nations, 2005) through making social communication easier and more affordable and by enabling speedy and secure economic transactions. 'As accelerator, driver, multiplier and innovator, ... ICTs are powerful if not indispensable tools in the massive scaling up and inter-linkage of development interventions and outcomes' in the 21st century (United Nations, 2005: 48). ICT in the context of governance may also play a critical role in speeding up the flows of information and knowledge between the government, citizens and business. This assumes regular interaction and feedback, as envisaged in the community participation requirements for the municipal integrated development plans. However, there is no guarantee that ICT will deliver development outcomes if this is not the explicit objective.

Electronic governance (e-governance), then, relates to the use and impact of ICT in governance systems. It involves new channels for accessing government, new styles of leadership, new methods of transacting, and a new purpose for information and services. Various models are used to assess the progress governments make towards achieving e-governance. Approaches that review progress through successive phases of maturity have been widely adopted. The phases refer to a sequence that starts with publishing government information on the web, and extend to increasing the quantity, quality and value to the citizen over time. This is followed by the addition of interactive features for users, moving progressively towards offering full transactional capabilities. These early phases are often followed by the integration of services across departments and levels of government for multi-channel 'one-stop' service delivery. From the perspective of this study, the most valuable forms of e-government are those related to governance and that entail creating online governance experience through channels for citizen participation and for public comment on government planning. Through them, it is possible to access information as input for social or economic decision-making, using electronic media for development purposes.

Whether the intended results of e-governance have been achieved or have failed to be achieved is a matter for debate, informed by a growing body of research, indicating that results vary dramatically from one country to another and within countries. The list of studies, reports, benchmarking exercises, evaluations and measurements undertaken to explore relationships between the results and the resources invested reveal there is explicit concern for the manner in which public money is spent (European Commission, 2006). The studies generally seek to learn lessons from the policies of other governments, measure e-government progress relative to other governments, identify and learn from best practice, and discover global trends, apart from evaluating underlying e-government concepts to identify points of leverage (Jansen, Rotthier and Snijkers, 2004). The indicators that have been used to measure e-governance include input (resources invested), output (number/type of applications available), usage (citizen and business usage), impact (benefits to users/society) and readiness indicators (degree to which a country has the necessary infrastructure and services) (Booz-Allen-Hamilton, 2002; Graafland-Essers and Ettedgui, 2003; European Commission, 2006). These indicators, typically, give little insight into the value of e-governance for social and economic development. Such insight is usually revealed through in-depth case studies or longitudinal studies.

The research study on which the chapter is based explored the relationship between e-governance initiatives and social and local economic development objectives and how these initiatives promote the selected good governance characteristics of strategic vision, responsiveness and transparency. In the context of this study, *social development* refers to the sense of maximising the capacity of the individual, the family or the household and the community to participate productively in society, both socially and economically (Gauteng Provincial Government, 2006). The notion of *local economic development* refers, on the other hand, to the sense of facilitating an appropriate environment for establishing economic projects and programmes. These would ensure that the economy as a whole works better for all residents, to foster growth and accelerate employment (City of Johannesburg, 2004; Ekurhuleni Metropolitan Municipality, 2007b).

The South African study

The study was shaped by the context in which it took place. Gauteng is the most economically productive and densely populated province of the nine that constitute South Africa. The population of Gauteng in 2007 was 10.3 million people, living in 3.1 million households. The 14 municipalities that operate within the province contend with high levels of inequality, expressed through joblessness and low levels of essential services to poor communities. Given that the provincial government is oriented towards promoting Gauteng as a competitive 'global city region', it aims to reduce the existing social inequalities in a region characterised by a combination of wealth and poverty.

Each municipality has its own particular social and economic realities to manage. Ekurhuleni Metropolitan Municipality has a population of 2.1 million people, about a quarter of the total population of Gauteng, while Metsweding District Municipality has a population of 164,000 people, or approximately 1.8 per cent of Gauteng's population (Statistics South Africa, 2001; Development Bank of Southern Africa, 2003). While both share a rural landscape, Ekurhuleni has pockets of high industrial activity that produces metals, machinery, chemicals and plastics, while Metsweding is largely agricultural, with limited tourism activity. The presence of globally integrated industries in Ekurhuleni attracts labour from across South Africa, leading to a high proportion of informal settlements which need significant investments in infrastructure and services.

The municipalities formulate growth and development strategies (GDS) to promote long-term objectives for planning and budgeting and to respond to social and economic needs. These strategies are supported by integrated development plans (IDPs), which are reviewed on an annual basis and resources allocated accordingly.

The GDS and IDP documents are required to identify social and economic development objectives. Ekurhuleni's GDS, for example, indicated that its industries had underperformed under globalisation. Consequently, its objective was to stimulate the local economy through infrastructure investments that would give citizens and businesses affordable access to broadband services.

The digital divide was as prevalent in Gauteng as elsewhere in South Africa, with high levels of access to voice and data communications in the middle to high income range and very low levels of ICT access for the majority of the population, except for mobile communications based on SMS messaging and 'please call me'. Community survey results show that approximately half of households in Gauteng (49 per cent) had access to a mobile phone, nearly double the number of households that had access to landlines (28.5 per cent). These results would need to be disaggregated to a municipal level and further to a community level to understand the trends in the penetration of ICTs, in order to design highly specific access and delivery strategies for e-governance, connectivity and digital inclusion. It is possible that there was slightly higher household Internet access in the three metros and practically none in the three districts.

Nonetheless, the statistics show that a substantial number of households had the potential to go online through mobile or fixed-line Internet. In spite of the available infrastructure, the rate of Internet usage was constrained by the lack of affordability (World Wide Worx, 2008). This had prompted the metropolitan municipalities and the provincial government to consider facilitating broadband access. As an example, the Ekurhuleni 'Digital City' strategy contemplated providing broadband access to the home for all households.

In summary, the potential of the government of Gauteng to offer citizens and businesses an experience broadly similar to that in any global city (whether London or Mumbai) requires, among other things, innovation in using ICT to contribute to greater social inclusion of poor communities, by improving access to social services and through the impact of ICT on local economic development. ICT also has the potential to build and sustain good governance. A development agenda cannot be achieved without establishing an explicit relationship between e-governance, on the one hand, and social or local economic development, on the other hand. Furthermore, attempts at innovation in the use of ICT must take into account the cultural and economic factors that influence the use of technology and, by extension in this case, the flow of communication for e-governance to be successful.

Status of e-governance for development

In the case of some metros and districts, social and local economic development objectives were clearly articulated, but this was not uniform with respect to all municipal functions. In other cases, the objectives were not clearly articulated. In the Ekurhuleni Metro, selected e-government programmes were being implemented, but had no written status in the growth and development strategy, the integrated development plan or the digital inclusion strategy. Elsewhere in Tshwane Metro, the Smart City project had created significant infrastructure, including fibre-optic cable and wireless infrastructure, but there was limited connectivity and usage because of the lack of content, content developers and content management in relation to the respective functions of the metro government.

The 'e-Government Blueprint' of the Gauteng Shared Services Centre addressed a range of policy, organisation and technology issues, but did not align e-government with social and economic objectives that were set out in GDS and IDP documents. In fact, the blueprint did not take cognizance of the 'global city region' perspective through which provincial and local government would combine their respective resource planning, infrastructure and staff capabilities to create a province-wide e-government strategy. However, managers in the Centre and in government departments were progressively working to situate their planning and activities in the city-region frame. Information from metro and district governments regarding the G-Link programme, which aimed to build a broadband strategy for Gauteng province, suggested that significant further discussion was needed to design a strategy that addressed the strengths and weaknesses of each metro, district and local municipality. This must be done in order to guarantee affordable access and usage for households, local government services, small and medium enterprises, and large businesses. Its benefits would include facilitating the necessary economic expansion that was required for greater economic participation of the poor and unemployed sections of society.

The lack of explicit objectives made it difficult for the many institutions of municipal and provincial government to select relevant inputs such as focus areas for e-governance, content management or for the development of human resources. The most explicit specifications were for infrastructure *inputs*, but the specifications for expected infrastructure *outputs* and *impact* were poorly stated. In the findings of this study there was no indicator-based framework in place to highlight gaps or weaknesses, though the provincial government was formulating a monitoring and evaluation framework.

Status of municipal websites

Web content is an indicator of the level of development of e-governance and needs to be checked, among other things, in relation to the objectives for social and local economic development and also in relation to the characteristics of good governance. The study considered the content, functionality and phase of development of selected municipal websites, and examined whether there was adequate information regarding the functions each municipality is legally obliged to fulfil. Table 9.2 is a summary of the functions the metropolitan municipalities are supposed to fulfil to contribute to local development at the social and economic levels.

The exercise was straightforward for the metropolitan municipalities as they were expected to fulfil the entire social and local economic development functions. Sites for metropolitan municipalities therefore contained information on the majority of the functions. It was, however, more difficult to assess the district and local municipalities because they shared these functions. The sites

TABLE 9.2   Functions of local government

Social development	Local economic development
Childcare facilities	Local tourism
Municipal health services	Municipal public transport
Free basic service: water	Trading regulations
Free basic service: electricity	Control of sale of alcohol
Free basic service: sanitation	Control of sale of food
Refuse removal	Markets
Local amenities	Street trading
Sports facilities	
Municipal parks and recreation	
Indigent policy	

Source: Republic of South Africa 1998, 2000.

for district and local municipalities did not contain the functions in Table 9.2, with two local municipalities having no website. The review was thus narrowed to two functions: municipal health services (social development) and local tourism (local economic development). Three key findings can be reported based on the review of the municipal websites.

The first finding was that in most cases the information on municipal health services was limited to databases of clinics and only a few sites supplied complete information. To a large extent, there was little or no information on local health matters. The content on local tourism also showed great variation. Information on local tourism can target tourists (local, national, international) and emerging and established tourism operators. It is necessary to note that dedicated agencies such as the Gauteng Tourism Authority and South Africa Tourism operate to promote South Africa as a tourist destination. In this context, municipal websites can fulfil two additional functions to promote local tourism. One is to promote micro- and small local tourism businesses that may not have coverage on commercial websites, and another is to supply information/advice on how to start up a business in the tourism industry.

On one site, a press release was available on the establishment of two township tourism authorities, but the contact details of the authorities were not available. From the perspective of information for emerging tourism operators, only one of the 12 sites had information directed at this target group. In considering whether websites had information on local tourism, it emerged that three sites had comprehensive information, five had limited information while four had no information.

The second finding was about the functionality of the sites. This concerned issues of the user interface (language, look and feel), the variation in the presentation of information, the lack of navigational necessities (search functions, site maps) and some serious technical errors (which contributed, for instance, to the failure of previous web pages to load). There was great variance in the look and feel of the sites, ranging from *professional* to *clumsy*. The functionality of the sites was generally compromised by the lack of effective search functions and, with one exception, there were no site maps. The effect of this is that it takes a long time to find information, potentially creating high costs for residents and businesses that use dial-up access.

Language was another concern, as information is generally presented in English. One site had a language policy, advising that it would publish information in the four dominant languages found in the corresponding municipal area. It can be argued that the dominance of English corresponds with the main language of the current user groups and that there is low demand for local languages, due to low levels of Internet access in the majority of Gauteng's households. This illustrates yet another aspect of the digital divide.

The final finding concerned the phases of maturity. The study found that most sites straddled the early phases of publishing static content, including public relations and services features, to providing for basic interactivity via email. Only one site was found to provide transactions capabilities for online customer services and payments. The overall impression was that the level of maturity of the majority of sites was information publishing.

Case studies on e-local governance for social and local economic development

Despite the limitations revealed in the study, some parts of government were developing relative sophistication in e-services, as exemplified for instance by mobile and Internet-enabled emergency services. The Gauteng Emergency Medical Services (GEMS) and the South Africa Police Services (SAPS) relied on ICT to offer their services effectively to the public and to respond to an emergency within the shortest possible time frame. The SAPS Call Centre had been operational for more than eight years, while the GEMS, which functioned under the auspices of the provincial health department, was established in 2008.

In both these cases (GEMS and SAPS), the electronic system made a difference, since among other things it improved capability and business intelligence, it was difficult to remove information from it, and the time and date of incidents was known. This enabled the agencies to bridge human limitations and manage the effectiveness of operations. Furthermore, the e-systems facilitated coordination across sections of government. Most of the services that the government provides require collaboration. Lessons from the emergency medical services (EMS) and the design of the SAPS Call Centre system can be applied to e-governance approaches to promote other aspects of social or local economic development.

Gauteng Emergency Medical Services

Emergency medical services (EMS) are a core function in the context of social development objectives and community safety. In Gauteng, these functions were health-related (planned patient transport or PPT), accident-related and benefited approximately 10 million citizens. PPT services alone handled up to 150 patients per day. Historically, emergency medical services operated at the municipal level of government, but the services were to be transferred to the provincial government by 2010. The Metsweding (district) services were transferred to the provincial government in 2008. Even when the EMS responsibility is migrated, there will still be a need to link to local government services, such as fire, local police and traffic services.

At the operational level, the control centre used the Gauteng EMS electronic system (GEMS) to manage incoming calls and dispatches. In addition, the control centre communicated with local government when required through SMS, email and centralised radio. The Call Centre staff had undergone intensive training, including training on the GEMS system, and in listening skills and stress management. At the workstation, the dispatcher viewed two screens, one for incoming calls and for dispatching and the other for tracking vehicles through a Geographic Information System (GIS). Ambulances were fitted with tracking devices, which made it possible for the dispatcher to see vehicle movements on the GIS map. In future, the ambulance attendant would log into the control centre via a console in the vehicle and would be able to send and acknowledge receipt of calls electronically.

The control centre was in contact with the SAPS operations centre, and often calls were referred from the SAPS, due to greater public awareness of the 10111 (SAPS) emergency number, as compared to the 10177 the national number for ambulance and fire services. It was common for the local government EMS to send ambulance, fire and traffic management services in major incidents. In the new arrangement, provincial traffic staff would also sit in the EMS control centre and have electronic access to traffic information in the system. The study also noted that it was possible to conduct data modelling based on historical data and to build scenarios for resource allocation. These capacities offered a high level of anticipation and preparedness for large events, such as the FIFA World Cup 2010.

This computerisation initiative promoted good governance from the standpoint of the factors of strategic vision, responsiveness and transparency. In this regard, it was possible to achieve responsiveness where the EMS could ensure rapid transport to the nearest appropriate hospital or hospitals for stabilisation or treatment.

The electronic system had distinct advantages over radio and telephone, as the control centre could have accurate information on a vehicle's positioning and movements, thus ensuring transparency of the operation. In comparison, the radio and the telephone could present inaccurate information and positioning. The foresight that was evident in the GEMS initiative indicated strategic visioning and orientation.

The SAPS Operations Centre

The SAPS Operations Centre took and screened calls related to policing issues. The Centre recorded details and registered complaints, some of which were non-police-related complaints that were referred to other departments. The dispatchers analysed the priority of the complaints and dispatched police service vehicles accordingly. The electronic operations centre, established in 2000, had introduced continuous system upgrades, after replacing analogue technologies with digital systems and encryption technology. This minimised corruption, since two-way radio users could no longer tap into information exchange. The mobile data system was faster than the case-based analogue system. When a call was taken, information was sent through to the dispatcher's screen instantaneously. This had improved reaction time, thus making it possible for the supervisor to receive comprehensive information on which to base a decision.

The upgrading of the electronic systems was based on the need to address difficulties and to ensure rapid response to all calls. This was made possible through high bandwidth that enabled the processing of very high volumes of data. Radio, phones, vehicle tracking and GIS system were all integrated. As such, a bulletin board could show all the important statistics and keep the staff informed about their call response times, which improved efficiency and responsiveness. The maximum required reaction time for a SAPS vehicle to respond to a dispatcher's call was five minutes and the SAPS vehicle could send reports via digital radio, phone or SMS.

E-governance in Gauteng province

While the national government had acknowledged the importance of e-governance, there was no guiding framework for local e-governance, or for the municipalities that were assessed in relation to their e-governance capabilities. This may have contributed to the slow pace at which e-governance has developed at the local sphere. Evidence indicated that the evolution of e-governance had not followed a logical path from the formulation of strategy and common standards necessary for interoperability and quality of service to infrastructure and content development, despite the fact that the province had the most sophisticated IT systems in the country. A number of strengths and weaknesses were observed.

The provincial government's announcement that it would invest in infrastructure (G-Link) and the formulation of the e-government strategy (eGovernment Blueprint) resulted in a massive connectivity programme and intentions to introduce e-services. However, the lack of detailed planning for e-governance projects raised the risk of a misalignment between infrastructure spending and the attainment of development objectives. Furthermore, attention to content had been an ongoing weakness. As an example, the aim of the Gauteng online education project was to build computer laboratories with email and Internet access in around 1,100 schools. However, it did not have an effective education portal with locally developed curriculum content.

The main avenue for accessing content was the link to the independent Mindset Network website and the curriculum learning spaces on the Thutong national government education portal. Instead of placing links to curriculum content on a page with links to a wide range of websites for general knowledge, curriculum content, youth advice and edutainment, material could be posted on dedicated pages with attractive and interactive web design. It was the case, however, that the online application process for jobs in provincial government showed a general measure of success. Locating the G-Link project and the Gauteng online project in the Gauteng Shared Services Centre (GSSC) created the opportunity to build the necessary synergies by bringing under one umbrella the supply-side aspects of access networks, information management and content provision.

From the perspective of infrastructure and e-governance content for promoting social and local economic development, the study concluded that the GSSC was a key role-player for both provincial and local spheres of government. However, it needed to address the absence of an explicit social and economic underpinning for e-governance in its philosophy and strategies. Other challenges it faced in targeting the achievement of a coordinated e-governance approach across provincial and municipal levels concerned the need for the following: institutional collaboration; having a common vision for operational staff; competition for limited resources; and slow progress towards maturing e-governance. Institutional coordination may improve in future with the inclusion of municipal chief information officers in the CIO Council and the expansion of the e-government subcommittee to include municipalities.

The Provincial Department of Local Government collaborated with the 14 municipalities to ensure that the content of the integrated development plans is aligned to legislative requirements and to the plans of the national and provincial governments to promote harmonisation across municipalities and across the three levels of government. However, this focus had not been extended to cover e-governance. As a consequence, there were weaknesses in relation to the alignment of strategies with the broad capital expenditure plans for e-governance across the three levels of government. The department had documented an overview of social and local economic development objectives across Gauteng Province and this must be used to inform e-governance strategy, including strategic vision, and the parameters of responsiveness and transparency.

E-governance in metropolitan municipalities

Gauteng's metropolitan municipalities, City of Johannesburg, Ekurhuleni Metropolitan Municipality and City of Tshwane had unique approaches to e-governance. None of the three had a clearly articulated e-governance strategy, though elements of such a strategy existed in various strategy and planning documents. The City of Johannesburg had developed three related strategies, each of which could contribute to local e-governance for social and economic development, namely a municipal broadband plan, a 2010 ICT plan based on the FIFA ICT requirements for the city to host the World Cup 2010, and a digital city strategy aimed at leveraging the 2010 ICT legacy for a range of purposes that included e-governance support to small and medium enterprises. This latter strategy was yet to be approved by the Mayoral Council. Furthermore, the precise nature of the interconnectedness among the three approaches was to be defined. The city administration was still grappling with these complexities.

The 2010 ICT strategy addressed the ICT requirements for a limited number of football venues and for the following: a local transport system; tourism; marketing and communications. These demands created an enabling 'digital skin' which could accommodate sophisticated levels of e-governance, once attention was given to the day-to-day services that were available in the city, not just for those intended for the FIFA requirements. The ICT infrastructure for tourism, transport and sport, including networks and content, could contribute to local economic development, as they provided ease of access to information and ease of access to services not previously available in the city. That is why, as an example, the 2010 ICT strategy document was intended to promote tourism business objectives by '[Inspiring] and [mobilizing] citizens to contribute in areas such as tourism' and by 'unlocking social and economic development opportunities' (City of Johannesburg, 2007: 22). Such strategic measures, when effectively implemented, could create efficient communications as a strong platform for local economic development, and as the foundation for tourism information services offered by both the city government and citizens.

Ekurhuleni Metropolitan Municipality (EMM) had probably most strongly articulated its vision of a digitally connected city, one in which all citizens had access to affordable broadband services and where ICT development was part of the 'economic transformation and development' of the municipality. This strategic approach was set out in the *Growth and Development Strategy 2025*, the *Integrated Development Plan*, the *EMM Digital City Blueprint* and the plan for Customer Care Centres. Furthermore, the metro recognised the contribution that a vibrant ICT sector could make to its manufacturing-oriented economy, which had been lagging behind in global terms. It also accepted that its role was to facilitate this process, as it created opportunities for the private sector to step in and provide the infrastructure and services.

With reference to e-administration, Ekurhuleni had made great strides as it had to build a wireless network that connected nine administrative centres. It was now focusing on improving individual administrative processes and aimed to create a single view of its customers. While the municipality had no e-services, apart from a website that was weak in having little on social and local economic development information, it had a major project on, building customer centres throughout Ekurhuleni as a primary vehicle for e-services. The *EMM Digital City Blueprint* illustrated extensive knowledge of and insight into the characteristics and future requirements of the local economy, local realities and inequalities and aimed to address these identified needs, including digital inclusion and e-governance. While an e-governance strategy was embedded in the Digital City Strategy, it could be more explicitly stated, particularly in relation to the purpose of supporting social and economic development.

The City of Tshwane had made perhaps the greatest advances from an infrastructure point of view, with 470 km of fibre-optic cable around the city. However, the potential to provide citizens with cheap broadband services had not materialised. Thus, it was comparable to having a road network without any vehicles driving on it. Tshwane planned to focus initially on providing connectivity to a selection of facilities (424 schools, hospitals and clinics). Challenges included content development (once schools were connected), and the integration of the connectivity strategy and programme into key planning regimes (GDS, IDP) so that its many departments (emergency services, safety and security structures) could harness and build on the existing infrastructure. Tshwane also planed to implement at least 10 ICT-related initiatives by 2011 that would take government closer to communities. This would require exploring and facilitating opportunities for content development. In this regard, as an example, connecting local schools to the Internet may present the opportunity for a selected group of teachers to be trained as content developers.

E-governance in district and local municipalities

The local municipalities were at far earlier stages of e-governance and were working to establish effective e-administration, having not yet embarked on e-services projects. E-services were currently less likely to be web-based and more likely to take the form of call centres and/or walk-in centres, since in the absence of affordable broadband connectivity the majority of the local populations found it easier and cheaper to contact the municipalities telephonically or to visit satellite offices. Emfuleni Local Municipality respondents noted that they 'are nowhere near thinking about e-governance'. Emfuleni made extensive use of information management and information systems and a number of applications were in place to enhance the administration of the municipality.

Yet, a number of routine processes were still being performed manually. The Emfuleni IDP 2007–08 discussed the challenges and strategies for local economic development and the present impediments to IT, but did not acknowledge the role of ICT as an enabler for local economic development. In order to promote good governance and institutional capacity building, projects listed in the plan included introducing an electronic documentation management system, emailing electronic statements to residents, and linking all libraries and clinics to the wide area network (over a two-year period). Emfuleni expressed the desire for greater support from the district, provincial or national governments at the level of sharing resources that were commonly required by municipalities. These were often described as an 'online real-time repository that could reduce the time for reporting and facilitate access to policies'.

The findings of the study also show that the Mogale City IT function was under-resourced. Apart from having a good website, the municipality had no e-services and was planning to establish a call centre with a toll-free number. Furthermore, e-administration was impaired as the network was incomplete. The IDP 2005–11 and the *Master Systems Plan Investigation Report 2003* reveal that there was no specific aim to foster social or economic development through electronic media. Neither connectivity nor digital inclusion for citizens was expressed as a key development challenge. Moreover, ICT was not mentioned in relation to providing sustainable community services. While ICT was seen as a means to ensure sound governance practices, the performance indicator related to the Master Systems Plan (MSP) rather than to good governance. A number of IT projects were listed as priority local economic development (LED) projects, including an integrated land use management system and a project on digitising building plans. However, there were no specific plans that were listed to improve ICT access and relevant content for citizens as part of the LED strategy.

In Sedibeng District Municipality (incorporating Emfuleni, Lesedi and Midvaal), IT was a centralised function. The rationale for treating IT as a shared service was diluted by the fact that the systems were not integrated. In an area with high levels of unemployment combined with poor skills levels, Sedibeng and its local municipalities could benefit from e-governance, but were hamstrung by the current low levels of municipal infrastructure, citizen connectivity and content development. The Sedibeng GDS identified improved ICT connectivity as a key ingredient for increased growth and for the attraction of investors to the area. Over the plan period, key deliverables included: developing an ICT connectivity master plan; reviewing effectiveness and considering improvements to the deployment of CCTV cameras; exploring the creation of a centralised call-centre service for all municipal services.

Sedibeng happens to be a transport corridor situated on the southern border of Gauteng, in an area which, of all the municipalities in Gauteng, has the largest number of heavy commercial vehicles passing through it. The municipality thus has the potential to become a hub for e-services by attracting drivers and their companies to utilise its location for driver and vehicle licensing. It can do so by providing physical access for drivers to use the electronic resources needed for motor vehicle licensing. 'Capturing' this audience can create opportunities for the governments of Gauteng to provide other e-services to the drivers, such as health information, while on the road. Linking e-governance services to the physical redesign of spaces being utilised by long-distance vehicles could inform the formulation of an ICT connectivity master plan that might entail locating connectivity in key nodes as an initial step before creating a district-wide network over the longer term. The financing model for such initiatives would require a collaborative approach among municipalities and the provincial government.

Good governance: strategy, responsiveness and transparency

Typically, no dedicated e-governance unit existed within municipalities. Initiatives were driven by chief information officers (CIOs) in the larger municipalities, while the smaller municipalities mostly did not have CIOs. This meant that the emphasis tended to be on technology solutions, rather than on strategic vision, responsiveness and transparency or on other features of good governance.

Project characteristics

The wide range of e-governance and ICT infrastructure investment projects across the provincial and municipal governments were not commonly known or collaboratively organised. Moreover, each project had limited funding and other resources. Due to the fact that the projects were typically small, the potential for significant impact on large numbers of citizens was lost. Opportunities to transfer lessons, to emulate projects or to share resources across the many institutions of government were not currently provided for in intergovernmental arrangements. Consequently, introducing e-governance was a costly and risky exercise and the risk was increased by working in isolation. Pitfalls included vendor lobbying, lack of (thorough) feasibility studies resulting in white elephants, poor contract management, low levels of staff capacity to use ICT, a focus on tools rather than systems, and poor take-up rate by end-users, due to inadequate computer literacy and/or lack of affordable access. These were some of the reasons why e-governance had not taken root or flourished, even in the metropolitan municipalities. The findings suggest that greater attention should be given to building the strategic vision and responsiveness of e-governance projects in the provincial and municipal governments.

In order to foster collaborative efforts in building purposeful e-governance, a co-coordinating entity was vital to create relationships with an extended array of potential contributors from inside and outside government. For this reason, a key objective of the intergovernmental leadership role should be to promote *transparent* government through the many opportunities presented by electronic media and to draw the players together to share emerging lessons.

Connectedness

While ICT infrastructure was seen to be a key element of many growth and development strategies, the many infrastructure plans that had been mooted since 2003 had not significantly increased government or citizen connectivity and usage. Ekurhuleni had plans to provide the infrastructure and services that would enable widespread Internet access, while Sedibeng had plans to provide limited connectivity to the citizens living in the urbanised parts of the district. However, for these plans to become a reality, the distinct and complementary roles of the various actors at provincial, metropolitan, district and local municipality levels in initiatives intended to create 'connectedness' needed to be clearly defined. This could be done by mapping the respective roles, responsibilities and constraints.

To build 'connectedness', municipalities and the provincial government have to increase their *responsiveness* to the real needs of citizens and businesses. In particular, municipalities require support to harness e-governance for social and local economic development as one of many ways of reducing the economic divide between rich and poor. To build a cohesive society, in which economic attractiveness and employment are increasing and poverty is decreasing, the actors at local government level have to address the need to disseminate social and economic development data to local communities and to small businesses by offering electronic resources to promote local economic development.

Conclusions and recommendations

On the basis of the findings of this study on e-governance, the study has some conclusions and recommendations for the design of local e-governance strategies. They are as follows:

Local government reform and citizen participation

Ongoing policy, strategic, institutional and operational reforms are needed to ensure that local government is able to address the changing demands of urban and rural populations. This applies in particular where new and complex approaches such as e-governance hold the promise, though not the guarantee, of contributing to development. Clear objectives for local government reform and e-governance must be made explicit in strategies and in integrated development plans. National policy enjoins municipalities to develop strategies and mechanisms to continuously engage with citizens, business and community groups and argues for citizens' active participation at four levels: as voters; as citizens expressing their views publicly in relation to policy; as consumers and end-users entitled to quality services; and as organised partners involved in development. All of these forms of participation can be supported by e-governance.

The majority of municipalities in South Africa are peri-urban or rural municipalities, and their main challenges in the adequate provision of essential services are lack of funds and backlogs due to historical underspending. This funding scarcity may be the reason for the widespread failure by municipalities to acknowledge information poverty as a form of poverty and their current emphasis on the provision of *essential* services that typically excludes access to ICTs. The contribution of e-governance to addressing poverty and to facilitating the acceleration of services requires strengthening. In addition, the perception that access to ICTs by the poor is a luxury rather than an essential set of services needs to be challenged. This is a necessary feature of future work in the arenas of public-sector reform and good governance.

e-Local governance and development

Local governance is concerned with whether citizens are able to interact with their respective municipalities using ICT media and channels, in affordable and convenient ways. There needs to be an alignment between the technology medium for providing e-services and the method employed by users to access communications. For example, the supply of information via website requires people to have easy and affordable Internet access, while providing services via toll-free numbers over fixed lines requires people to have access to affordable fixed-line services. This has implications for e-governance as the channels available to facilitate interaction between citizens and local government depend heavily on the penetration of affordable ICT services.

The majority of the municipalities in Gauteng had websites, yet only a small percentage of the population had ready access to the Internet. Moreover, while all of the municipalities could be contacted via fixed-line numbers, most people relied on mobile technology for regular communication and interaction. It was beyond an average citizen's financial ability to contact municipalities via mobile phones. Consequently, most people used their phones mainly for text messages. It can be concluded therefore that citizens were not yet able to interact with municipalities in an affordable and convenient way, due to a broad policy failure in the country to achieve universal service and access.

Even where municipalities had introduced broadband infrastructure, there was still no guarantee that such projects would achieve the social and economic objectives expected from them, in the absence of an e-governance strategy that made the objectives of good governance and of social and local economic development explicit.

The following conclusions can be made for local government officials and policymakers:

- Web presence will have no value for poor communities as long as there is limited access to the Internet; hence the need to develop e-access strategies (more than just infrastructure).
- While larger municipalities with a larger tax base can implement advanced infrastructure plans, these plans must be aligned to social and local economic development priorities.
- Municipalities with a low tax base will struggle to build e-administration and e-services and will require funding from other spheres of government.
- Investments in ICT infrastructure require partnerships with the private sector, but municipalities need to have identified their purpose and objectives and employ effective partnership management skills to ensure that funds are well spent.
- Good governance, including public participation in decision-making, should be a major objective, given the opportunities offered by multimedia channels.

Recommended strategic initiatives

From the study, the following strategic initiatives to promote social and local economic development through local e-governance can be recommended:

Strategic Initiative 1 E-governance strategies must identify the particular focus for e-governance for a municipality as a whole, as well as for its constituent parts, based on particular social and economic development priorities. These focal areas could, for example, be health and schools in one municipality, emergency services in another, and local transport and tourism in yet another. The choice should be based on a service or groups of services that would make a significant impact in the lives or on the livelihoods of a large percentage of a population living in a province or municipality. The choices should be limited to two or three manageable projects per municipality and should emphasise the objectives of good governance.

Strategic Initiative 2   E-governance strategies should include an e-governance monitoring and evaluation framework to provide government with insights into the following: the appropriateness of the choice and level of desired outputs and outcomes (or usage); the levels of operational effectiveness and the relevance and quality of inputs; the short-, medium- and long-term impact of a given particular area of activity.

Strategic Initiative 3   A well-supported content management system that offers a collaborative platform for municipalities is necessary to continuously provide content that citizens and businesses need. Appropriate content management policies will be needed to promote transparent and responsive government. Public servants, teachers and communities can become content creators.

Strategic Initiative 4   E-governance strategies should be underpinned by infrastructure access strategies, which could be digital city strategies incorporating approaches such as municipal broadband interventions aimed at promoting connectivity over a defined time period, ten years for example. A GIS map of the infrastructure strategies of respective municipalities and their interlinkages should be prepared. This would show the gaps in a province-wide picture.

Strategic Initiative 5   A demand-side analysis should be carried out and a comprehensive budget prepared for groups of municipalities in a particular province or region, with individual breakdowns per municipality for current capital expenditure and running costs.

The analysis can be used to explore options for funding e-governance and infrastructure development, as well as for utilising e-governance applications across municipalities.

Strategic Initiative 6   Provincial and municipal governments must foster effective e-governance implementation, leading to project, budgetary and human resource planning that meets stated social and economic development objectives. If, as it may be expected, different governments decide to choose different focal projects, such a move would introduce opportunities for sharing lessons across the many institutions of government.

Strategic Initiative 7   An independent, non-partisan advisory panel on e-governance should be constituted that can be called upon as required to provide relevant strategic and technical expertise.

Strategic Initiative 8   The provincial sphere of government should facilitate regular and ongoing consultation and collaborative planning across the institutions of the provincial and municipal governments.

Implications for policymakers

The eight strategic initiatives may be viewed as general recommendations applicable and relevant to local government in a variety of contexts. The main lesson that emerges is that the local and provincial levels of government require a common strategy that views the purpose of e-governance as being that of generating social and local economic development. This is generally the case with other tools, such as those that apply to finance and to human resources which promote social and economic development. To attain this status, 'e-governance' or the utilisation of ICT in the governance and development processes can be stimulated by a clear specification of priority projects that use new technologies to serve large segments of a population in ways intended to have a significant impact on the lives and livelihoods of communities. This approach can be fostered by incorporating e-governance as a component of broader growth and development strategies at local government level and by making explicit the connection between development objectives and ICT-for-development approaches.

While ICT infrastructure and connectivity are a necessary condition for e-governance, they are not a sufficient condition for e-governance to enable social and local economic development. Therefore content development and infrastructure development strategies need to proceed in parallel, the one feeding the other, for people and communities to realise and experience the value of ICT in their economic and social activities. This suggests that government information and government services must be made easily accessible in the online environment.

People and communities can provide the content required for community information services, and for information services for the informal sector. Unleashing the power of new technologies through this approach can create 'social capital' and 'informational capital' currently only available to those segments of the population that can afford the relatively expensive mobile and Internet-based communications. In addition, it will succeed in placing such social and informational capital in the hands of poor households and communities.

10

ICTs in local governance: a case study of the Local Government Information Communication System (LoGICS) in Uganda

Narathius Asingwire, Christopher Muhoozi and Jennifer Angeyo

Uganda has been implementing a decentralisation policy for local governance since 1993 guided by the Local Government Statute (1993), the Republic of Uganda Constitution (1995) and the Local Governments Act (1997). Decentralisation in Uganda hinges on the need to increase local autonomy, while strengthening upward and downward accountability, so that the autonomy is used to meet the needs of the population. However, the implementation of decentralisation in Uganda – intended to improve local governance – has been criticised as poorly financed and as an overly centralised technocratic approach and system of local patronage (UNDP, 2003).

The Uganda local government system comprises five tiers, all referred to as local councils (LCs). LC I, representing the village level, is at the base of the ladder, while LC V, representing the district level, is at the top. Most executive decisions are taken at the LC III level, sub-county/lower local government (LLG) level, and at LC V, the district/higher local government (HLG) level. The last two are mandated by the decentralisation policy to act as corporate entities. The Ministry of Local Government (MoLG) oversees the decentralisation process, while fiscal mechanisms are the responsibility of the Local Government Finance Committee (LGFC).

Local governance system

The system of local government in Uganda, subject to Article 176 of the 1995 Constitution, is based on the district as a unit, under which there are lower local governments such as counties, sub-counties and parishes. The local governments (at LLG and HLG) are led by directly elected persons, who form local government councils. The LCs have both legislative and executive powers. They assist in the resolution of disputes, monitor the delivery of services and assist in the maintenance of law, order and security. Local Council III (sub-county local government) and the district council (LC V) are the main focus of this research, due to their pivotal role in local governance under the decentralised structure of local government in Uganda.

Under decentralisation, HLGs and LLGs have been empowered by the Uganda Local Governments Act 1997 (Cap 243) to be self-governing. This means that planning and implementing projects, identifying revenue streams and managing revenue, hiring and firing human resources, budgeting and budget control are done by the local governments and not the central government. In the local government structure, the district acts as a focal point for accounting of resources, while lower councils act as centres for implementing district programmes. The overall management of a local council requires that the council makes considerable investment in human resources and infrastructure, including ICTs.

National ICT policy and e-government strategy

In October 2003, the Uganda government produced a draft National ICT Policy.[1] This policy envisions Uganda as a country where national development – especially human development and good governance – are sustainably enhanced, promoted and accelerated by efficient use of ICTs. Despite these good intentions, the government is yet to produce a final ICT policy. However, in a positive move seen as an indicator of commitment to promote

ICTs, the government created the Ministry of ICT, almost three years after the draft National ICT Policy was produced.

Although it gives a framework for the integration of ICTs in national development, the draft policy seems to have been overtaken by events. It requires revision to include the current technological innovations and trends. More significantly, however, the National ICT Policy does not address the uniqueness of sectors. This can be evidenced in the overlaps between the mandates of the ICT Ministry, the MoLG, the Ministry of Education and Sports (MoES), the Ministry of Health (MoH) and the Communications Commission. These overlaps create conflicts in standards and affect initiatives in the use of ICT in local governance. Furthermore, in the absence of a harmonised legal and institutional framework, compliance with IT systems (such as LoGICS[2]) becomes a problem, especially when these systems are designed to cut across sectors, as in the case of LoGICS. The implications of this problem has forced the MoLG to prepare an Implementation Policy Framework that will be derived from the main National ICT Policy.

Despite these problems at the policy level, the government believes that ICT will improve its relationship with the country's business sector and citizens, and with its own employees (Government of Uganda, 2006). Uganda's acknowledgement and commitment to e-governance is reflected in its draft E-government Strategy where ICT is viewed as a tool and enabler for reforming government service delivery and for achieving transparency, accountability and credibility. In addition, it is regarded as a tool for providing effective access to information and in the provision of efficient and cost-effective service delivery. Other benefits associated with ICT include its potential to broaden public participation, promote democracy, facilitate research and development, and enhance competitiveness in the global economy.

ICT and local government context

Developments in ICTs have dramatically changed the way information is collected, stored, processed, disseminated and used, thus making it the most powerful tool for modernisation and development. E-government has emerged as one of the key initiatives to enhance efficiency and reduce corruption in the public sector, besides providing state-of-the-art services to citizens and businesses (Society for the Promotion of eGovernance, 2006). The investment climate in any country is partly dependent on the e-government readiness index of the country.

The Uganda government recognises ICT as a tool for social and economic development. For the government to implement the long-term national development programmes – such as the Poverty Eradication Action Plan (PEAP) and the Plan for Modernization of Agriculture (PMA) – it was realised that timely and relevant information must be available at all levels of implementation. In light of the catalytic role that information plays in national development, the Uganda government set up a policy framework to ensure optimum utilisation of ICTs towards socio-economic development. This policy framework was intended to stimulate more participation in the socio-economic, political and other developmental activities, so as to lead to improved standards of living for the majority of Ugandans and enhance sustainable national development.

To show its policy support for ICT development and for the integration of ICT in national development, the government launched several IT systems to enhance service delivery. Among these are HealthNet, DistrictNet and LoGICS.

An overview of LoGICS

LoGICS is a Microsoft Access-based system designed to facilitate local government monitoring and evaluation (M&E) and compliance inspection. Available literature (Government of Uganda, 2004) shows that LoGICS has specific objectives. These include:

- Ensuring the availability of timely, reliable and accurate information in the local governments to facilitate evidence-based decision-making and inform policy, thereby improving govern-ance standards.

- Strengthening decentralised service delivery by automating the local government planning process through service delivery monitoring and evaluation and project cycle management.
- Formulating a standardised way of monitoring the level of adherence to national standards and guidelines of the councils through compliance inspection. Through this process, best practices are disseminated and weak areas addressed.

These specific objectives of LoGICS have influenced the design of the system in relation to what it covers. The system collects data on local government profiles; monitors resource usage and availability; tracks project implementation and completion; reports on compliance of implementers with set rules, regulations and

TABLE 10.1   Planning and monitoring by LoGICS

Planning and monitoring aspects	Description
Area profiles	Provides descriptive information about a local government, e.g. the population and the number of cases of illegal lumbering in a particular local government area.
Resource usage and availability	LoGICS monitors available finance, staffing and vehicles.
Activity completion and planning	LoGICS monitors the building of classrooms, the spot maintenance of roads, and the training of staff (capacity building).
Compliance inspection	The compliance inspection database monitors the adherence to rules, regulations and processes.
Service delivery	LoGICS looks at coverage, usage, efficiency and other performance measures.

Source: Government of Uganda, 2004.

processes; and tracks coverage and usage of local government services, as illustrated in Table 10.1.

According to the Ministry of Local Government (Government of Uganda, 2004), LoGICS is flexible and allows for partial implementation based on local capacity and for customized analysis and reporting in response to local needs. Designed as a shared management tool for LGs and the MoLG, LoGICS makes information available to other ministries and stakeholders through the web-enabled *One Stop Resource Centre*. At LG level, simple performance reports can be made available on local bulletin boards. This functionality and operation of LoGICS is graphically explained in Figure 10.1.

As shown in the figure, information collected by LoGICS is stored in three main databases:

FIGURE 10.1   Operations of LoGICS

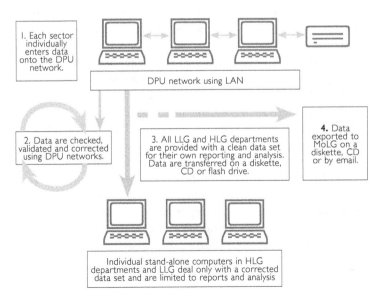

1. Each sector individually enters data onto the DPU network.

DPU network using LAN

2. Data are checked, validated and corrected using DPU networks.

3. All LLG and HLG departments are provided with a clean data set for their own reporting and analysis. Data are transferred on a diskette, CD or flash drive.

4. Data exported to MoLG on a diskette, CD or by email.

Individual stand-alone computers in HLG departments and LLG deal only with a corrected data set and are limited to reports and analysis

- The District Database, which contains data about facilities like schools and health centres. It also has data on LC IIIs (sub-county councils) targeting, for example, agricultural extension areas in sub-counties. Other available data are on school construction, road maintenance, and results of district or municipal compliance inspection of LC IIIs.
- The MoLG Inspections Database, which records the ministry's inspections of LCVs (district councils) and municipalities.
- The One-Stop Information Resource Centre at the MoLG, which is an Oracle 9i-based database that compiles information from all district databases. It is available to the MoLG and other stakeholders for the purpose of improved decision-making at national level. It attempts to reduce repeated requests for information in the LGs. The system is therefore designed to help decision-makers to pinpoint or to flag problem areas.

Research objectives and methodology

The main objective of the research was to assess the effects of ICTs on service delivery among local governments, specifically investigating the effects of LoGICs on the good governance constructs of participation, transparency, and efficiency and effectiveness. More specifically, the study sought to determine the contribution of LoGICS to improved service delivery at the local government level, as per the three good governance constructs.

The research was exploratory and utilised a largely qualitative methodology covering two districts which had been implementing LoGICS since its inception. These were Kayunga, located in central Uganda, and Mbale in the eastern region of the country. There were 9 sub-counties covered in Kayunga and 11 in Mbale. These districts were also piloting other ICT projects, such as the District Administrative Network Project (supported by IICD and the Uganda government) as part of the support for the decentralisation process. The districts were therefore selected because they already had existing ICT infrastructure and services.

Both primary and secondary data were collected to address the study objective. Data collection was divided into two phases. In phase one, initial data were collected and analysed. This enabled the research team to participate in the LOG-IN online discussions and contribute to the development of a draft e-Local Governance Africa Road Map. The second phase of data collection took place six months after the first one and, more importantly, three months after LoGICS had been upgraded to LoGICS Plus. The main objective of the second phase was to establish whether the gaps identified in LoGICS had been addressed by LoGICS Plus, especially with respect to impacts on governance. Study participants were purposively selected at different levels. These included lower local government (sub-county) staff as well as civil and political leaders at the higher local government (district) level. At the national level, key informants were selected from the MoLG.

Most of the collected data were qualitative, which required use of qualitative data analysis methods. Thematic and content analysis was therefore used, whereby data were grouped into themes as per the research objectives.

Findings

Effects of LoGICS on participation

The following categories of stakeholders participated: lower local governments (LLGs), made up of sub-counties, parishes and villages; civil society organisations (CSOs); the private sector. The participatory planning process from the village through parishes and sub-counties to the district is one of the critical aspects of Uganda's decentralised local government system. Participation in planning is gauged by the availability and quality of sub-county development plans, which incorporate submissions from village-level units and parishes.

This research focused on the application of LoGICS in LLG planning processes to determine the extent to which the use of LoGICS facilitated the participation of key stakeholders.

Involvement of the rest of the LLGs was through collecting and sending data to the district/municipality. At the LLG, the sub-county accountant, the community development assistant (CDA), the agricultural extension worker and the health assistant (HA) were listed as data providers for their role in filling forms sent to the LLG from the District Planning Unit (DPU).

The study findings reveal that the roll-out of LoGICS only involved the participation of local government stakeholders, as this was largely an internal system. At the time of the research, CSOs, as external stakeholders in district projects, had not yet been involved in LoGICS, whether as suppliers of information to the DPU through LoGICS or as recipients of LoGICS reports.

Theoretically, citizen participation under LoGICS is possible through the LLG, and the CSOs. It was revealed that there was no electronic link between civil society, the private sector and the LLG. The major reason was related to resource constraints on activating and actualising this link. Design problems also existed, since the CSOs were not treated as data providers and could not participate in validating the data. This created some inconsistency because the CSOs were represented on the district planning committee by virtue of their stake in planning and in implementing development projects in the district.

The version of LoGICS permitted CSO, and by extension citizen, participation by allowing them to publish reports on LLG issues to be shared with the public. They could also use civil society noticeboards or meetings as participation channels. However, the option of publishing reports faced challenges traceable to the design of LoGICS. This meant the system could not produce useful reports for the various stakeholders. In effect, therefore, 'users' of LoGICS data or reports existed only in theory because the system did not produce reports. Even where claims were made that the system could produce reports (as was the case for the Mbale municipality) there was no evidence to back up such claims.

In the study districts, there was no evidence of a district database which was a repository of information facilities on local

FIGURE 10.2   The data collection process

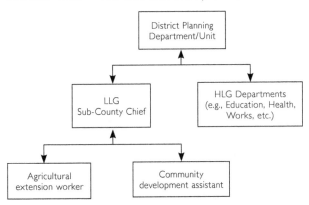

councils, projects or even on district inspections. It is from this database that reports would be produced and shared with stakeholders. In effect, the findings of the study cast doubt on the ability of LoGICS to promote the participation of key external stakeholders, including citizens.

The data collection process started with the printing of data collection forms (over 40 different forms exist) from the DPU, which were then sent to other HLG departments and LLG (see Figure 10.2). Data providers at various points, which included schools, prisons, police stations, health units, HLG and LLG head of departments and accountants, then filled out the forms. The completed forms were validated by the heads of department and/or LC III chiefs, as the case required. After this validation exercise, the forms were sent back to the DPU for entry into the system and for report production.

There was no evidence that LoGICS forms were completed in all the LLGs that were visited, although some HLG departments reported late submission of completed forms to the DPU. It was worth noting that filling in LoGICS forms and sending them to the DPU (in time) was an assessment area, which attracted a reward if complied with, or a punishment in case of non-compliance or underperformance. Mbale district received a reward for its implementation of LoGICS, because it 'made an attempt to use LoGICS' by filling out forms. Awards came in the form of an increase in central government financing of the winning district.

Although LoGICS provided for the validation process, to involve sharing of reports (software versions) with all units that sent in data, this activity was found inactive. The operation of LoGICS, represented in Figure 10.2, was very weak. For instance, the DPU did not send LoGICS reports to the parent ministry simply because these reports did not exist.

However, the failure of LoGICS to produce useful reports was addressed in the course of the research. Six months after the first field visit, LoGICS was upgraded to LoGICS Plus. The latter was easy to use and easily produced reports. The upgrading of LoGICS also rendered the system able to measure several parameters. In essence, it was no longer 'a closed system', where the LGs did not have access and power to add areas of assessment as their needs dictated. This meant that LGs were now able to use LoGICS to collect data on all parameters as they deemed necessary. However, this focus was still in trial mode by the end of the study.

The researchers found that the 'reports' were only dispatched in Mbale and Kayunga municipalities when there was a visit from the national local government assessment team. On such occasions, the DPU of the municipality submitted reports, for instance in the form of export data to the MoLG (see Figure 10.1, box 4). However, all the preceding processes (Figure 10.1, boxes 1, 2 and 3) were conveniently bypassed. In the case of Mbale district, most of the data that were collected using the LoGICS forms remained unsatisfactory, due to the inadequacy of the system.[3] The shortage of computers also meant that the computers that were given to the LGs to kick-start implementation of LoGICS ended up being used for ordinary local government work. Besides, the research findings showed that even if LoGICS in its original version had been able to generate reports, the parameters under which it monitored and reported were not in tandem with the monitoring and evaluation parameters of several departments or sectors.

While all departments at the HLG had computers, only a very small number of LLGs had them (only two LLGs in Mbale and two in Kayunga). It was revealed that even those with computers, including some departments at the HLG, faced difficulties because these computers were 'incompatible' with the specifications of the end-user equipment for LoGICS. The system was a Microsoft Access program which required the end-user to have at least a Pentium 100 MHz, 64MB RAM, 500 MB free space, SVGA and a working CD-ROM drive. In addition, its minimum software requirement was a Windows 95/98 or a Windows 2000 operating system. Some of the computers supplied, in comparison, did not have a functioning CD-ROM drive, floppy drive or USB port. These problems were frequently cited as a limitation to the sharing of software reports to enable validation – a key component in the operation of LoGICS. Lack of validation undermined the validity and reliability of the data collected and consequently that of LoGICS. Some respondents cited the threat of computer viruses as a barrier to electronic sharing of reports.

The study reveals that despite the rich potential that LoGICS carried, its implementation had met challenges that other ICT programmes also faced in their roll-out. In Uganda's case, these included characteristics associated with rural areas, such as remoteness, poor or absent proper communications infrastructure, and the shortage or complete lack of electricity. Other challenges were inadequate resources and the lack of computers and accessories.

It was clear from the study that to improve participation in decision-making through the use of systems such as LoGICS, it would be necessary to remove the barrier of lukewarm appreciation of its usefulness by a majority of its potential users. This response was a direct outcome of the lack of active involvement of technocrats and political leaders following the introduction of LoGICS. Other researchers, such as Tusubira (2004), have also argued that rural communities need to learn about the opportunities offered by technology in order to know how to put it to use. The engagement of rural communities also promoted ownership and sustainability.

LoGICS was also affected by the perception that it was basically a 'data entry' system meant to carry out the work of a copy typist. Due to this, training opportunities were often given to the lower cadre of staff. That was why several technocrats at the HLG level failed to take up these opportunities and passed them on to their secretaries. Such staff could not appreciate the benefits of the system in the way their bosses would have done.

In addition, most of the local government respondents agreed that LoGICS was viewed by the majority of implementers and users as a computer-based system to be used by those with computer knowledge. Sometimes information technology projects failed because they are termed and understood as 'IT projects', and not as government change projects (Society for the Promotion of eGovernance, 2006).

A further challenge for LoGICS, which also affected the implementation of other LG programmes, was the creation of new districts. This destabilized staffing arrangements. As an example, the creation of the District of Manafwa out of Mbale resulted in fewer staff in Mbale district as some moved to the new district. Among those who were transferred were people who had been trained in the use of LoGICS.

Despite the upgrading of LoGICS, implementation was still at the 'business-as-usual level', a foundation level that provided a limited framework for decision-making. Earlier research (Tiamiyu, 2000) had shown that at this level there was no opportunity to interrogate the transactions of government. Thus the level did not provide a basis for decision-making. In effect, LoGICS did little to enhance participation or facilitate transparency in LG operations. This suggested that it could face challenges also in enabling efficiency and effectiveness.

In summary, there was very little to show that LoGICS was helping to improve participation, either in the processes of LG performance evaluation or in access to LoGICS information by stakeholders. Besides, very few political leaders in local government were aware of LoGICS. This lack of awareness was largely responsible for the small number of political leaders who used LoGICS data as a basis for decision-making.

Effects of LoGICS on transparency

The design of LoGICS shows that its monitoring areas included resource usage and availability; compliance inspection; activity completion and planning. The implementation level of LoGICS by the time of the study did not fully enable authorities to use the system to release all relevant information to their stakeholders.

Apart from the challenge of printing reports, transparency would be possible if LoGICS had the capability to interface with other sectoral management information systems (MIS). Interface with systems owned by other sectors reduces duplication of effort, thus contributing to efficiency and effectiveness, as well as to transparency, as each sector can track what the other is doing.

In this regard, it was the case that at the HLG, each department (representing a sector or ministry) had its own stand-alone MIS provided by the mother ministry. For example, the Health Department had the Health Management Information System (HMIS) while the Education Department had the Education Management Information System (EMIS). In such a situation, there was bound to be conflict, especially in relation to the use of sector-level specific indicators. This was the reason for the perception that the introduction of LoGICS marked an extension of the Ministry of Local Government MIS, which was perceived to 'interfere' with other existing systems.

While it was true that LoGICS was primarily designed to help LGs to monitor their performance, it was also designed to be of use to other ministries and donors (Government of Uganda, 2004). Further, while some staff decided to 'add' LoGICS to their own MIS, they soon realised that LoGICS lacked various key indicators that were present in their sectoral MIS. This realisation created scepticism regrding the usefulness of LoGICS, since it did not monitor all the relevant ministry-specific performance indicators. It was noticeable, for instance, that in the Works Department (responsible for roads, water, housing, district construction equipment and vehicles), the LoGICS form covered only the name and length of a given road. It did not include key monitoring aspects such as road condition, drainage factors, traffic density and road location. The narrow scope of LoGIC's indicator coverage had created an ambivalent group of users and relegated the system to a secondary M&E system, able to attract a penalty or a reward from the MoLG, after the annual compliance assessment.

LoGICS was proposed by Uganda's Poverty Reduction Strategy Paper (PRSP) as the main M&E system for the PEAP at the local government level and fed into the country's national M&E. It was recommended that compatibility issues of LoGICS in its ties with other sectoral MIS be addressed if LoGICS was to make a meaningful contribution to the success of the National Integrated Monitoring and Evaluation Strategy (NIMES). This was the framework for harmonising existing M&E systems to reduce duplication of efforts and enhance quality data generation.

The case study findings demonstrate the interoperability challenges within LoGICS. Interoperability can be viewed from three perspectives (Society for the Promotion of eGovernance, 2006): the technical perspective refers to interoperability in the transfer of data across operating systems; semantic interoperability refers to challenges at the level of communicating concepts across operating systems; and the third is organisational in nature and occurs when there is an impediment in aligning information architecture with organisational roles. LoGICS faced these challenges to differing degrees in the various perspectives, severely compromising the attainment of transparency in monitoring the performance of local authorities.

The research findings also indicate that although LoGICS had been upgraded to LoGICS Plus in order to close the design gaps, the system needed to be able to run on a local area network (LAN). This could not be achieved because in some HLGs there was no LAN and no link between the ministry and the local governments. The LAN option would be an expensive venture since most of the HLG offices were scattered in different locations. Mbale was one of the few exceptions in that seven of its eight departments were

FIGURE 10.3   The ideal path of LoGICS

Base	**Transition**	**Functional**
• Assessment/baseline study • System launch • Recruitment and training of technical staff • Procurement, distribution and installation of computer software and hardware at Centre, HLG and LLG • Guaranteed access to uninterrupted power supply	• Mobilisation for political support at Centre, HLG and LLG • Follow-up, monitoring and mentoring • Refresher training for LG staff • Replacement of malfunctioning system • Attempts at utilizing data and reports generated	• All levels utilizing the system as per the design • All levels with technical financial ability to run the system • All levels with adequate budget lines for sustaining the system • System helping LGs in achieving set development goals

on a LAN, although the link with the parent ministry was not reliable. The existence of a local government LAN infrastructure and a reliable link to the ministry would enhance online transfer of information and contribute to the sharing of information, apart from reducing costs. It would also boost transparency in the use of public resources.

Effects of LoGICS on efficiency and effectiveness

One of the indicators of the impact of LoGICS on efficiency and effectiveness was the time taken by LLGs and HLG departments to file information to the DPU using the system. It was thought that since LoGICS contained resource and planning information, timely provision of such information was of fundamental value in helping LGs to allocate available resources properly and quickly. Timely access to information was important for an effective M&E of LG projects. Most of the LoGICS forms were filled on a quarterly basis, except for some that were needed for planning purposes, which were submitted annually.

At the HLG, the filing and reporting process was often erratic. This situation prevailed in Mbale where some departments could not recall when they last filled in the forms. Others could not even trace the forms.

The efficiency and effectiveness of LoGICS in improving local governance was constrained by low usage of LoGICS. For instance, only one technocrat at Mbale HLG was reportedly using LoGICS as a source of planning information. The majority claimed they extracted some information from the LoGICS forms that they used in planning. They added that if the system could produce reports, it would be much more useful. As stated earlier, the LoGICS system could not easily supply planning information due to its inability to cover all parameters required by planners.

Figure 10.3 is a schematic representation designed by the research team and is intended to illustrate the ideal operationalisation path of LoGICS. Some LGs were at the 'base' level, while others were in 'transition'. Within the framework of the illustration, no LG could claim to be at the 'functional' stage, essentially because the roll-out of LoGICS was still in its infancy in most districts. Technical, funding and budgetary challenges, among others, were standing in the way of almost all LGs to move to the functional stage.

Conclusions and recommendations

The realisation of the full potential of LoGICS was partly in enabling stakeholders to understand and use the system. Lack of knowledge of LoGICS among citizens was to an extent an outcome of less involvement in the planning and implementation design feature in LoGICS. The study found that the system did not have any significant effect on participation of stakeholders, whether in the operational aspects of LoGICS or in accessing information produced by the system. This was due to a number of reasons. The chief ones were: a faulty system design, which lacked useful reports and did not take account of all the requirements of the line ministries (sectors); lack of appropriate local area network infrastructure; and a prevalent perception that the system was appropriate only for techies and low-level data entry staff (e.g. secretaries).

Nevertheless, LoGICS had the potential to achieve a lot in terms of participation of stakeholders. The study therefore recommends a redesign of the system to take account of all the requirements for monitoring the performance of line ministries and to include appropriate management information and reports. In addition, the government needs to encourage user involvement. This may require orienting these users to LoGICS by pointing out its uses and benefits and implementing a change management programme to ensure increased adoption and usage. Finally, the Ministry of Local Government should enforce and maintain the existing system of incentives and penalties.

Although LoGICS has been upgraded to LoGICS Plus to address technical gaps, there was still much to be done to interest other sectors to use it. The study found that LoGICS faced interoperability challenges that severely compromised the attainment of transparency in monitoring the performance of local authorities. It is therefore recommended that the system should be redesigned and integrated with other sectoral management information systems and enabled to generate detailed information that can be directly used for planning and decision-making in all sectors. Legislation should also be instituted to ensure that other sectors are obligated to feed information into the system and to access information from it.

Furthermore, there is a need to sign a memorandum of understanding (MoU) with all central government agencies or sectors to streamline the roll-out of the system to the districts. This would help to harmonise and build interfaces between the various systems in local governments, since each department at the local government level tends to use its own sector MIS. This would also ensure that the roll-out of LoGICS is well planned and conducted to maximise its impact and uptake in local governments.

LoGICS was also found to have little or no effect on the efficiency and effectiveness aspects of governance. This was largely due the low usage of the system. This in turn was due to the poor technical design, poor system implementation and other challenges cited earlier.

The study also makes other recommendations, which, if implemented, would improve governance in local governments. One is that the government and its development partners should make available start-up funds to operationalise the system. At the same time, the government should encourage LGs to allocate revenue to maintain LoGICS after the launch. Further, the study recommends increased spending for infrastructure and facilitation for data collection, as well as provision of training and sensitisation activities to create a system that enables LGs to be efficient and effective. Increased investment in IT infrastructures, especially at the HLG level and gradually at that of LLG, needs a supportive environment. Establishment of a robust e-governance system will need strong budgetary commitment. The MoLG should also have budgetary provision for facilitating data collection using the LoGICS forms.

On ICT capacity in local governments, the study recommends the establishment and filling of ICT positions in all LGs to boost the capacity of the local governments to use LoGICS. Instead of using the district planner as the focal person for LoGICS at the HLG, a fully fledged section under the District Planning Unit should be created to take charge of the implementation of LoGICS. Additionally, there is a need to conduct training regularly, focusing on ICT preventive maintenance and troubleshooting of computer-related problems.

In order to complement the ICT capacity at local government level, the study recommends that the Ministry of Local Government should expand its staff and provide additional ICT support personnel to support LoGICS at the HLG (district) level. At the same time there is need to recruit appropriately trained ICT staff, and develop and implement an ICT staff retention strategy, at the Ministry of Local Government level.

Notes

1. See www.ucc.co.ug/nationalIctPolicyFramework.doc. The draft is still under review by the ICT ministry, which aims to embrace the many ICT initiatives in the country.
2. In January 2008, the Ministry of Local Government launched an upgraded version of LoGICS under the name LoGICS Plus. The researchers will maintain the use of 'LoGICS' for purposes of consistence and clarity. However, and where necessary, reference will be made to LoGICS Plus, especially to draw attention to particular modifications made in the system.
3. Six months after the first field visit, the LoGICS system was upgraded and its ability to produce usable reports was enhanced, implying that it is now possible for Mbale district to generate reports from LoGICS.

11

ICTs for political inclusion and good governance in northern Ghana

John Gasu and Jonnie Akakpo

The return to democratic rule in Ghana in January 1993 required the adoption of fresh modes of engagement between political actors to nurture the new democratic dispensation. The elitist cultural attributes associated with previous authoritarian regimes needed to be removed at all levels of governance for effective participation to take root.

Democracy is effective when it creates room for the participation and free expression of the preferences of the citizenry. Political participation, in this context, includes the involvement of previously excluded groups. In addition, participation is viewed as meaningful only when the social system is able to provide an information flow that allows the acquisition of knowledge on the workings of civil government. Since participation is a goal-directed activity, those in leadership positions are subject to the demands and preferences of the citizenry. The limitations on resources to meet the vast number of demands are often overlooked by the people, who are hard pressed; hence leaders need to find acceptable means of keeping the population informed on the state of the economy. If this does not happen, an overload created by demands may wreck the whole system.

The approach adopted in this chapter for civil–state engagement is one that entails the dualisation of communication channels. It is acknowledged that political participation in a democratic environment should go beyond the periodic plebiscitary systems that electoral democracies represent. In Ghana, however, what constitutes 'political participation' had been confused with populism in the aftermath of the December 1981 coup. The challenge of transcending a narrow conception of participation in favour of one where the citizenry see themselves as partners in the decision-making process became obvious in the early years of the new democratic dispensation. At the time, the freer democratic environment invigorated civil society and, due to the continuous demands made on political leaders, it became necessary to rethink the modes of political engagement by utilising e-government opportunities. It is from this perspective that e-government became relevant in the Ghanaian context.

The policy framework for utilising electronic media for the participation of citizens in the governance process is captured in the Ministry of Communication's *Information Communication Technology for Accelerated Development* (ICT4AD) document (Government of Ghana, 2003). The policy regards the e-government process as a way of improving the quality of governance and life. In the scheme of governance, the local level government structures are the closest to the populace. The decentralisation process demands that the local governments should be able to respond quickly to grassroots needs. The ICT4AD policy, therefore, recognised the importance of an effective e-government at the local level. This recognition did not translate into its comprehensive adoption principally due to infrastructural and human capacity constraints that a poverty-ridden country can experience.

Northern Ghana is economically backward and the limitations imposed by infrastructural and human capacity deficiencies assume exaggerated proportions in this part of the country (Bening, 1990; Songsore, 2003). It is for this reason that the IDRC-sponsored e-local governance project, on which this chapter is based, focused on Tamale Metropolis and Tolon-Kumbungu district. The project focused on the uses of ICTs for political inclusion and good governance in Northern Ghana. The project was carried out by the Centre for Information Technologies and Research Development (CITRED) based in Tamale. The primary data for the chapter were based on the field study that CITRED conducted in 2006. The research was based on the premiss that it is possible to utilise ICTs innovatively, even in deprived areas, to bridge the political gap between political leaders and their constituents.

National ICT context and the ICT4AD policy

According to the World Bank's gross national income (GNI) classification, Ghana is a low income country (LIC) with a per capita income of US$520 World Bank, 2007a). The country's low income status is also reflected in its ranking as a 'low average' country in the International Telecommunication Union Opportunity index. The low status of Ghana in ICT rankings appears in addition in the UN e-government readiness (United Nations, 2008) ranking of countries, where Ghana occupies position 133. The low placement of Ghana in ICT readiness and penetration generally is a reflection of an underdeveloped country phenomenon where infrastructural limitations as well as high levels of illiteracy, among other factors, act as barriers to capital-intensive ICT projects.

The realisation of opportunities that the ICTs provide in bringing efficiency and effectiveness in government and in governance played a role in the dissemination of the policy paper on ICT4AD in 2003. This policy aimed to streamline the use of ICTs for national development as it was clear that ICTs could bring about socio-economic development and changes in the governance systems of the country. In so doing, it would serve as an instrument for closing the gap between civil society and government.

The policy document is clear that enhanced knowledge of a people would change the way they do business. The expanded knowledge at the disposal of a society would become an asset in changing horizons and shaping conceptions of how the world systems run. In pursuit of that vision, the policy seeks 'To improve the quality of life, for the people of Ghana by enriching their social, economic, and cultural wellbeing, through the modernization of the economy and society' (Government of Ghana, 2003: 1). Within this broad vision, there are 14 pillars for defining priority areas and focus that were seen as crucial for national development. Among these pillars is 'Facilitating Government Administration and Service Delivery: Promoting Electronic Government and Governance.'

ICTs can play a crucial role in the delivery of government services, bringing government closer to the people, and facilitating the implementation of a decentralisation policy to support the activities of regional and district administration units. According to the policy, 'the government is committed to deployment and exploitation of ICTs to support the operations and activities of the Civil and Public Services to facilitate administrative cost reduction and the promotion of effectiveness and efficiency in the delivery of government services to the people of Ghana' (Government of Ghana 2003: 36–7).

The intentions and the visions enshrined in the ICT4AD policy are clear. Hence, efforts by the government to achieve the policy objectives have been earnest since 2004. In this regard, the Ministry of Communication has been working with local government to set up community information centres (CICs) that serve as portals across the country. The Ministry of Education has also been keen to set up ICT laboratories, especially in high schools, to equip the young with the requisite capacities to make them competitive in this digital age. The Advanced Information Technology Institute (AITI), established in 2003, at the Kofi Annan Centre of Excellence in Accra, is at the apex of the programmes in capacity building.

Ghana Telecom (GT) manages the fibre-optic backbone of the country, which now covers eight out of the ten administrative regions of Ghana. It is envisaged that the remaining two regions, which are in Northern Ghana, could be covered in the near future. It is also noticeable that in the past few years mobile telephony has been quite vibrant and competitive in ways that have contributed to the expansion of ICT coverage in the country. The coverage can be utilised for the purposes of e-governance and related electronic applications.

Despite these advances, a gulf exists between initial policy intentions and implementation realities. That is probably the reason for the silence in the ICT4AD document on what to do to bridge the digital divide between Southern and Northern Ghana through mechanisms that would enhance the establishment of viable e-government systems in the country.

Northern Ghana in perspective

Northern Ghana, which accounts for 41 per cent of the country, is noticeable for its pervasive poverty (Ladouceaur, 1979: 20). A combination of colonial and post-colonial neglect impacted negatively on the socio-economic development of this area to such an extent that the territorial limits of Northern Ghana coincide with the country's poverty map (Bening, 1990). The persistence of pauperised existence in this area is shown by the statistics in the various survey reports of the Ghana Statistical Service (GSS) on living standards in Ghana (Ghana Statistical Service, 2000).

In these reports, the three administrative regions of Northern Ghana occupy the unenviable first three positions on the poverty league table. Whereas poverty is not an unknown phenomenon in underdeveloped Ghana, what distinguishes poverty in the north from that in the rest of the country is the fact that in the south poverty is largely a scattered case, but in the north it is a near absolute situation. Figures from the Ghana Living Standards Surveys (GLSS) have since 1999 demonstrated this reality. By income measure, poverty levels are highest in the three administrative regions: Northern Region, Upper West and Upper East. In real statistical terms, this means that seven out of every ten people in the Northern Region are classified as poor.

With reference to literacy, as judged from the perspective of the ability to 'read or write a simple letter in English or in a local Ghanaian language, the savannah rural regions (which denote rural Northern Ghana) have rates below the national average. Whereas the average national literacy figure is 50 per cent, the average for the rural savannah is 41 per cent (Ghana Statistical Service, 2000: 11). These figures indicate lower levels of adult school attendance and literacy for the north compared to the average for the rest of the country.

Beyond the basic arterial (mostly untarmacked) routes that connect the principal settlements, Northern Ghana remained largely unconnected by road infrastructure during the colonial period. For reasons having to do with paucity of economic resources, even post-colonial Ghana has not done much to change this skewed infrastructural development. The denial of basic transport infrastructural development in the north since the colonial period has generally affected access to the rest of the country. This is especially so in the rainy season when swampy terrains render non-engineered routes impassable, thus thwarting attempts to reach the people.

The poverty imposed by the inadequate road infrastructure is worsened by the backwardness of the alternative channels of communication that electronic media provides in the contemporary world. The national radio and television networks are poor in terms of coverage, and unreliable in terms of reception. Reception of the only private television channel that reaches the north from Accra, Metropolitan Television (METRO), is limited to Tamale, Wa and Bolgatanga, which are the administrative regional capitals.

The gap is filled to a degree by radio, especially FM stations, which provide the readiest means of accessing news and other forms of information. The communal mode of existence in communities has also made it possible for large households to use a single radio set to receive programmes. Obviously, this arrangement limits individual programme preferences, since choice is determined by whomever is in charge of the radio. The Ghana Broadcasting Corporation (GBC), a public service broadcaster, operates three FM stations in the capitals of each of the three administrative regions: Savannah Radio in Tamale (Northern Region); URA Radio at Bolgatanga (Upper East Region); Radio Upper West in Wa (Upper West Region). A number of private, profit-driven stations are also to be found broadcasting in the regional capitals. The north is also thinly covered by the print media. Daily newspapers are normally published in the nation's capital, Accra (in the south), but do not reach Northern Ghana until the evening. The poor state of roads, and the sheer distance from the nation's capital, principally account for the late delivery of newspapers.

The distribution of telephones and other data communication services in Ghana is largely confined to the urban south. For instance, Accra alone accounts for 50 per cent of all telephone lines and more than 85 per cent of Internet service providers (ISPs) in the country. The second largest city, Kumasi, also in the south, accounts for about 30 per cent of all telephone lines (Government of Ghana, 2004). Rural fixed line telephony is almost non-existent in the northern sector. However, the mobile phone system has made significant inroads in opening up Northern Ghana. Three of the five mobile phone companies that currently operate in the country are in the north with reasonable coverage, which is still expanding. These mobile phone operators are MTN, TiGo and Onetouch. Fixed-line telephone services are provided by Ghana Telecom (GT), a quasi-state company. Call drop rates in the phone system are high, however, which produces a perpetual state of frustration among customers.

In addition to the challenges posed by the socio-economic backwardness of the area, there is also the problem of cultural elements associated with traditional notions of patriarchy. Despite the ethnic diversity of the north, males remain predominant in traditional governance structures and in decision-making positions. Unfortunately, a patriarchal order thrives by depreciating the value of women, supported by a culture that places them at the margin of society (Apusiga, 2004). This is a position that women, through socialisation and traditional modes of acquiescence, come to accept without question.

The CITRED e-government project and political engagement

It is against the background of the challenges posed by socio-economic backwardness – a subculture that is in tune with tradition, a parochial political culture and gender sidelining – that the CITRED e-governance project was undertaken in Tamale and Tolon-Kumbungu. The task entailed employing the available ICTs in the two districts to reduce socio-cultural as well as other impediments that affect participation in the local governance process.

The effort to identify the kind of ICT tools to be used and their suitability for optimum results began in 2006 through a baseline data collection approach. The task included identifying the existing ICTs that were in place, as well as assessing their usage, the capacity of the users, and the purposes for which they were being used. These objectives illustrate that the study was an inquiry to find out whether such ICTs were being used in the governance process at the local level.

Running a decentralised local government system in Ghana has always been associated with challenges. One of these is the realisation that opening up governmental activities to prying eyes, in most cases, would negate the very reason why people enter politics in the first place, namely to make money through political entrepreneurship (Bayart, 1993). Furthermore, the feebleness that poverty imposes on its victims invariably makes the poor and the marginalised reluctant to confront their social superiors. Instead, they are often quite willing to form client relations (Nugent, 1995). In such situations, compliance is considered a social virtue to be encouraged, and adopting a view divergent from the mainstream is considered insulting and an act of insubordination (Gasu, 2007). People without influence are thus confronted with hard choices if called upon to contribute to the ongoing discourse. Faced with this reality, they have the option of ignoring the prevailing social culture of compliance or of withdrawing and remaining mute. Neither option is in the interest of democratic participation. This can be achieved by using the avenues that ICTs currently offer. The open system that e-government portends for governance at the local level is well understood by political managers and thus is only minimally employed to run the affairs of the area.

The CITRED (2006) baseline studies in 2006 in Tolon and Tamale show that, except for occasional use of local FM radio

TABLE 11.1   Usage of community Internet facility

Do you use the Internet facility in your community?	frequency	%	valid %	cumulative %
Yes	160	22.6	47.2	47.2
Not at all	170	24.0	50.1	97.3
Sometimes	9	1.3	2.7	100.0
Total	339	47.9	100.0	

Source: CITRED, 2006.

stations for announcements about activities of the district/metropolitan assemblies, there was no mechanism for non-physical engagement with political leaders. The political leadership's preferred mode of contact with its constituents was through durbars channelled through chiefs, especially in the rural district of Tolon-Kumbungu. This was because the influence of the chief was felt most strongly in rural communities. The purposes of these durbars were mainly to convey government communications through local representatives without raising corresponding platforms for feedback. In Tamale, whose urban nature diluted the influence of chiefs, information dissemination was mainly done through the radio. In both cases, no serious effort was made to elicit proposals for the attention of local or national leaders.

The employment of the medium provided by computers for e-government was limited due to the low level of literacy in computing in the two areas. In the rural district of Tolon-Kumbungu, computing knowledge was only available to a small core of workers in the district administration. Computing knowledge in the Tamale Metropolis was noticeable, but mainly among the youth. The adult population remained largely stuck in the past, as basic computing skills and the application of that knowledge for such fundamentals as accessing the Internet and sending email remained a mystery.

TABLE 11.2   Purposes of Internet use

What do you usually use the Internet for?	frequency	%	valid %	cumulative %
To participate in online discussions	8	1.1	4.3	4.3
To send and receive emails	158	22.3	85.9	90.2
To do research	9	1.3	4.9	95.1
Education	9	1.3	4.9	100.0
Total	184	26.0	100.0	

Source: CITRED, 2006.

Evidence from the field study also shows that even the clerical staff in the district/metropolitan assemblies who keyed correspondence on computers for their bosses had not deployed their knowledge to access information on the Internet.

The general scenario as revealed in the baseline report was one of impoverished knowledge in the use of computers. Since the problem was pervasive, one can understand why that medium could not become the choice for the mobilisation of views for decision-making. Table 11.1 provides information on the use of Internet facilities in Tamale. It is based on responses to a question that sought to find out whether the respondents used Internet facilities in their communities.

Of the 339 who responded to the question, 50.1 per cent indicated 'not at all', 47.2 per cent responded 'yes', while 2.7 per cent checked 'sometimes' in response. Since Internet usage has many purposes, the study sought to find out the reason for using an Internet facility. The responses that were given are captured in the statistics in Table 11.2.

From the table, it is clear that most respondents used the Internet to send and receive electronic mail messages (85.9 per

TABLE 11.3   Restraining factors in the use of Internet facilities

What restrains you from using the Internet facility?	frequency	%	valid %	cumulative %
Cost of the service	75	10.6	29.2	29.2
Lack of computing knowledge	97	13.7	37.7	66.9
Not Interested	19	2.7	7.4	74.3
Lack of Time	66	9.3	25.7	100.0
Total	257	36.3	100.0	

Source: CITRED, 2006.

cent of respondents). The percentages for other modes of use were: to participate in online discussions, 4.3 per cent; for research purposes and for education, 4.9 per cent each.

Since Internet access was not as widespread as access to the radio or television, the researchers sought to find out from the respondents the factors that restrained their utilisation of the Internet services. Table 11.3 gives a summary of their responses.

The statistics reveal that 37.7 per cent specified 'lack of computing knowledge' as the reason, while 'cost of the service' was the reason given by 29.2 per cent of respondents. 25.7 per cent gave 'lack of time' as the reason for their inability to use the services. From these figures, it is quite clear that Internet use was not a popular activity among the people.

Even in areas where no specialised skills are required for reaching the people on a broader scale, as is the case of radio, lethargy on the part of local leaders in applying themselves to this medium is clear. During election periods the power of the radio is exploited fully for campaigning, but such conscious efforts for the utilisation of radio end immediately the last vote is counted. The mushrooming of various talk-shows that review newspapers in the mornings carry a rather deceptive view that these discussions are

TABLE 11.4   Statistics on radio ownership

	frequency	%	valid %	cumulative %
Yes	495	69.9	72.8	72.8
No	185	26.1	27.2	100.0
Total	680	96.0	100.0	

Source: CITRED, 2006.

targeted at the leaders. No agencies are created for the collation and transmission of information to the leaders, and for feedback to the populace. The widespread ownership of radio sets could easily be exploited in this regard. The statistics on ownership of radio sets are presented in Table 11.4.

Some 72.8 per cent of respondents indicated they owned a radio set, while only 27.2 per cent did not. It is noteworthy that non-ownership did not necessarily mean lack of access to radio. Table 11.5 provides statistics on access to radios.

Some 78 per cent of respondents indicated some access through friends, parents or other family members. However, 21 per cent indicated that they did not have any access to radio at all.

It is useful to note that mobile telephony had been outpacing other communications channels in the two local government areas.[1] Competition among providers had driven down rates, making it possible for more customers than before to get connected. These ICT facilities could be harnessed to establish and run e-governance systems.

At this juncture, it is necessary to recall some core issues concerning the concept 'political participation' in order to come to terms with the way it was applied to the e-governance project in Tamale and Tolon. Political participation, in this regard is seen to entail the following:

- inclusion;
- information flow;
- access and acquisition of knowledge regarding what is happening in civil government;
- establishment of a social auditing system between the leadership and its followers.

However, the limitations on resources to meet the numerous demands are often not clear to the hard-pressed people and hence there is a need for leaders to find acceptable means of conveying information on the state of the economy. If this is not done, an overload of demands could break down the whole system. As already indicated, the approach that was adopted in interpreting the nature of civil–state engagement is the one that reflects the dual nature of the communication channels that link leaders to citizens. This kind of representation is similar to the input–output political model of Easton (1965). Figure 11.1 demonstrates Easton's input–output model of political analysis.

In the model, there is a feedback mechanism that links the output with the input for a rerun of demands that re-enter a

TABLE 11.5   Access to radio

Access to radio through others	frequency	%	valid %	cumulative %
Access through parents	67	9.5	32.7	32.7
Access through friends	65	9.2	31.7	64.4
Access through other family relations	28	4.0	13.7	78.0
No access at all	43	6.1	21.0	99.0
Total	205	29.0	100.0	

Source: CITRED, 2006.

FIGURE 11.1   Eastonian input–output model

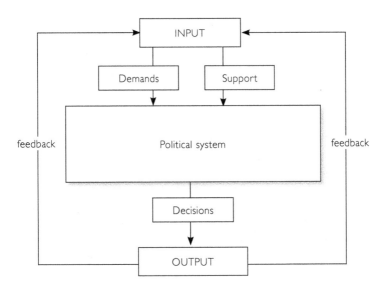

political system for consideration. In the contemporary situation, ICTs provide the easiest means for the population to link up with their leaders, and also the means for establishing a feedback mechanism. The project therefore ran on the notion that it is possible to dualise the channels of communication between civil society and the political leadership, and vice versa.

Implementation of the interventions in the project was guided by the results-based management approach. In this regard, it examined the extent to which such interventions had produced outcomes in the way people communicated with their political leaders. More specifically, the RBM approach informed the various interventions that CITRED embarked on in the Tamale and Tolon-Kumbungu local government areas to enhance political inclusion and participation.

Project interventions

In view of the state of socio-economic underdevelopment of Northern Ghana, it was found necessary to blend very basic ICT tools like radio with more sophisticated channels like interactive websites. The popularity of radio in terms of ownership and access determined its selection as the starting point for information dissemination on issues, and also as the medium for channelling demands to the authorities in the two local government areas. CITRED subsequently sponsored interactive 'breakfast shows' from March to September 2006 on Radio Savannah and Justice Radio. Bureaus were also created in the assemblies to receive collated information from radio stations and to give feedback on the information. The interactive nature of the radio programmes was facilitated by the use of mobile phones for the call-ins.

The medium provided by the Internet was useful, but since capacities were low, community members and local government officials had to be trained to use the facility. In this regard, CITRED trained 18 gender-balanced community members and local government officials over a two-month period. Ten men and eight women benefited from the training programme in the basics of computing and techniques of Internet access and usage. These trainees were in turn to train at least 10 others to expand capacities.

To enhance the flow of communication, CITRED procured materials for its technical team to wire up the offices of the two local government areas and to link Tolon to a VSAT facility in Tolon. CITRED also donated two desktop computers, multimedia projectors and tripod projection screens to the two districts. These were used to establish bureaus in the conference rooms that workers and the public could use for Internet access.

In Tamale, CITRED secured Internet connectivity for offices through Ghana Telecom. This was because the Broadband4U facility was available in Tamale at a cheaper operational cost than what VSAT could offer. The connectivity for internal usage and to the Internet became operational in November 2007. It facilitated transactions within district administrations and on the World Wide Web. CITRED paid for the website with an understanding that the government would take over by the end of December 2008. An interactive website (www.citred.org) became operational and served as a virtual interactive medium between the political leadership and constituents. It was possible for those who did not have direct access to computers to communicate their views through text messages, which were captured on the website. This option helped to close the gap between the people and their leaders.

The challenge of involving the non-literate group remained. Such people had a morbid fear of what the state represented. As a consequence, they would rather choose to be on the margin. For this group, the task began with breaking myths regarding the state and its leadership. This was done by using the medium of drama to illustrate the role of government and that of members of parliament (MPs) in a civic education activity. It was facilitated by officials of local government who volunteered to do the docu-dramas in the local vernacular (Dagbani) in ways that would enable the people to be excited by it and to appreciate its content. To achieve the desired effect, CITRED contracted professional scriptwriters and directors to help the volunteers. It was possible for community members to access the three docu-drama clips that were produced through a touch-screen activation process.[2] The touch screen was chosen because it could overcome difficulties associated with illiteracy. The videos had been successful in drawing the interest of the villagers due to their user-friendly characteristics.

The challenges took many forms, with varying impacts on the rate of work and on the complete realisation of project goals. Since the e-governance project challenged the status quo, the reaction of leadership reflected their fears about the likelihood of being inundated with demands. After the initial enthusiasm of political leaders, who perhaps had misread the exercise and assumed it was solely for the provision of Internet services, there was a change of attitude when they realised it represented a new avenue for political inclusion and for participation in governance. The political leadership that is represented by the district and metropolitan chief executives is the key implementer of the policies of the local government. In carrying out this role, the civil servants in the local administration execute what had been agreed upon. The subculture on which this system of administration works was borrowed from the British and in many ways had remained calcified in its application norms, which relied on physical contacts. When these key players realised there was a challenge to the status quo, they became evasive and failed to honour scheduled meetings.[3]

Discussions with civil servants showed they preferred physical contacts with people they dealt with, since the approach had the potential of giving them personal rewards. For this group of workers, physical contacts created opportunities for supplementing their income. Since they formed the core of the implementers, one can understand the foot dragging that they often demonstrated.[4]

Social conflict is quite endemic in Northern Ghana and the rate of progress had been halted several times as the national government had to impose a state of emergency to maintain law and order. In addition, there were prolonged breaks associated with religious fasting periods.

Conclusion

Despite the low level of economic development of Northern Ghana, this area is now the pacesetter in the e-local government system in Ghana. The populace, in particular, are enthusiastic about the opportunities that ICTs has provided. The use of interactive radio programmes helped local government officials in the two districts to appreciate the problems their constituents face and how to address them. The bureaus that were set up at the district offices also provided quick feedback that helped the officials to determine what was most urgent and achievable.

In addition, the project succeeded in building capacities in computing and in the application of that knowledge. The initial 18 trainees helped to expand the competence network. It was also the case that active participation and interaction on the CITRED website was proof of the advantage of adopting a dualised channel for communication between leaders and the population.

From this chapter, it is quite clear that there is a movement away from the rhetoric of participation to the utilisation of an effective mode of participation, one that is dependent on ICTs. Through this mode the illiterate and the previously excluded have the means to overcome some of their traditional impediments as they move into the mainstream. Such impediments include patriarchy. The chapter has therefore established that with the appropriate choice of ICT tools and the requisite ICT and non-ICT support to suit the realities of a community, it is possible for ICTs to increase the participation of citizens, even illiterate and rural citizens, in governance.

Notes

1. There is tremendous competition among mobile phone providers in Ghana, such that national coverage is now nearly achieved. At the start of the project in January 2006, the Tolon-Kumbungu area was not covered by mobile phone, but by June 2006 this area and many others had been covered by MTN, Onetouch and TiGo phone networks. Stiff competition among the mobile phone providers had helped in linking people to call-in interactive programmes on the electronic media.
2. Two of the three docu-drama clips are: (a) 'Be a Member of Parliament'; (b) 'Local Governance: The Chief Executive, the Assembly Person, and the Constituents'.
3. Several appointments that had been made by the CITRED research team with the Northern regional minister and the Tamale Metropolitan chief executive (mayor) failed to be honoured, as excuses rolled out, after one another, on their inability to be available.
4. In the many forums that the research team held with local government officials in the two areas, it was evident that pecuniary concerns regarding out-of-station allowances and benefits were one of the main reasons for the perpetuation of modes of physical contact when dealing with clients.

12

Summary of findings
and e-local governance roadmap

Timothy Mwololo Waema

One of the key aims of LOG-IN Africa was to develop a 'Roadmap for e-local Governance in Africa'. This can be achieved by synthesising the experiences and research findings of the individual national projects. The results can be used to sensitise and inform national governments, multilateral agencies and local authorities, as well as civil society, on broad guidelines for future investment and development in this area. The network chose to develop a roadmap based on a framework of questions derived from strategic management literature, as shown in Table 12.1.

The following sections contain a description of what was synthesized from the findings of the various research projects described in the previous chapters.

The national e-governance context

Answering the first question on the status of e-governance involved assessing the existing e-governance policy and strategy situation at national and local government levels, as outlined in this and the following sections.

Overview

Three main parameters were used to get a general overview of the status of the countries that were studied. The first was gross

TABLE 12.1   Framework of questions for the roadmap

Key questions	Outline description
Where are we?	Assessment of the existing e-governance context at national and local government levels.
Where do we want to go?	An expression of the overall aim of African countries with respect to e-local governance in the longer term.
How do we get there?	Developing a set of suitable strategies on how to address key issues from the assessment of e-governance context and to meet the vision.
	Methodologies and tools that are useful in the implementation of e-governance projects to accomplish the vision and objectives.
How do we know if we are getting there or not?	Monitoring and evaluation framework for the implementation of e-local governance projects.

national income (GNI) per capita, which the World Bank uses to classify countries into the following categories (World Bank, 2007b):

- Low-income countries (LIC) ≤ US$875
- Middle-income countries (MIC) US$876–10,725
- Lower middle countries (LMC)
- Upper middle countries (UMC)
- High-income countries (HIC) ≥ US$10,726.

The second parameter used was the ICT Opportunity Index (IOI). The index is derived from the merger of ITU's Digital Access Index (DAI) and Orbicom's Digital Divide Index (DDI). Its ten indicators seek to measure access to and usage of ICT by individuals and households (ITU, 2007). According to ITU, countries are classified and ranked into low, medium, upper and high average categories depending on their computed IOI values using 2005 data as shown below:

- High average IOI ≥ 249 (country ranks 1–29)
- Upper average IOI 150–248 (country ranks 30–57)
- Medium average IOI 68–149 (country ranks 58–120)
- Low average IOI 12–67 (country ranks 121–183)

The final parameter used was the United Nations e-government readiness index and associated ranking. The index and ranking are derived from a survey that was carried out in October and November 2007. The period corresponds with the timeframe for the LOG-IN Africa project.

It is possible to assess the status of a given country by creating a composite index comprising the web measure index, the telecommunications infrastructure index, the human capital index and the e-participation index (United Nations, 2008). When three of these parameters are used, as was the case for the LOG-IN Africa project that covered eight countries, the resulting classification would be as shown in Table 12.2 for 2008 and 2005.

From Table 12.2, it can be observed that the upper middle-income countries (Mauritius and South Africa) have the best e-government readiness indices and perform equally well from the perspective of the ITU ICT Opportunity Index.

Although the parameters outlined have some shortcomings, they nevertheless provided relevant information on the status of the countries that were studied. The efforts of these countries towards e-local governance benefited from a number of enabling conditions in the national context. However, they also had to contend with several constraining factors.

Enabling conditions in the national context

The research found that the national context was generally enabling of e-local governance in all countries. One of the enabling conditions is the fact that all the countries recognised the importance

TABLE 12.2   Overview of countries using selected parameters

Country	WB GNI	ITU ICT Opportunity Index	UN e-gov readiness 2008 (2005)	
			rank	index
Egypt	LMC	Medium average	79 (99)	0.4767 (0.3793)
Ethiopia	LIC	Low average	172 (170)	0.1857 (0.1360)
Ghana[1]	LIC	Low average	138 (133)	0.2997 (0.2866)
Kenya	LIC	Low average	122 (122)	0.3474 (0.3298)
Mauritius	UMC	Upper average	63 (52)	0.5086 (0.5317)
Morocco	LMC	Medium average	140 (138)	0.2944 (0.2774)
Mozambique	LIC	Low average	152 (146)	0.2559 (0.2448)
South Africa	UMC	Medium average	61 (58)	0.5115 (0.5075)
Uganda	LIC	Low average	133 (125)	0.3133 (0.3081)

of local governments in national socio-economic development and had developed a governance policy that was enshrined in certain laws and regulations, including national constitutions. The degree of autonomy of the various levels of local governments varied, depending on the extent to which a country had implemented the governance or decentralisation policy.

In general, it was found that governance policy is inextricably tied to legislative reform and that it was in the process either of being developed or of being reformed. The implementation of this policy was generally slow and incomplete in all countries (except in Kenya, where it had stalled; Mitullah and Waema, 2007), with a lot of power, resources and responsibilities remaining vested in the central government. This incompleteness in policy implementation may partly be explained by the great amount of restructuring associated with implementing a governance policy and the attendant resistance. Other reasons include the length of time it takes to implement a decentralisation policy, including the time it takes to enact the necessary pieces of legislation; and the intense politics that decentralisation often evokes.

Despite the incompleteness of the decentralisation policy, local governments in the various countries were still able to implement relatively successful e-governance initiatives. This implies that it is possible to implement e-governance without necessarily having a decentralisation policy. A decentralisation policy therefore is not a necessary condition or even a panacea for effective e-governance. Instead, what is needed is a supportive context for e-governance to exist. This perspective is exemplified by the situation in Kenya where there is no decentralisation policy or even a local government strategy. However, there was a relatively successful implementation of an Integrated Financial Management Information System (IFMIS) in the two local authorities in the country that were studied as described in Chapter 5. In this case, a number of policy initiatives succeeded in creating an enabling governance context for implementing LAIFOMS – the e-local governance initiative. The influencing elements in shaping this context were as follows: the report of the Commission of Inquiry into LAs in Kenya in 1995; the concept paper on empowerment of LAs; the policy initiatives contained in the budget speeches of 1997/98 and 1998/99; the Kenya Local Government Reform Programme (KLGRP), focusing on improvements in financial management in LAs; the fiscal transfer through LATIF; the results-based management and associated performance contracting that are part of public service reform (Waema and Mitullah, 2008). In addition, the national development plan and the Economic Recovery Strategy Paper also played a significant role in creating an enabling strategy context. At the implementation level, other elements came into play to ensure success. These included the contribution of the Ministry of Local Government's Kenya Local Government Reform Programme (KLGRP).

In most of the countries, e-local governance systems were being implemented as part of the shift towards reforming the public service sector. In some of them, e-local governance initiatives were driven by local government reform programmes, as a segment of the reform packages in the wider public service sector. For example, in Kenya and Mozambique, the devolution of power, resources and responsibilities to the lower levels of government was driven by the local government reform programmes in the ministries in charge of local government (Mitullah and Waema, 2007; Macueve, 2007). In others there was a mismatch of initiatives. This was the case in Uganda, for example, where the implementation of LoGICS and DistrictNet preceded the draft e-governance strategy. In neighbouring Kenya, the implementation of the IFMIS preceded the e-government strategy of 2004, although in this case the implementation was guided by local government reforms (Asingwire et al., 2007; Mitullah and Waema, 2007). It also happened that in some of the countries, the e-local governance initiatives gained direction from the national ICT policy. This was the situation in Uganda where LoGICS was certainly guided by the National ICT Policy of 2002 (Asingwire et al., 2007). A similar scenario applied to Egypt. In some of the countries, the e-local governance initiatives received impetus from the national e-government strategy, as was the case in Mozambique.

Another condition that enabled e-local governance is the recognition that ICT is a critical or strategic resource in national development, coupled with the existence of a national ICT policy and an e-government strategy, as was the case in all the countries, except in Ethiopia, where both were in draft form. In most of the countries, the planning and/or implementation of the e-governance policy and strategy is vested in an agency or in a unit in an appropriate ministry. The relevant ministry varies from country to country. Examples of such ministries include the Ministry of Capacity Building in Ethiopia, the Ministry of IT and Telecommunications in Mauritius and the Ministry of State for Administrative Development in Egypt.

A further enabler of e-local governance is the tie between the national ICT policy and governance initiatives in most of the countries. As an example, the Egyptian Information Society Initiative (EISI) enhanced the decentralisation of service delivery in government by providing multiple communications delivery channels and service provision centres (Fahmy et al., 2007). EISI had the aim of achieving three major outcomes: raising productivity, reducing costs, and ensuring efficient allocation of resources. Another example can be found in Kenya where one of the aims of the national ICT policy is to redefine the relationship between the government and citizens by empowering them. This would be done by providing increased and better access to government services (Mitullah and Waema, 2007). A final example can be traced to Mozambique where two key goals of the national ICT policy are 'to raise the efficacy and efficiency of public and private services' and 'to improve governance and public administration' (Macueve, 2007).

The link between e-government strategy and governance is unequivocally clear in most of the countries. In Kenya, for example, the 2004–07 e-government strategy had the aim of delivering government information and services efficiently to the citizens, in addition to empowering and encouraging their participation in government (Mitullah and Waema, 2007). As a further example, in Morocco the e-government policy targets online access to public information and services and the automation of the workflows of public administrations. The aim in this country is to improve governance by increasing the transparency, effectiveness and speed of public administrations in processing citizens' requests (Kettani, 2007). A final example is from Mozambique, where the key objectives of the e-government strategy are: to improve efficiency and effectiveness in the delivery of public services; to ensure transparency and accountability of government; to provide access to information as a way of improving business and simplifying citizens' lives (Macueve, 2007). The examples indicate that the e-government strategy has to be consistent with the national ICT policy. That is why in most of the countries the e-government strategy had been derived from the national ICT policy.

A final condition that had a role in enabling e-local governance is the effect of the successful implementation of e-government projects, as is inferable from the impact of some isolated examples.

TABLE 12.3   Necessary conditions for e-local governance roadmap

---

Necessary conditions at the national level

- Existence of a governance policy

- Recognition that ICT are strategic resources in national socio-economic development

- E-local governance linked to and implemented as part of wider public service or local government reforms

- Alignment of e-government with the national ICT policy

- Appropriate government agency or unit in charge of ICT

- Successful pilot implementation of e-government projects

In this regard, one of the key projects that had been rolled out in most countries was the development of an ICT backbone infrastructure, linking central government ministries to create effectively a government intranet. There was, however, no country that had rolled out this infrastructure in all ministries or at all levels of local government. It was observed, nevertheless, that all countries, ministries and government departments had created websites to provide public information and online services. Furthermore, they had made it possible for senior officers to have email accounts. In certain countries, some of the larger and more progressive local governments had begun to computerise selected priority business applications to inject efficiency in areas such as customs clearance and in citizen or civil registration. Other areas that were targeted included: electoral registration and tax, financial, land and human-resource management depending on the priority sectors of each country. However, such projects created isolated sectoral systems or databases. The situation was different in countries such as Egypt which had started to integrate systems.

In general, the implementation of projects, although varied in scope and in their level of success, had created an awareness of the role of ICT in development. It had also established usage of ICT in government, which had in turn created a readiness for e-local governance systems. In addition, it had provided useful lessons that can be drawn in the implementation of e-local governance systems. The factors that have been outlined create the necessary enabling context at the national level for an e-local governance roadmap. Table 12.3 summarises these factors on the basis of the LOG-IN Africa research.

Constraining conditions in the national context

The research found challenges at the national level that constrained or could potentially constrain the realisation of e-local governance. The key and common challenges were in relation to the following aspects.

ICT infrastructure There were two facets to this challenge. The first concerned the limited penetration of the infrastructure in central and local governments and at the household level. The second had to do with the poor quality of the infrastructure. As an example, in Mauritius, which has one of the highest ratings on the continent, less than 18 per cent of the population had access to the Internet from their homes as at 2006. In South Africa, only about 4 per cent in Gauteng province had a working Internet connection at home (Abrahams and Reid, 2007b).

E-government strategy In most countries, e-government strategies did not address local government and there were no e-government policies/strategies at the local government level.[2] In Kenya, for example, the existing central e-government strategy did not explicitly address local governments. Instead, e-government initiatives at the local level were guided by a local government reform programme (Mitullah and Waema, 2007). A further example is that of South Africa, where there was no e-government policy framework at either the national or the provincial government level (Abrahams and Reid, 2007a). A final example is the case of Mozambique, where many were ignorant of an e-government strategy in local governments, despite the fact that the implementation of e-government projects at that level was guided by a national e-government strategy (Macueve, 2007). This demonstrates an apparent disconnect between the policy/strategy level in central government and the local government level in e-government project implementation. Thus there is a need to promote and publicise e-government strategy and projects at all levels of government through various media channels to remove the possibility of such occurrences. In Kenya there was an inconsistency between the country's e-government strategy and the national ICT policy largely because the e-government strategy was developed before the preparation of the national ICT policy. This was also the case in Ethiopia, where the national ICT policy remained in draft form until it became irrelevant.

Centralisation   A great deal of power was still vested in central government in most of the countries. In Egypt, for example, although local authorities had a certain degree of administrative authority, they were still financially and politically managed by the central government. A further example can be seen in Kenya, where local governments have very limited autonomy and rely quite significantly on the central government, especially for funding and for financial management (Mitullah and Waema, 2007). Elsewhere, in Morocco, there is a high degree of centralisation of financial management (Kettani, 2007).

Financial resource allocation   In most of the countries there was inadequate budgetary allocation to local governments in national planning. In Kenya, for example, the government only allocates 5 per cent of the national income tax to local authorities. In addition, it was also observed that there was insufficient financial resource allocation to ICT at the national level in all the countries. In this regard, in Morocco, which is a lower middle-income country with a medium average ICT Opportunity Index, as shown in Table 12.1, the ICT budget is less than 1 per cent of the government's total operational budget (Kettani, 2007). This inadequacy in financial resource allocation affected budgetary allocations to ICT at the local government level.

Cost of ICT equipment and services   Most countries, including Kenya and Uganda, have ICT policies on universal access/services and/or strategies to enable underserved and marginalised communities to have easily accessible, available and affordable ICT infrastructure and services. However, the study came across cases of widespread unavailability of ICT infrastructure and relatively expensive ICT equipment and services. This means that local governments cannot provide e-services. This also makes it impossible for citizens to have online access to local government information and services or to have online interactions. Another study (Waema et al., 2007) found that the cost of dial-up Internet access in Kenya was 233 per cent of the gross national income (GNI) per capita. In South Africa the decision by some municipalities to acquire a class licence from the regulator to operate electronic communications networks for commercial purposes can be attributed to the failure of the universal service and access agency (USAA) to provide universal access/services to underserved areas and disadvantaged households (Abrahams and Reid, 2007b). Whether these municipalities will be able to provide local communities with affordable broadband ICT infrastructure and services and readily provide e-services remains to be seen.

Coordination   There was ineffective or poor coordination in e-government implementation. For example, in South Africa there was lack of support from institutions that have been set up to address and facilitate ICT penetration (Abraham and Reid, 2007b).

Others   Other challenges were the lack of adequate basic ICT skills at all levels of government, uncoordinated ICT investment, lack of integration of existing systems, lack of political will for e-government, and the shortage of relevant local research and human capacity in e-governance.

TABLE 12.4   Obstacles to effective e-local governance implementation

---

Obstacles at the national level

- Limited penetration and poor quality of the national government ICT infrastructure
- E-government strategy not addressing local governments
- Failure to promote and publicise e-government strategy and projects at all levels of government
- Inadequate basic ICT skills at all levels of government
- Inadequate financial resource allocation to local governments and to ICT
- Incomplete decentralisation of government
- Inadequate implementation of universal access to ICT
- Poor coordination in e-government implementation
- Lack of political will

These constraints can be considered to be the obstacles at the national level facing the effective implementation of e-local governance. Table 12.4 gives a summary of the constraints that were identified by the LOG-IN Africa research.

The e-local governance context

The defining characteristics of this context can be derived from a summary of the prevailing situation in the countries that were studied and from a synthesis of the key issues and challenges in the implementation of e-local governance systems.

Summary of findings on e-local governance

Results indicate that local governments in most of the countries had started to implement e-government applications, although they often lagged behind the implementation of e-government in central government. In Ethiopia, for example, the e-government applications that were studied had not been automated; while in Kenya, Morocco and Mozambique the applications that were assessed were the pioneer e-government systems at the local government level. It also emerged that in almost all the countries where e-government applications had been implemented, the local governments had created the necessary local area networks, Internet connectivity and web presence. However, from an e-government perspective, the focus had predominantly been on e-administration.

A few local governments had moved to providing services and information to key stakeholders electronically (e-services) through web portals. However, this move faced challenges in most countries. In Morocco, for example, the government portals did not take into account the socio-economic and cultural characteristics of the target users. The characteristics included language background, literacy level, and level of ICT knowledge. The oversight tended to indirectly enhance e-exclusion (Kettani, 2007). In South Africa it emerged that the web content was generally presented in English, while Gauteng province has four official languages. To compound the problem, some of the content was difficult to understand, out of date or poorly written and irrelevant (Abrahams and Reid, 2007b). Moreover, in most of the countries, the provision of information through the web portals tended to be frustrated by the poor state of e-readiness of most local governments. It was therefore common to find poor penetration of ICT infrastructure, limited access to the Internet at the household level, and a low level of ICT literacy among local community members. This was the case in Mozambique, Uganda, Ghana and Ethiopia.

In local governments that had web presence, the websites were at the publishing stage of the staged e-service content development model (Chan et al., 2007) or at stage 1 (emerging stage) of e-government readiness categorisation (United Nations, 2008). At this stage the focus is on rolling out informational content, which is largely static, concerning for example the procedures of and guidelines on various public services offered by respective government agencies. Only the city of Johannesburg in South Africa had online services. This would be expected in other big cities such as Cairo. However, hardly any local government had moved to the point of achieving electronic interactions between government actors and civil society (e-society).

A second finding of the LOG-IN Africa research was the revelation that championship of the implementation of e-local governance depended largely on officials in central government in several countries. In Kenya, Uganda and Mozambique, for instance, it was clear that the implementation of e-government at the local government level was still driven or championed by the central government. That is why in Uganda respondents from both higher and lower local governments revealed that LoGICS was basically a 'ministry [of Local Government] thing', implying that it had been planned and its implementation directed by the central government (Asingwire, et al., 2007).

A third finding concerned the technical quality of the imple-mented e-governance systems. In four of the countries the techni-cal quality of the implemented e-local governance systems was deemed to be unsatisfactory, with the quality suggesting poor system implementation or inability of the system to interface with other e-government systems. In Uganda, for example, the system functionality for LoGICS was found to be inadequate for generating detailed information that could be used for planning and decision-making. In addition, the system could not be inter-faced with other systems in government (Asingwire et al, 2007). Elsewhere, in Mozambique the network infrastructure had either been poorly installed or was very poorly maintained. This is a plausible explanation of why even though the Provincial Directo-rate of Agriculture in Pemba and Beira had installed the Internet, it only worked for a few months before ceasing to operate. Faced with this reality, the staff had to rely on Internet cafés and other available Internet sources to maintain communications links. One characteristic of e-governance implementation at the local level in most of the countries was the general lack of business process re-engineering (Macueve, 2007).

In addition, the research found that most local governments relied heavily on external consultants and/or contractors to provide a host of ICT services such as maintenance of ICT systems due to the lack of in-house technical capacity. This had significant financial implications.

Finally, and most importantly, the effects of ICT systems on good governance were found to vary from country to country depending on local and national contexts. The following is a synthesis of the effects of ICTs on different characteristics of good governance.

Participation

The study found that this varied depending on the governance context, with ICT having minimum to no effect on the participation of citizens in the affairs of the local governments. In Mozambique, only the top-level managers had been involved in land management system implementation. The users indicated they had played a very passive role and only got in touch with the top-level managers when something in the released modules was not working properly. It seemed in the case of Mozambique that the focus was on improving internal processes related to land management, overlooking the importance of improving external processes which link the system to citizens and other stakeholders.

In Kenya, although the study showed a significant increase in citizen participation following the implementation of the system, this change could not be attributed to system implementation. Interviews with key informants and focus group discussions revealed that the increase was due to the introduction of local authority service delivery action plan (LASDAP) as a requirement for accessing the Local Authority Transfer Fund (LATF) (Mitullah and Waema, 2007).

In Gauteng, South Africa, the majority of the municipalities had websites. However, only a small percentage of the population could use ICTs to interact with the municipalities. The key reasons were lack of access to the Internet by the majority of the citizens and that the total cost of ownership of a mobile phone was beyond the ability of most citizens. This was attributed to a broad policy failure in the country to achieve universal service and access.

There was very little evidence that implementation of LoGICS in Uganda had helped improve participation, either in the processes of local government performance evaluation or in access to LoGICS information by stakeholders. This was due to a number of factors. The chief ones were a faulty system design where the system did not have useful reports and did not take account of all the requirements of the line ministries (sectors), lack of appropriate local area network infrastructure, and a prevalent perception that the system was appropriate for techies and low-level data entry staff (e.g. secretaries). In addition, very few political leaders at the local government were aware of LoGICS. This lack of awareness was largely responsible for the small number of political leaders who used the LoGICS data as a basis for decision-making.

Only in Ghana did ICTs have significant effects on participation. The use of the various ICT tools, with the requisite ICT and non-ICT support to suit the realities of the communities, had helped to enhance effective participation of illiterate citizens in the decision-making processes of two local governments in Northern Ghana.

Responsiveness

In Kenya, the implementation of LAIFOMS had increased the responsiveness of both councils. For example, the system had hastened the issuance of business licences, there were fewer errors in payroll processing, and expenses were being monitored in real time. In addition, the number of complaints went down tenfold in Mavoko municipality, while in Nyeri municipality the number reduced by about 50 per cent. Most of the complaints were associated with errors in billing and with delays in the issuance of business permits, which LAIFOMS reduced remarkably. After LAIFOMS, customer satisfaction levels were relatively high, as is inferable from the low number of complaints.

In Mauritius, RMS implementation had improved the quality of service provision, including reminders that were easily generated and the detailed amount due provided on claims, reduced application processing time, improved response time to events and improved interactive communication, particularly between government and remote communities. However, these gains in responsiveness were negated by the lack of adequate and up-to-date information on local authority websites, the limited education level of some of the citizens, and the obsoleteness of the e-governance application and the platform on which the system was running.

In Mozambique, the Land Management Information System had helped to organise land information better and simplified the process of carrying out information searches. However, the response time or the time for issuing land tenure did not reduce after the implementation of the LMIS. This was due to the incomplete nature of the LMIS – land surveyors had to deal with both the electronic and manual systems simultaneously. In addition, most of the procedures on land registration were performed manually, while the LMIS was used to digitise the paper-based land tenures.

Efficiency and effectiveness

In Kenya, staff and consumers in both municipal councils acknowledged that the implementation of LAIFOMS had enhanced financial management and the efficiency and effectiveness of the councils' operations. Specifically, the system had enabled a marked improvement in revenue collection, increased business registrations, enhanced staff productivity, increased outstanding debt collection, reduced turnaround time from lodging payment request to receiving payment, and increased payroll accuracy.

In Mauritius, the effects of the revenue management system on efficiency and effectiveness were mixed. The more positive effects were negated by a number of system and institutional factors, including lack of regulations governing resource allocation and use, outdated/obsolete software and platform, lack of integration of RMS with other systems and resistance to change by users.

Efficiency and effectiveness were not improved by implementing LMIS in Mozambique. This was largely attributed to the fact that the system was still at the development stage due to lack of internal technical capacity in GIS. The system had been developed and partially implemented by foreign consultants, who left after resources ran out. They left only a few modules partially deployed in the provinces. The implemented modules were used to enter text data into the database, while maps of land processes were sent via email from the provinces to the national level, where the land cadastre was updated.

In Uganda, LoGICS was also found to have little or no effect on the efficiency and effectiveness aspects of governance. This was largely due to the low usage of the system. This in turn was due to poor technical design and poor system implementation, among other challenges.

Transparency

In Kenya, staff and consumers in both municipal councils agreed that the implementation of the financial management system had led to increased transparency. For example, the system had facilitated all payments to be receipted and the issuance of business permits to be transparent, consistent and straightforward; rendered staff overspending without approval difficult and reduced corrupt practices; and increased openness in the tendering process.

In Mauritius, the implementation of RMS improved transparency by clearly showing the rate applicable on claims and the proposal made by the Valuation Office, and increasing public access to information on revenue collection procedures and on specific rates. However, these improvements in transparency were negated by the lack of adequate and up-to-date information on local authority websites, the limited educational level of some of the citizens and hence ability to interpret the information on bills, and the obsoleteness of the governance application and the platform on which system was running.

The study in Uganda found that LoGICS faced interoperability challenges that severely compromised the attainment of transparency in monitoring the performance of local authorities.

Accountability

In Kenya, staff and consumers in both municipal councils agreed that the implementation of LAIFOMS had enhanced accountability. In this connection, the system had enabled all business permit licences to be tracked very easily; the keeping of a record of all properties; the monitoring of revenue collection; the tracking of payrolls to ensure there were no ghost workers; and the tracking of all payments made by the councils from the time they were authorised to the time they were received.

Equity

The implementation of the revenue management system in Mauritius had no negative effects on equity. However, a significant proportion of citizens believed that other forms of disparity had been created. The system discriminated between educated and less educated citizens, low and high income earners, and young and old citizens. This can be explained by the elitist nature of ICTs, the associated high costs and the apparent alignment of the culture embedded in ICTs to the culture appreciated by most youth.

Key challenges

Thematically, the key challenges at the local government level according to the research findings can be summarised as follows:

E-governance strategy   In almost all the countries where e-government systems had been or were being implemented (Ethiopia, Kenya, Morocco, Mozambique, South Africa and Uganda), there was no guiding e-governance or e-government strategy at the local government level. It was only in the highest levels of local government (large city directorates in South Africa, Egypt and Ethiopia) where there were e-governance strategies at that level.

E-readiness   The e-readiness of most local governments that were studied was low. The key issues leading to this state include the lack of technical ICT human capacity (Ethiopia, Kenya, Uganda and Mozambique); low ICT literacy and usage (Ethiopia, Kenya, Mauritius, Mozambique, South Africa and Uganda); lack of ICT units or functions (Ethiopia, Kenya, Mozambique, Morocco, South Africa and Uganda); little or no access to ICT infrastructure (Ethiopia, Mauritius, Morocco and Uganda); limited, slow or non-existent Internet connectivity (Ethiopia, Kenya, Mauritius and Uganda) for the staff of local authorities or the community.

ICT funding There was inadequate financial resource allocation to ICT in most of the countries (Ethiopia, Kenya, Mozambique, Senegal and Uganda). Although this challenge could be considered to be a part of poor e-readiness, it is an important issue in its own right as nothing can be meaningfully achieved without financial resources.

Human resources capacity In addition to the lack of technical ICT skills, which also affects e-readiness, most local governments did not have the requisite in-house managerial ICT skills. In addition, they lacked the training programmes to create a sustainable pool of staff with basic ICT literacy, technical and managerial skills. The key consequence of this was the use of external consultants and contractors (in Kenya, Mozambique and Mauritius), who make e-governance roll-out very expensive.

Institutional governance structure There were no institutional governance structures in most local governments that were studied. In South Africa, for example, there was no institutional framework to drive e-governance in the municipalities at national and regional levels. The metropolitan municipalities would typically employ chief ICT officers (CIOs), who would be part of executive management. In comparison, the smaller municipalities would employ IT managers or directors, who would not be strategic. This made it impossible for them to influence ICT direction (Abrahams and Reid, 2007b). In the other countries, local governments did not have either an ICT structure or staff. ICT issues in these countries tended to be handled by management or by appropriate departments, depending on the initiatives being implemented. In the Kenya case study, for example, the accounting department was responsible for the roll-out of the Integrated Financial Management Information System in both municipal councils (Mitullah and Waema, 2007). The status of ICT staffing and institutional governance structure in the local authorities in the various countries is a reflection of the stage of ICT development at that level of government.

Business processes　Business process re-engineering has been identified as critical in e-government implementation. In Egypt and Morocco, for example, business processes were not documented, as well as being ineffective or inconsistent.

Change management　Change management has been identified in relevant literature as one of the key challenges in e-government implementation. In this research, resistance to change associated with e-government implementation was found in Egypt and Mauritius.

Cost and affordability　The high cost of training and of ICT equipment in Mauritius and Mozambique, respectively, were a great challenge to the implementation of the e-government systems that were studied. From a consumer perspective, a different study in Kenya (Waema et al., 2007) found that the Internet was relatively expensive. This affected e-access. More specifically, the average dial-up Internet cost was 233 per cent of gross national income per capita.

The proposed roadmap

The proposed roadmap is made up of the answers to the remaining three questions of the adopted framework of the research, as outlined in Table 12.1. This roadmap for the implementation of e-local governance projects is supported by the following fundamental requirements:

Vision

In order to implement e-local governance projects, it is important to consider where e-governance will take us. The answer to this question would be an expression of a vision for e-local governance, or for the desired end-state in the longer term. A vision for e-local governance according to the recommendation of this research can be expressed as:

> E-government implementation resulting in good local governance outcomes and contributing to local economic and social development.

Strategies and methodologies

From the research results the means of achieving the desired end results for the countries that were studied can be synthesised. The synthesis is relevant for other countries in the same development stages as the countries in the LOG-IN Africa research, especially those in the low-income category. It focuses on three main areas: e-governance strategic direction; business process re-engineering methodology; e-governance implementation methodology.

E-governance strategic direction

The first step is to establish an e-governance strategic direction. To establish this direction for the countries in this research, certain steps were taken: identifying issues based on assessment of the existing situation in the various countries; specifying the reasons governing their conceptual status as issues (such as an inadequacy in the existing situation or being inconsistent with the vision); assessing what the consequences would be if a given issue was not addressed; developing a set of suitable strategies to address the issues. Details of how the strategic direction and strategies were developed are presented in Appendix 5. The recommended strategies for the issues that were identified in the research include:

1. *National ICT infrastructure*
   - Build and maintain high-quality national backbone infrastructure with adequate Internet connectivity.
2. *Governance policy and e-governance strategy*
   - Devolve decision-making power and resources to local governments.

- Create a clear e-governance vision and strategy linked to the wider governance reform programme and to the national development plan.
- Develop clear priority sectors (e.g. judiciary, education), and start implementation with those carrying minimum risks of failure.
- Engage citizens at all stages.
- Communicate the e-governance vision and strategy across government and to the public.

3. *Human resources*
- Build the capacity of local government personnel.
- Improve the quality of councillors through higher education requirements.
- Develop required hybrid human capacities: technological, commercial, management and e-literacy.
- Carry out continuous in-service training on ICT skills and usage.

4. *Funding*
- Increase the level of funding to local governments.
- Increase the budget allocation to ICT at both national and local government levels.
- Mobilise resources for developing and sustaining ICT infrastructure and services which would be undertaken by local governments.

5. *Affordability*
- Develop and implement a policy for lowering the cost of ICT equipment and services in sectors dealing with universal access/services.

6. *Political will*
- Create e-leaders or e-champions with authority, willing to take risks, willing to mobilise resources, able to commit time and act as advocates for e-governance.
- Organise e-governance competitions nationally and regionally where awards are given by the highest political figure to acknowledge innovative efforts of active e-governance actors/teams.

- Develop an e-governance strategy in local governments.
- Educate policymakers in local governments on e-governance.

7. *Communication*
   - Promote and publicise projects through various media channels.
   - Organise regular events nationally/regionally with citizens and entrepreneurs to communicate the importance of successful e-governance projects; celebrate what was achieved, shed light on what was not achieved, identify underlying obstacles, and readjust the action plans.
   - Issue proceedings/publications through reports on events.

8. *Business processes*
   - Reform public administration processes and culture in support of e-business governance.
   - Reduce the number of hierarchical levels and departments/institutions a citizen has to deal with in transactions.

9. *E-governance projects management*
   - Plan e-governance projects as socio-technical systems.
   - Plan and implement e-governance projects that cater for local needs as perceived and identified by local stakeholders.
   - Develop test-bed e-governance experiences (pilots) in order to demonstrate and prove the feasibility and benefits of the concept.
   - Scale up e-governance projects successfully.
   - Assess e-governance projects on a systematic basis throughout different phases and carry out continuous monitoring and regular evaluation of project progress and outcomes.
   - Involve the public in implementation, monitoring and evaluation using a citizen evaluation tool.
   - Readjust project implementation to take account of evaluation findings

The research recommends that these strategies should be appropriately devolved to the various levels of local governments based on their contexts.

FIGURE 12.1   Methodological framework

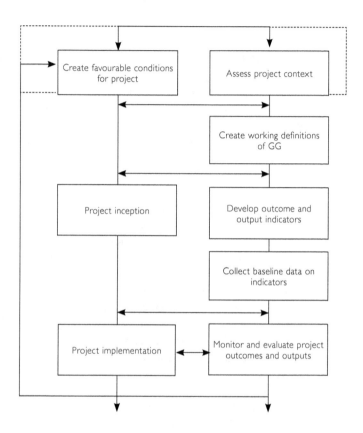

Business process mapping and re-engineering methodology

In most of the countries it was found that business processes had not been re-engineered. It is not desirable to automate inefficient systems. Consequently, business process re-engineering/reform is an important requirement. Once an e-governance strategy has been developed and priority e-governance projects selected, it is important to re-engineer the business processes of the projects to be implemented. Egypt, which is one of the leading countries in Africa in implementing e-governance systems, has focused on delivering services to citizens, at both central and local government levels for a long time. A business process mapping methodology was developed by the Egyptian LOG-IN Africa team to respond to the business process challenges found in e-government implementation. The methodology aims to document effectively and efficiently all aspects of service delivery processes. Details of this methodology and the associated automated tool are provided in Chapter 3.

The business process mapping tool has been tested in two sites. Further testing by different users is needed to improve the tool and to attract suggestions on potential enhancements. Although the tool is still under development and needs to be extended to include optimisation of the business processes (the re-engineering aspect), this research believes it could be useful to many governments in the roll-out of e-governance projects.

E-local governance application implementation methodology

The methodology was developed as part of the implementation of e-local governance projects in Morocco (Kettani et al., 2006). It was used in the LOG-IN Africa project in Morocco that is described in Chapter 7. The original model has been improved significantly and includes a feedback loop. The proposed methodology is shown in Figure 12.1. The activities to be carried out are outlined in the table. They include:

Creating favourable conditions for project   Once the project to be implemented is agreed upon with the local authorities, in consultation with the relevant ministry or e-government authority, the first phase involves creating and sustaining the conditions that will favour the project's progress. It mainly involves the various concerned stakeholders, among which the most critical are the project's champions (called e-champions) that promote and support the project at all the critical levels of the organisation's hierarchy. The project's management team must be aware that certain stakeholders and e-champions may change from one phase to the other and act accordingly in order to maintain favourable conditions for the project, given the changes taking place in the organisation. The key outputs are identified e-champions and other stakeholders, as well as an initial vision for the project. The creation of a favourable climate is a continuous process, as shown in the methodological framework.

Assessing project context Conduct an assessment of the context of the e-government project to gain a deeper understanding of the context of the implementation for the e-government intervention being studied. The context may include the e-government/e-governance policy environment, business and ICT environment, political commitment, ICT infrastructure and connectivity, human resource skills and budget allocation. This context is important in explaining why certain outcomes were or were not realised.

It is to be noted that the context of an e-government project is ever-changing. This stage therefore involves making regular updates on any significant contextual changes that may occur. This is why the assessment of project context is shown as a continuous process.

Project inception The e-champions and the development team must develop a clear and structured vision of the e-governance system to be developed and/or deployed and of the outcomes it must provide to the organisation and to its clients. This will be achieved through workshops with the local government staff as well as citizens. The favourable conditions created in the earlier stage should be sustained and built up during this phase.

The inception phase is paramount in helping e-champions to shape their vision and refine their expectations with respect to the project's outputs and outcomes. It is also during this important phase that the most critical stakeholders are led to share the project's vision and reach a consensus on its main targets (outputs and outcomes). This increases the favourable conditions for the project. The main outputs of this phase are:

- updated project vision
- expected outcomes and outputs

- system quality requirements
- the project plan
- project resources requirements

Creating working definitions of 'good governance' Choose the key good governance constructs relevant to the project and create contextualised or 'working' definitions. These localised definitions would inevitably be linked to the national government and/or local government concepts of good governance, as well as the specific context of the e-government project.

Developing outcome and output indicators Translate the working definitions of good governance into identifiable and measurable (or at least observable) outcome indicators for the chosen good governance constructs in the previous stage. This translation is carried out for each of the three dimensions of e-government. Outcome indicators can be further specified or associated with identifiable and measurable output indicators which are meaningful in the specific context and directly linked to the e-government project-based intervention.

Collecting baseline data on indicators Collect baseline data on the developed indicators to establish the status of the various outcome and output indicators before the implementation of the e-government intervention. This status sets the reference against which future changes can be assessed. These data can be collected through participant observations, review of official documents, focus group interviews and other data-collection methods. In all cases, research designs must identify the sources of data, specify the data-collection methods and how to minimise biases associated with the chosen data-collection methods.

Project implementation This phase starts whenever the GO decision has been made by the local authority management after the completion of the project inception phase. A critical success factor is that favourable conditions are maintained during this phase. All the inception phase's outputs are available during the development and/or deployment of the e-governance application. It mainly consists of activities similar to those found in traditional information systems development, including:

- information requirements analysis (both business and information systems)
- business process redesign and development of new workflows
- development of a strong system architecture
- interface and system design
- implementation and testing
- deployment and adjustments

The above activities should be carried out through appropriate participation of both the local authority staff and citizens. They should also be guided by the project's vision and with the aim of achieving the key outcomes and outputs developed during the previous phase. The key output is a working e-governance application.

Assessing project outcomes and outputs   This phase is the action research component and is carried out in parallel with the other phases. Its goal is systematically to assess and monitor the evolving situation during the course of the project and establish the effects of the implemented e-government intervention on good governance. This involves collecting data on the status of the outcome and output indicators to establish the changes from the baseline position established earlier.

In general, outcome measurement is a challenge (Mayne, 2005); indeed this is where the greatest challenge lies. In particular, determining the extent to which an e-government intervention can be associated with observed outcomes is quite a challenge, largely because of the attribution problem. Further, the long periods from the times outputs are produced to the time 'allegedly' associated outcomes are realised creates an additional problem of attribution. In order to deal with these challenges, we propose that researchers focus on the degree to which an e-government system under study has contributed to the status of the outcomes in question, and, at the same time, establish other factors that have contributed to the realisation of the outcomes.

During this phase, favourable conditions should be maintained and they may be different/complementary to those that prevailed during the earlier phases, since the right setting must be established in order to conduct the various investigations needed to carry out the various assessments. This phase should be carried out through participant observations, review of official documents, focus group discussions and interviews with local government staff, citizens and other key stakeholders.

This research supports the position that this implementation methodology would be useful in guiding the roll-out of e-governance projects, in addition to contributing immensely to successful implementation.

Monitoring and evaluation

The monitoring and evaluation of the implementation of e-local governance projects can be done through a framework derived from the LOG-IN Africa conceptual framework. This framework, together with a list of generic good governance outcome indicators, is the focus of Appendix 6. The good governance indicators should be developed during the project planning phase.

In addition, the research recommends the involvement of policy-makers in developing the outcome indicators. Their involvement is also necessary at the project planning stage and in the evaluation process. The participation of citizens is also recommended in all the stages of monitoring and evaluating the implementation of e-governance projects.

Conclusions and recommendations

The effects of ICT systems on good governance were found to vary from country to country depending on local and national contexts. In all cases it was possible to explain these mixed effects of e-local governance from a rich understanding of the contextual information, from the application system design and implementation to institutional, local government and national contexts. Indeed, contextual information from e-governance projects provides a rich foundation for e-local governance.

The research established that it was not possible to explain e-local governance outcomes without the e-local governance context (what we have referred to as favourable conditions). That is, the outcomes are inextricably tied to the context in which they are created or form, in line with a social-informatics view of information systems (Kling, 2000). This was amply demonstrated by the huge differences in the implementation of the citizen registration system in Fez and Larache in Morocco. It was not possible to replicate the Fez success of the e-local governance system in Larache largely because the contexts were different. This reveals clearly how ICT-mediated organisational change cannot be determined based on other ICT projects' experiences. Experiences from other projects should only serve to inform researchers and practitioners on how to condition desired organisational change fostering good governance practices. The key insight in this case of Morocco is that no organisational change could take place in ICT projects unless the public mindset is correspondingly changed.

The research projects reveal that in some of the countries there were average to modest enhancements in local good governance, resulting in improved efficiency and effectiveness, better customer service provision and increased transparency and accountability. However, most countries had not experienced positive good governance outcomes. It is plausible that this can be explained by the fact that the projects in most countries were in the initial/first stage of e-local governance implementation. At this stage, the effects on good governance are expected to be low and to increase with experience in implementation of such systems. At the same time, these results cannot be divorced from the governance context of the various countries and local governments, which provided critical explanatory power.

In addition to the e-local governance outcomes, there were also other developmental outcomes brought about by researchers using the e-local governance implementation to influence policy and practice. These included adoption of the prototype on life-events services for implementation by the city government of Addis Ababa, Ethiopia; the decision to replicate the Fez e-governance platform for automation of civil registration in several local governments in Morocco, including Marrakech, Essaouira, Midelt, Casa, Taza, Jerada, Mekness, and Sefrou; the use of the LOG-IN e-local governance roadmap to inform national e-government strategy in Kenya; the development of an e-local governance course for non-IT decision-makers in Ekurhuleni metropolitan municipality, South Africa; the invitation of one of the Mauritian research team to participate in a major national e-national e-government project; and the adoption by the Egyptian government of the business processing mapping methodology (BPM) and tool developed by LOG-IN Africa's Egypt team. In addition, LOG-IN Africa researchers presented their findings in numerous forums and published over 30 peer-reviewed journal and conference papers.

One of the interesting findings was that ICTs had no effect on participation in all countries, except in Ghana. Even in Ghana, the success can be attributed to the researchers' creation of an enabling environment and their appropriate choice of ICT tools to suit the specific realities the communities faced. Another interesting finding is that the use of revenue management in Mauritius discriminated between educated and less-educated citizens, low and high income earners, and young and old citizens. This can be explained by the elitist nature of ICTs, the associated high costs and the apparent alignment of the culture embedded in ICTs with the culture appreciated by most youth.

Another further finding is that a prototype of a working system is a very powerful tool to persuade (local) government policymakers to make a decision to implement a certain e-local governance application. This was the case in Morocco where, after showcasing eFes to the managers in Larache, the eLarache project was readily accepted. This was also the case in Ethiopia, where the researchers, after demonstrating the KLESS prototype for automating life event services in local governments, the decision-makers of the city government of Addis Ababa decided to convert the prototype into an operational system and implement it in a few *kebeles*.

A final finding concerns the championship of the project and its effects on the successful deployment of e-local governance applications. The replication of eFes in Larache (Morocco) came to a standstill when the leadership that supported this project was appointed to a different position outside the local government. This underscores the importance of a sustained e-local governance leadership throughout the life of a project. This was also illustrated in Kenya, where the success of rolling out the Integrated Financial Management Information System was partly attributed to the sustained leadership provided by the local government reform programme in the Ministry of Local Government and consistent leadership from the accounts departments of the two municipal councils studied.

In the case of Morocco, the emergence of an alternative champion for the eLarache project and the restarting of the stalled project, although after a long, three-year wait, demonstrate that e-governance projects in our African context, and indeed other development contexts, can be derived from a demand perspective. Most of the projects reported in information systems and e-governance literature tend to have a supply push. Given the importance of context, as argued above, perhaps what merits more research are the circumstances in which a 'demand-pulled' e-governance implementation is successful or unsuccessful.

The lessons from the projects in the LOG-IN Africa research inform the proposed e-local governance roadmap. This roadmap entails achieving the following:

- Developing an e-governance strategic direction that is consistent with the wider governance reform programme and the national development plan.

- Developing good governance outcome indicators for e-governance projects to be implemented as part of project planning using the framework shown in Appendix 6.
- Re-engineering the business processes for the priority e-governance projects to be implemented, using a specific business process mapping methodology, such as the one developed by the Egyptian team.
- Rolling out the e-governance projects by using the methodological framework described in this chapter (Figure 12.1).
- Using the good governance outcome indicators to monitor and evaluate the implementation of e-governance projects.
- Ensuring the participation of policymakers and citizens in all these activities.

We recommend other researchers try out either the whole proposed roadmap or some of its elements to evaluate its significance and relevance in e-governance research and practice. Although not reported in detail in this book, the author effectively used the e-local governance roadmap guidelines to inform the development of a national e-government strategy for Kenya.

Notes

1. Although Ghana was not one of the countries in the LOG-IN Africa project, a Ghanaian project on e-governance was incorporated into the LOG-IN Africa research network.
2. The only exceptions were the large city councils in the more developed economies of South Africa and Egypt. These tended to have e-government strategies.

Appendices

Processes and outputs in public and private

Issue	Government	Private
Staff		
Education	Most employees have commercial, agricultural and industrial secondary school certificates. The small proportion who hold a degree are mostly engineers.	Employee education level and specialisation will depend on the requirement of the position held
Level of experience	Employees get promoted on time basis regardless of practical experience	The level of experience must satisfy job requirements
Work environment	Poor work environment due to: places, facilities, low salaries, and clashes with citizens	Good environment; there are no direct interactions between the employees who do the service and customers
Speed of assimilating requirements	Low, since the communication channels with the citizen are bad	High, since there are many ways to communicate with the citizen
Speed of service	Slow (routine/red tape)	Faster
Executing laws	Employees in government establishments must execute services according to certain regulations	More flexibility
Gender	In some government establishments most employees are female (in tourism and petroleum, for example, the ratio can be 90% female to 10% male). Most are married and have family responsibilities, so they have no time to make an extra effort.	Male or female according to position requirement

Issue	Government	Private
Age	Most employees above 40. Since the government has not hired employees for a long time, there are no juniors. Employees fear new technology and success; the result is resistance.	According to position requirement
IT skills	Low or non-existen; governmental establishments join ICT project later	More advanced than government establishments

Customers

Time	Customers' time spent in government establishments is not taken into consideration because there are no deadlines	Customers' time in business and industry is critical: customer service deadlines mean lost time produces criticism
Customer rights	Customers can't discuss with employees at service location, but there are procedures for complaints. The slogan at government establishments is pay, then complain.	Customers can discuss possible improvements in service with the employee
Customer reactions	Bad, because the service is time-consuming, and the customer must take responsibility for follow-up. There is direct interaction between the customer and the employee; as a result, there tend to be clashes.	Good, because the customer knows when the service is finished; in business environment the customer takes responsibility for following up his/her service
Service fees	The citizen wants services with minimum fees. One important consequence of expensive fees at government establishments is the high number of objections, especially to building licences.	Service fees not considered

Issue	Government	Private
Process		
Steps	Sequential steps to do specific service	The process in a business environment may be sequential or parallel, depending on the type of service, and may change
Change rate	Higher rates of change in business process since more privileges delegate to the governor and the president of the municipality. Each municipality governor has their own vision of services provided; governors may add extra documents or steps, or may curtail specific services.	Most business environments affected by changes in governmental establishments
Variability in process duration	Highly variable. From the backlog of requests for specific services, we found extremes in time taken. These variations related to the absence of documented business procedures, and the existence of favouritism.	Low or non-existent
Work cycle	One process may have different work cycles. The procedure is affected by the individual employee providing the service, and may differ from one district to another in the same region.	One work cycle for one process
Organisation chart	There is no unified and updated organisation chart for all municipalities. For example, that for Alexandria municipalities differs from that for Cairo.	Unified organisation chart for similar sectors

Issue	Government	Private
Existence of work cycle documentation	Low or non-existent	Mostly exists
Control over employees	Low or non-existent control on employees	Full or semi-full control on employees
Existence of employees' KPI(s) (key performance indicator)	Low or non-existent employees' KPI(s)	Make efforts in human resource development and have KPI(S)
Resources available	Limited resources available from the state	More resources, since based on profit model, not public service model
Customer satisfaction	Low customer satisfaction; not a strategic goal of governmental establishments	Customer satisfaction strategic goal for business environment

Outcome and output indicators for computerising
financial processes (e-administration)

GG constructs	Outcome indicators	Output indicators
Participation	Increased participation in LA decision-making Increased participation in programme implementation	Adequacy of fiscal, revenue and expenditure information provided to enhance participation in decision-making and implementation of programmes Institutionalised forms of participation
Transparency	Extent to which financial policies, processes and procedures are clear and open	No. of financial policies and procedures documented and disseminated No. of financial processes documented and shared
	Enhanced financial transparency	Reduction in number of corruption cases in procurement Extent of openness in tendering Readily accessible financial details
Responsiveness	Extent of feedback from staff and response given to staff	No. of responses and feedback
	Extent of satisfaction with computerised financial services	Reduced complaints from staff Reduced queues at council counters or less waiting time
	Community satisfaction index: council's responsiveness towards resolving problems and inquiries	Reduced complaints Reduced queues at council counters or less waiting time
Effectiveness and efficiency	Completeness in rolling out the financial management system	No. of modules rolled out No. of users (internal) using the system Extent of integration with other systems

GG constructs	Outcome indicators	Output indicators
Effectiveness and efficiency *contd*		No. of stakeholders having access to financial services
		No. of users trained
		No. of ICT technical staff trained
		No. of accounting staff trained
	Enhanced financial performance	Percentage increase in revenue collection
		Percentage reduction in cost of financial operations
		Growth in revenue base
		Rates collected as a percentage of total revenue
		Effectiveness of transfer of tax collections from tax collectors
		Increased debt collection ratio
	Improved budget performance	Expenditure out-turn compared to approved budget
		Revenue out-turn compared to approved budget (tests accurate forecasting of revenue and revenue collection methods)
		Comprehensiveness of information included in budget documentation
	Enhanced financial management	Reduced unauthorised spending
		Increased ability to track financial transactions
		Increased ability to monitor revenue collection in all income streams
		Tighter financial controls (payroll, procurement, etc.)
		Accuracy and timeliness of payments
		Recurrent operating expenditure as a percentage of total expenditure
		Ratio of administrative expenditure against total recurrent expenditure
		Ratepayers' assessment of quality of administration and public inquiry
		Accuracy of payroll processing

GG constructs	Outcome indicators	Output indicators
Effectiveness and efficiency *contd*		Extent to which cashflows are forecast and monitored
		Payroll audits to identify control weaknesses and/or ghost workers
	More efficient and effective delivery of public services	Resource allocations and utilisation are consistent with priorities
		Outputs represent value for money
		Procurement is timely, economical and effective
		Timelines in processing bills
	Increased productivity of financial staff	Increase in revenue per staff
		Reduced turnaround time in producing standard financial reports (budgets, balance sheets, p/l accounts, accounts reconciliation)
Accountability	Enhanced financial accountability	Effectiveness of expenditure commitment controls
		Improvement in accounting for programme/project funds
		Reduced turnaround in producing financial returns
		Comprehensiveness, relevance and understanding of other internal control rules/procedures
		Degree of compliance with rules for processing and recording transactions
		Evidence of follow-up on audit recommendations
	Regular and adequate feedback to management on performance of internal control systems	Coverage and quality of the internal audit function (bank reconciliations, financial statements, accounting standards used)
		Frequency and distribution of reports on internal control systems
		Extent of management response to internal audit findings

GG constructs	Outcome indicators	Output indicators
Participation	Increased gender participation in service access	No. of women and men accessing services
	Increased involvement of stakeholders (customers, private sector, civil society, etc.)	No. of other stakeholders accessing services
		No. of women and men inputting into the council processes
		No. of residents participating in decision-making and programme implementation
	More democratic participation	
Transparency	Effectiveness of means used to facilitate public access to information	Effectiveness of information posted in press, websites or public noticeboards (language, structure, layout, size, etc.)
	Improved access to information and public services	Adequacy of financial information accessed by citizens (annual budget, in-year budget execution, year-end financial statements, external audit reports, contract awards, resources available to service units)
		Frequency of access to financial information
Responsiveness	Extent of feedback from external stakeholders and response given to them	Use of feedback
	Extent of customer satisfaction with service provision	No. of complaints and compliments
	Extent of access to services	Percentage of residents using services

GG constructs	Outcome indicators	Output indicators
Effectiveness and efficiency	More efficient and effective delivery of public services	No. of complaints and compliments
	Better quality of services	Increased number accessing services
	Extent of customer satisfaction	No. of complaints and compliments
	Reduced cost and time in accessing services	No. accessing services and clear procedures of access
Accountability	Extent to which direct service providers can be held accountable for their actions	No. of residents engaging councils and censoring services

APPENDIX 4   Outcome and output indicators for society
interactions (e-society)

GG constructs	Outcome indicators	Output indicators
Participation	Improved interactions with stakeholders (central government, business, industry, customers, public, etc.)	Timelines in sending (specific) financial reports to MoLG Timeliness in sending bills to customers Increased level of feedback from residents Procedures for feedback
	Increased inclusiveness in society interactions/ consultations (with business, industry and citizens)	Participation of citizens and customers in deciding on projects to be undertaken through LASDAP (e.g. from minutes of LASDAP meetings)

Issue	Why is it an issue?
National ICT infrastructure	Limited penetration Poor quality Poor Internet access
Governance policy and e-government strategy	Lacking or unclear governance policy Lack of alignment between governance policy and government strategy Incomplete decentralisation e-government not cascaded to LG (most LGs have no e-gov strategy) Ineffective coordination in e-government implementation Inability to provide a framework of reference for citizen engagement
Human resource capacity	Inadequate e-literacy skills and ICT usage Low ICT skills (technical and managerial)
Funding	Inadequate resource allocation to LGs Inadequate resource allocation to ICT Inadequate resource mobilisation
Affordability	High cost of ICT equipment and services affect the public

Consequences if not addressed	Strategies
Constrained provision of services and information to citizens Negative effect on local economic development Stakeholders cannot participate in activities Poor e-readiness	Build and maintain high-quality national backbone infrastructure with adequate Internet connectivity
E-local governance will not have a driver/basis Implementation is likely to falter, negatively affecting good governance realisation	Devolve decision-making to local governments Create a clear e-governance vision and strategy linked to the wider governance reform programme and the national development plan Develop clear priority sectors (e.g. judiciary, education), starting implementation with those with minimum risk of failure Engage citizens at all stages Communicate the e-governance vision and strategy across government and to the public
Resistance to change No capacity to implement and use e-governance systems, leading to unrealised good governance outcomes	Build capacity of local government personnel Improve the quality of councillors through higher education requirement Develop human capacities: technological, commercial, management and e-literacy In-service training on ICT skills and usage
No required investment in e-governance systems E-governance systems cannot be sustained	Increase the level of funding to local governments Increase the budget allocation to ICT at both national and local government levels Mobilisation of resources by local governments for development and sustenance of ICT infrastructure and services
Limited number of end-users will use the e-governance systems	Develop and implement a policy for lowering the cost of ICT equipment and services, e.g. universal access/services

Issue	Why is it an issue?
Political will	Inadequate political will
	Failure to understand ICT due to low levels of education among councillors
	Lack of ICT strategy at the local level
Communication	E-government projects are stand-alone and not integrated
	Inadequate promotion and publicity of e-government projects
Business processes	Not documented, ineffective or inconsistent
Change management	Resistance to change
	Requirements for change not known
	Prerequisites for change management not in place
	Lack of shared vision for change

Consequences if not addressed	Strategies
Implementation is likely to falter, negatively affecting good governance realisation	Create e-leaders or e-champions with authority, willing to take risks, willing to mobilise resources, able to commit time and who can act as advocates for e-governance
	Organize e-governance competitions nationally and regionally where awards are presented by the highest political figure to acknowledge innovative efforts of active e-governance actors/teams
	Develop an e-governance strategy in LG
	Educate policymakers in local governments on e-governance
Lack of efficiency/effectiveness	Promote and publicise projects through various media channels (e.g. radio, posters, public meetings, newspapers)
Problems of 'reinventing the wheel'	
No improvement: repeating the same mistakes	Organise regular events nationally/regionally with citizens and entrepreneurs to communicate the importance of successful e-governance projects, celebrate what was achieved, shed light on what was not achieved, identify underlying obstacles, and readjust the action plans
No dissemination of lessons learned, good/best practices generated by practice on the ground	
Ineffective provision of services	Issue proceedings/publications to report on the events
Ineffective e-business governance systems.	Reform public administration processes and culture in support of e-business governance
	Reduce the number of hierarchical levels and departments a citizen has to deal with
Unsuccessful e-governance implementation, leading to wasted investment	Develop and share vision with key stakeholders
	Involve key stakeholders (invite, train and assign them responsibilities) to create trust and commitment
Inability to embrace change	
Different understanding of change by different stakeholders	Expose and sensitise governors, councillors, etc., on benefits of ICT in local economic development

Issue	Why is it an issue?
E-governance projects management	E-governance projects partially implemented, inappropriately implemented, completely abandoned, not used, or not maintained
	Most projects are not evaluated and hence no feedback on projects' progress status: success/failure
	Failure to involve the public adequately in developing vision and path for change

Consequences if not addressed	Strategies
Partial or complete e-governance project failure occurring at development, implementation, deployment or maintenance phase/stage	Plan e-governance projects as socio-technical systems
	Plan and implement e-governance projects that cater for local needs as perceived and identified by local stakeholders
No feedback on projects' progress status: whether the project objectives are being accomplished or not	Develop testbed e-governance experiences (pilots) in order to demonstrate and prove the feasibility and benefits of the concept
No feedback to know whether the project is succeeding or failing	Scale up successful e-governance projects
	Assess e-governance projects on a systematic basis throughout different phases: continuous monitoring and regular evaluation of project progress status and the outcomes/changes being generated
No way to identify, highlight and compile e-government obstacles (hard and soft)	
No way to capture lessons learned from the experience	Involve the public in implementation, monitoring and evaluation using a citizen evaluation tool
No way to extract good/best practices for learning/sharing purposes	Readjust project implementation to take account of evaluation findings

Good governance constructs	Working good governance definitions	
		e-administration
Participation	Stakeholders participate in local government decision-making processes and activities	Extent of participation in decision-making of staff at different levels
Transparency	The full disclosure of information, presentation of information in an easy and accessible format, and free access to LG operations and information by stakeholders	Access and understanding of e-governance policy and strategy by stakeholders
		Extent to which LG business processes and information are clear and accessible to stakeholders
		Visibility and trackability of LG internal operations
		Extent to which government institutions exchange and share information
Responsiveness	Two-way communication between LG officials and stakeholders	Degree of enhancement of feedback and response to feedback from staff
		Extent of staff satisfaction with computerised service

Good governance outcome indicators

e-services	e-society
Extent of involvement of customers, politicians, private sector and civil society in LG e-governance processes Extent of availability of electronic delivery facilities empowering citizens to serve themselves without being dependent on employee intermediaries and their 'goodwill' to do their job	Extent of improvement in interactions with central government, businesses, citizens and other key stakeholders Degree of joint planning between local government and civil society Extent of less privileged people, including illiterate and indigenous people, participating in LG decision-making
Improvement of public access to pertinent information and services Degree of ease for citizens to find/access procedures to follow in order to request and receive services Extent to which ordinary citizens can read and understand the language in which information and service are presented Degree of ease for citizens to post comments, questions and complaints on service delivery Response rate to citizens' comments, questions and complaints Availability of government official documents as electronic resources Availability of public servants' profiles	
Extent of enhancement of feedback from customers, central government, private sector, public and civil society Effectiveness of resolution of complaints from external stakeholders	

Good governance constructs	Working good governance definitions	e-administration
Responsiveness *contd*		Reduction in response time for internal transactions
		Degree to which peer or hierarchical communication is enhanced
Equity	Services provision or access on equal basis irrespective of gender, disability, socio-economic status or other forms of possible discrimination	Degree of equity in computerised service access by staff without discrimination
		Degree of equity in staff ICT training without discrimination
Effectiveness and efficiency	Optimal use of resources for the achievement of local governance purposes and objectives	Increase in efficiency and effectiveness of internal business processes
		Enhancement of institutional performance
		Degree of integration of e-governance applications
		Reduction in effort needed by LG employees in accomplishing internal business processes
		Improvement in the quality of services delivered
		Reduction in number of persons required to carry out internal operations

Good governance outcome indicators

e-services	e-society
Extent of customer satisfaction with service provision	
Increase in access to LG services and information	
Reduction in turnaround time for citizens to request and receive their services	
Improvement in the quality of services delivered	
Extent to which citizens can check progress of their service requests	
Degree of equity in service delivery irrespective of gender, country's geographical localisation and other forms of marginalisation	
Reduction in the frequency of 'favouritism' incidents in serving customers	
Availability of 'self-service technology' (e.g. touch-screen kiosks) to empower citizens by enabling them to serve themselves without being dependent on employee intermediaries as a way to further fight favouritism incidents and endorse the principle of 'first come, first served'	
Increase in effectiveness of service delivery	
Improvement in quality of services and information	
Degree of increased customer satisfaction	
Increase in access to public services and information	
Reduction in citizens' waiting time for the delivery of their services	
Reduction in citizen's effort to request and receive their needed services (e.g. time spent queuing)	

Good governance constructs	Working good governance definitions	e-administration
Accountability	LG managers and employees are accountable to citizens and other key stakeholders	Extent of accountability of LG managers and employees for their actions
		Extent of availability of ways to monitor and trace LG personnel activities (i.e. know who does what and when)
Rule of law	Laws and administrative procedures are applied fairly and objectively	Extent of increase in objectivity in applying legal instruments, policies and administrative procedures
		Increase in visibility and traceability of violation incidents of 'rule of law' due to back-office routinisation and automation
		Decrease unwillingness of staff to shoulder their responsibilities
Consensus orientation	Conflicts of interest of the various stakeholders are resolved	Reduction in internal conflicts of interest
		Extent of reduction in the possibility of alienation of staff that could be caused by minority vs majority of votes
Strategic vision	Managers and the public have a long-term view of governance but are aware of contextual obstacles and their solutions	Enhancement in long-term view of governance
		Existence of e-governance strategy
		Alignment of e-governance strategy to national socio-economic development priorities

Good governance outcome indicators

e-services	e-society

Extent to which LG staff can be identified
with their actions in service delivery and be held
responsible for them

Degree to which public servants and local
governors are accountable to citizens

Increase in objectivity in applying legal
instruments, policies and administrative
procedures

Reduction in conflicts of interest in service
delivery

Enhancement in long-term view of governance

Existence of e-governance strategy

Alignment of e-governance strategy to national
socio-economic development priorities

References

Aboagye, E. (2000). *Promoting the Participation of Women in Local Governance and Development: The Case of Ghana.* ECDPM Discussion Paper 18, Maastricht.

Abrahams, L., and Bhyat, M. (2007). *Designing Joburg's Digital Future: Leveraging the 2010 ICT Legacy.* Johannesburg: LINK Centre.

Abrahams, L., and Newton-Reid, L. (2007a). *eGovernance for Social and Local Economic Development.* LOG-IN Africa Mid-term Review Report.

Abrahams, L., and Newton-Reid, L. (2007b). *eGovernance for Social and Local Economic Development.* LOG-IN Africa Third Technical Progress Report, December.

Abrahams, L., and Newton-Reid, L. (2008). e-Governance for social and economic development. In *Proceedings of 'LOG-IN Africa e-Local Governance 1st Conference, June 5–6 2008', Cairo, Egypt,* Tangier: CAFRAD, pp. 43–65.

Accenture (2005). *Leadership in Customer Service: New Expectations, New Experiences.* Toronto: Accenture. www.accenture.com.

African Development Bank (2003). *To Serve and to Preserve: Improving Public Administration in a Competitive World.* www.adb.org/documents/manuals/serve_and_preserve/Chapter19.pdf.

African Development Bank (2004). *Mauritius 2004–2008 Country Strategy Paper.* September 2004. www.afdb.org/fileadmin/uploads/afdb/Documents/Project-and-Operations/ADB-BD-WP-2004-105-EN-MAURITIUS-2004-2008-CSP.PDF.

Aicholzer, G., and Schmutzer, R. (2000). Organizational challenges to the development of electronic government. In *Proceedings of the 11th International Workshop on Database and Expert Systems Applications.* New York: Springer, pp. 379–83.

Aliyu, A. (2003). Nigerian experience of decentralization as a means to improve governance and how it contributes to combating poverty. www.idrc.ca/en/ev-115659-201-1-DO_TOPIC.html.

Almond, G.A., and Verba, S. (1963). *Civic Culture: Political Attitudes and Democracy in Five Nations.* Princeton, NJ: Princeton University Press.

Apusiga, A. (2004). Gender vulnerability and the politics of decision-making in Ghana: The case of Upper East Region in Ghana. *Journal of Development Studies*, 1(2): 15–31.

Asingwire, N., et al. (2007). *ICTs in Local Governance: A Case Study of the Local Government Information Communication System (LoGICS) in Uganda*. LOG-IN Africa First Technical Report.

Atkinson, J. (1974). *Motivation and Achievement*. Washington, DC: V.H. Winston & Sons.

Atkinson, J., and Feather, N. (1966). *A Theory of Achievement Motivation*. New York: Wiley & Sons.

Atnafu, S., et al. (2008). ICT for local governance: A case study on the application of ICTs on life-event services at the kebeles of the City Government of Addis Ababa. In *Proceedings of 'LOG-IN Africa e-Local Governance 1st Conference, June 5–6 2008', Cairo, Egypt.*

Ayee, J.R.A. (2000). Decentralization and good governance in Ghana. Paper prepared for the Canadian High Commission, Accra, Ghana.

Bar-Tal, D., Frieze, I., and Greenberg, M. (1974). *Attributional Analysis of Achievement Motivation, Some Applications to Education*. Chicago, IL: American Educational Research Association.

Baum, C., and Di Maio, A. (2001). Gartner's four phases of e-government model. http://gartner3.gartnerweb.com/public/static/hotc/00094235.html.

Bayart, J.F. (1993). *The State in Africa: The Politics of Belly*. Harlow: Longman.

Bening R.B. (1990). *History of Education in Northern Ghana, 1907–1976*. Accra: Ghana Universities Press.

Bening R.B. (1999). *Regional Boundaries and National Integration*. Accra: Ghana Universities Press.

Bhatnagar, S. (2004). *E-government: From vision to Implementation*. New Delhi: Sage Publications.

Board of Investment Mauritius. (n.d.). Mauritius – A global island in the making. www.boimauritius.com.

Booz–Allen–Hamilton. (2002). International e-economy benchmarking: The world's most effective policies for the e-economy. www.itis.gov.se/publikationer/eng/ukreport.pdf.

Brain, D., Seltsikas, P., and Tailor, D. (2005). *Process Modelling Notations for eGovernment: An Assessment of Modelling Notations for Identity Management*. Paper prepared for the 18th Bled eConference, 'eIntegration in Action', Bled, Slovenia, 6–8 June.

Bridges.org (2005). The Real Access/Real Impact framework for improving the way that ICT is used in development. Cape Town. www.bridges.org/digital_divide.

Butcher, J.N., et al. (1989). *The Minnesota Multiphasic Personality Inventory–2 (MMPI–2): Manual for administration and Scoring*. Minneapolis: University of Minnesota Press.

Capurro, R. (2004). Sceptical knowledge management. In Hobohm, H.C.,

Knowledge Management: Libraries and Librarians Taking up the Challenge. Munich: Saur, pp. 47–57.

Carbo, T., and Williams, J.G. (2004). Models and metrics for evaluating local electronic government systems and services. *Electronic Journal of e-Government*, 2(2): 95–104.

Centre for Public Service Innovation (2003). *Citizen Access to E-government Services*. Pretoria: Mohlaleng Strategy Consultants.

Clement, A., and Shade, L. (1998). *The Access Rainbow: Conceptualising Universal Access to Information/Communication Infrastructure*. Working Paper No. 10. Toronto: Information Policy Research Program, Faculty of Information Studies, University of Toronto.

Chan, C.M.L., et al. (2007). e-Government implementation: A macro analysis of Singapore's e-government initiatives. *Government Information Quarterly*, 25(2): 239–55.

Cheng, B.S., et al. (2008). How openness to experience can facilitate knowledge sharing: An international perspective. http://gra103.aca.ntu.edu.tw/gdoc/D93227102b.pdf.

Ciborra, C., and Navarra, D. (2005). Good governance, development theory, and aid policy: Risks and challenges of e-government in Jordan. *Information Technology For Development*, 11(2): 141–59.

CITRED (2006). *CITRED Baseline Report*. Tamale: Centre for Information Technologies and Research Development.

City of Johannesburg (2004). *Joburg 2030*. www.joburg.org.za/content/view/123/58/1/1/.

City of Johannesburg (2007). *2010 Information and Communications Technology Strategy*. Johannesburg: Office of the Chief Information Officer.

City of Tshwane (2004a). *Global Digital Hub Scoping Reports*. Tshwane.

City of Tshwane (2004b). *Tshwane City Strategy Final Report*. Tshwane.

City of Tshwane (2007). *Tshwane spatial Development strategy 2010 and Beyond*. Tshwane.

CPINFO (2002). *Information and Communication Technology Policy Implementation Strategy: Towards the Global Information Society*. Maputo: Comissão para a Política de Informática.

Cresswell A.M., and Burke G.B. (2006). The Government of Israel, the Merkava Project. www.ctg.albany.edu/publications/reports/proi_case_merkava?

Cross, R., et al. (2001). Knowing what we know: Supporting knowledge creation and sharing in social networks. *Organizational Dynamics*, 30(2): 100–120.

Cyrus, F.G., and Nolan, R.L. (1974). Managing the four stages of EDP Growth. *Harvard Business Review*, 52(1): 76–88.

Dale, R. (2003). The logical framework: An easy escape, a straitjacket, or a useful planning tool? *Development in Practice*, 13(1): 57–70.

Davenport T.H. (1993). *Process Innovation: Reengineering Work through Information Technology*. Boston, MA: Harvard Business School Press.

Davis, W.S. (1983). *Systems Analysis and Design: A Structured Approach*. Reading, MA: Addison-Wesley.

Deloitte & Touche (2001). The citizen as customer. *CMA Management*, 74(10): 58.

Deloitte & Touche (2003). *Citizen Advantage: Enhancing Economic Competitiveness through E-Government*. New York: Deloitte &Touche. www.deloitte.com/dtt/newsletter/0,1012,sid%253D15288%2526cid%253D26079,00.html.

Dennis, A., and Wixom, B.H. (2000). *Systems Analysis and Design: An Applied Approach*. New York: John Wiley & Sons.

Deutsch, K. (1968). *The Nerve of Government of Government*. New York: Free Press.

Development Bank of Southern Africa (2003). *DBSA Provincial Report on Gauteng 2003*. www.dbsa.org/Research/Documents/DBSAActivitiesReport2004-2005.pdf.

Dugdale, A., et al. (2005). Accessing e-government: Challenges for citizens and organizations. *International Review of Administrative Sciences*, 71(1): 109–18.

Dutta, S., Lopez-Claros, A., and Mia, I. (2006). *The Global Information Technology Report 2005–2006, Leveraging ICT for Development, Insead & World Economic Forum*. New York: Macmillan.

Dzidonu, C. (2006). *The National ICT for Development (ICT4D) Five Years*. www.eictda.gov.et.

Easton, D. (1965). *A System Analysis of Political Life*. New York: Wiley.

Ekurhuleni Metropolitan Municipality (n.d.). *Digital City Blueprint*.

Ekurhuleni Metropolitan Municipality (2007a). *Ekurhuleni Growth and Development Strategy 2025*. Ekurhuleni.

Ekurhuleni Metropolitan Municipality (2007b). *Integrated Development Plan, Budget and Service Delivery Budget Implementation Plan 2007/8–2009/10*. Ekurhuleni.

Elkadi, H. (2007). Interview with Government Services Delivery Program Director, Ministry of State for Administrative Development. Cairo City Observation. March 2007.

Emfuleni Local Municipality (2007). *Emfuleni Integrated Development Plan 2007 – 2008*. Emufuleni.

Eskeles-Gottfried, A., Fleming, J., and Gottfried, A. (1998). Role of cognitively stimulating home environment in children's academic intrinsic motivation: A longitudinal study. *Child Development*, 69: 1448–60.

Ethiopia Telecommunications Corporation (2001). Official website of the Ethiopian Telecommunications Corporation. www.ethionet.et.

European Commission (2006). *Measurement Framework Final Version*. http://217.59.60.50/eGEP/Static/Contents/final/D.2.4_Measurement_Framework_final_version.pdf.

eUser (2004). Public online services and user orientation. www.euser-eu.org/Default.asp?MenuID=8.

Eysenck, H.J., and Eysenck, S.B.G. (1975). *Manual of the Eysenck Personality Questionnaire*. Sevenoaks: Hodder & Stoughton.

Fahmy, A.A. (2007). *An ICT Based Methodology and Software Tool for Local Government Services Delivery Process Modeling Adapted for African Country*. LOG-IN Africa Second Progress Report.

Fahmy, A.A., et al. (2008). A process modeling methodology for e-local government service delivery projects in Egypt. Paper presented at the 'LOG-IN Africa International Conference on e-Governance', Cairo, June.

Felts, A.A., and Jos, P.H. (2000). Time and space: The origins and implications of the new public management. *Administrative Theory & Praxis*, 22 (3): 519–33.

Finger, M. (2005). Conceptualizing e-Governance. Paper prepared for 'European Review of Political Technologies' conference, March. www.politech-institute.org/review.asp.

Flak, L.S., Olsen, D.H., and Wolcott, P. (2005). Local E-Government in Norway. *Scandinavian Journal of Information Systems*, 17(2): 41–8.

Fu, J.R., Farn, C.K., and Chao, W.P. (2006). Acceptance of electronic tax filing: A study of taxpayer intentions. *Information & Management*, 43(1): 109–26.

Gasu, J. (2007). Power and patrimonial order: The challenge to democracy in Africa. Paper presented at the '1st Congress of the African Association of Sociologists', Rhodes University, Grahamstown, South Africa.

Gauteng Provincial Government (2006). *Gauteng Social Development Strategy 2006–2014.* Gauteng.

Gauteng Provincial Government (2007a). *e-Government Blueprint Proposal.* Gauteng.

Gauteng Provincial Government (2007b). *Building Gauteng as a Globally Competitive City Region.* Gauteng.

GDRC (2004a). *Urban Governance* Global Development Research Centre (GDRC). www.gdrc.org/u-gov/index.html.

GDRC (2004b). *Understanding the Concept of Governance.* Global Development Research Centre (GDRC). www.gdrc.org/u-gov/governance-understand.html.

GDRC (2004c). *Governance: A Working Definition.* Global Development Research Centre (GDRC). www.gdrc.org/u-gov/work-def.html.

Ghana Statistical Service (1989). *Ghana Living Standard Survey: First Year Report (September 1987–August 1988).* Accra: Ghana Statistical Service.

Ghana Statistical Service (1991). *Rural Communities in Ghana: Report of a National Rural Community Survey.* Accra: Ghana Statistical Service.

Ghana Statistical Service (1995a). *Ghana Living Standards Survey: Report on the Third Round (GLSS 3): September 1991–September 1992.* Accra: Ghana Statistical Service.

Ghana Statistical Service (1995b). *The Pattern of Poverty in Ghana 1988–92.* Accra: Ghana Statistical Service.

Ghana Statistical Service (2000). *Ghana Living Standards Survey: Report of the Fourth Round (GLSS 4).* Accra: Ghana Statistical Service.

Gillwald, A., et al. (2005). Towards an African e-Index, household and individual ICT access and usage across 10 African countries. http://link.wits.ac.za/papers/e-index-front.pdf.

Glasser, B., and Strauss, A. (1967). *The Discovery of Grounded Theory.* Chicago: Aldine.

Gordijn, J., Akkermans, H., and van Vliet, H. (2000). Business modelling is not process modelling. In *Proceedings of ER 2000 Workshop*, Berlin: Springer-Verlag, pp. 40–51.

Gordon, T.F. (2004). eGovernance and its value for public administration. www.lefis.org/meetings/workshops/2004/munster/presentaciones/ legal_knowledge_based_systems_for_%20egovernance_and%20_public_ administration.pdf.

Government of Australia (2005). *Australians' Use of and Satisfaction with E-Government Services*. Canberra: Australian Government Information Management Office.

Government of Egypt (2008a). *Egyptian Information Society Initiative*. www.egypt. gov.eg/english/laws/download/Egyptian_Info_Society_Initiative.zip.

Government of Egypt (2008b). *The Egyptian Information Society Initiative for Government Services Delivery*. www.egypt.gov.eg/english/laws/download/ EISI_Gov_English_paper.zip.

Government of Ethiopia (1994). *The Constitution of the Federal Republic of Ethiopia*. www.ethiopar.net.

Government of Ethiopia (2003a). *Addis Ababa City Government Sub-Cities and Kebeles Establishment Proclamation*. Proclamation No. 1/2003.

Government of Ethiopia (2003b). *Addis Ababa City Charter*. Federal Government of Ethiopia. Proclamation No. 361/2003.

Government of Ethiopia (2004). *Addis Ababa City Government Sub-Cities and Kebeles Establishment*. Proclamation No. 13/2004.

Government of Ethiopia (2005). *The Official Website of the City Government of Addis Ababa*. www.addisababacity.gov.et.

Government of Ethiopia (2006a). *Addis Ababa City Administration Kebele Residents' Service Delivery Guideline*. Addis Ababa: Government Printers.

Government of Ethiopia (2006b). *Information Communication Technology Policy of the Federal Democratic Republic of Ethiopia*. www.eictda.gov.et/.

Government of Ghana (2003). *ICT for Accelerated Development Policy Document*. Accra: Graphic Communications Group.

Government of Ghana (2004). *Brochure on Telephony System in Ghana*. Accra: Ministry of Communication.

Government of Ghana (2005). *Growth and Poverty Reduction Strategy (GPRS II) 2006–2009*. National Development Planning Commission. Accra: Accra Assembly Press.

Government of India (2002). *Successful Governance Initiatives and Best Practices, Experiences from Indian States*. New Delhi: National Planning Commission and UNDP.

Government of Kenya, Ministry of Local Government (1999). *Report of the Rationalization and Staff Rightsizing for Effective Operation of the Ministry of Local Government*. Nairobi: Government Printer.

Government of Kenya (2001). *Economic Survey*. Nairobi: Government Printer.

Government of Kenya (2002a). *Economic Survey*. Nairobi: Government Printer.

Government of Kenya, Ministry of Local Government (2002b). *Kenya Local*

Government Reform Program Concept Paper. Nairobi: Ministry of Local Government.

Government of Kenya, Office of the President (2004). *E-Government Strategy: The Strategic Framework, Administrative Structure, Training Requirements and Standardization Framework*. Nairobi: Cabinet Office, Office of the President.

Government of Kenya (2006). *Information and Communications Technology Policy Guidelines*, Gazette Notice no. 2431.

Government of Malaysia (1995). *The Civil Service of Malaysia, Improvements and Development in the Civil Service of Malaysia 1994*. http://catalogue.nla.gov.au/Record/422878.

Government of Morocco (2007). *Strategie e-Maroc 2010: Realizations, Orientations & Plans d'action, Reussir*. Rabat.

Government of South Africa (2001). Electronic government the digital future: A public service IT policy framework. Department for Public Service and Administration. www.dpsa.gov.za/documents/acts&regulations/frameworks/IT.pdf.

Government of South Africa (2004). *Local Government Fact Book 2003–4*. Department of Local Government. www.thedplg.gov.za/index.php?option=com_docman&task=cat_view&gid=14&Itemid=27accessed.

Government of South Africa (n.d.) *Towards an Inclusive Information Society in South Africa*. Presidential National Commission on Information Society and Development. Pretoria: PNC ISAD.

Government of Uganda (2004). *Local Government Information and Communication System: Integrated M&E Manual*. Kampala: Ministry of Local Government.

Government of Uganda (2006). *Uganda E-Government Strategy Framework*. Kampala: Ministry of Information and Communication Technology.

Graafland-Essers, I., and Ettedgui, E. (2003). *Benchmarking e-Government in Europe and the US*. Santa Monica, CA: RAND. www.rand.org/pubs/monograph_reports/MR1733/MR1733.pdf.

Gupta, M., and Jana, D. (2003). E-Government evaluation: A framework and case study. *Government Information Quarterly*, 20: 365–87.

Gurstein, M., and Misuraca, G. (2006). Background paper for LOGIN Africa. http://unpan1.un.org/intradoc/groups/public/documents/CAFRAD/UNPAN023423.pdf.

Hammer, M., and Champy, J. (1993). *Reengineering the Corporation: A Manifesto for Business Revolution*. London: Nicholas Brealey.

Hanchinamani, B. (2000). The impact of Mozambique's land tenure policy on refugees and internally displaced persons. *Human Rights Brief*, 7.

Hansen, E. (1991). *Ghana under Rawlings: Early Years*. Oxford: Malthouse Press.

Harrington, J.H. (1991). *Business Process Improvement*. New York: McGraw-Hill.

Harrison, A.F., and Bramson, R.M. (1988). *InQ Inquiry Mode Questionnaire: A Measure of How You Think and Make Decisions*. Berkeley, CA: Bramson, Parlette, Harrison & Associates.

Heath, A. (2007). *Sedibeng IDP and Budget Lekgotla*. Drakensburg: Sedibeng

Heeks, R. (2003). Most egovernment-for-development projects fail: How can risks be reduced? http://idpm.man.ac.uk/publications/wp/igov/index.shtml.

Hiller, J., and Belanger, F. (2001). *Privacy Strategies for Electronic Government.* Arlington, VA: PricewaterhouseCoopers Endowment for the Business of Government.

Ho, A.T. (2002). Reinventing local governments and the e-government initiative. Public administration review, 62(4): 434–44.

Hogan, T.P. (2003). *Psychological Testing: A Practical Introduction.* Hoboken, NJ: Wiley.

Hood, C. (1983). *The Tools of Government.* London: Macmillan.

Hult, M., and Lennug, S. (1980). Towards a definition of action research. *Journal of Management Studies*, 17(2): 241–50.

Human Sciences Research Council (2005). *Poverty Pockets in Gauteng: How Migration Impacts Poverty.* Pretoria: Urban Rural and Economic Development, HSRC.

Huntington, S.P. (1991). *Third Wave Democracy in the Late Twentieth Century.* Oklahoma: University of Oklahoma Press.

Hyden, G. (1995). Public administration in developing countries: Kenya and Tanzania in comparative perspective. In Pierre, J. (ed.), *Bureaucracy in the Modern State: An Introduction to Comparative Public Administration.* Cheltenham: Edward Elgar, pp. 1–17.

Ibahrine, M. (2004). Towards a national telecommunications strategy in Morocco. www.firstmonday.org/issues/issue9_1/ibahrine/.

Information Communication Technology Authority (n.d.). Information and Communications Technology Authority: Secure Communications for all. www.icta.mu/icta/.

Intergovernmental Advisory Board (2003). *High Payoff in Electronic Government: Measuring the Return on E-government Investments.* www.gsa.gov/intergovt/iab.php.

Ipe, M. (2003). Knowledge sharing in organizations: A conceptual framework. *Human Resource Development Review*, 2: 337–59.

ITU (2001). *Effective regulation: Case study of Morocco.* www.itu.int/itudoc/gs/promo/bdt/cast_reg/79125.pdf.

ITU (2007). *Measuring the Information Society 2007: ICT Opportunity Index and World Telecommunication/ICT Indicators.* www.itu.int/ITU-D/ict/publications/ict-oi/2007/index.html.

Janssen, D. (2003). Mine's bigger than yours: Assessing international e-government benchmarking. In Bannister, F., and Remenyi, D. (eds), *3rd European Conference on eGovernment.* Reading: MCIL, pp. 209–18.

Janssen, D., Rotthier, S., and Snijkers, K. (2004). If you measure it they will score: An assessment of international e-government benchmarking. *Information Polity*, 9(3/4): 121–30.

Jeger, E. (2000). *Quality in Public Service Provision: The experience of São Paulo State Government.* George Washington University, School of Business and Public

Management and The Institute of Brazilian Business and Management Issues, XII Minerva Program.

Jeremy, G., Kenny, C., and Qiang, C.Z. (2004). *Information and Communication Technologies and Broad-based Development: A Partial Review of the Evidence*. Washington, DC: World Bank.

Jones, T. (1976). *Ghana's First Republic: The Pursuit of the Political Kingdom*. London: Methuen.

Kaboolian, L. (1998). The new public management: Challenging the boundaries of the management vs. administration debate. *Public Administration Review*, 58(3): 189–93.

Karagiannis, D., and Palkovits, S. (2002). *Prozessmodellierung in der öffentlichen Verwaltung – Ein ganzheitliches Rahmenwerk für E-Government*, October, for eGOV day 2003.

Keller, G., and Teufel ,T. (1998). *SAP R/3 Process Oriented Implementation*, Harlow: Addison-Wesley.

Kettani, D. (2007). *Larache e-Government Project*. LOG-IN Africa Mid-term Review Report.

Kettani, D., and Asmae, E.M. (2008). Proposition of a roadmap to 'e-Governance for Good Governance' in developing countries. In *Proceedings of 'LOG-IN Africa e-Local Governance 1st Conference, June 5–6 2008', Cairo, Egypt*, pp. 179–190.

Kettani, D., Moulin, B., and Elmahdi, A. (2005). Towards a formal framework of impact assessment of E-Government systems on governance. In *Proceedings of the 'Fourth WSEAS International Conference on E-ACTIVITIES (E-ACTIVITIES '05)'*, Miami, pp. 12–20.

Kettani, D., et al. (2006). An approach to the assessment of applied information systems with particular application to community based systems. In Meersman, R., Tari, Z., and Herrero, P. (eds), *On the Move to Meaningful Internet Systems 2006: OTM 2006 Workshops*. Montpellier: Springer-Verlag, pp. 301–10.

King, S., and Johnson, O. (2006). VBP: An approach to modelling process variety and best practice. *Information and Software Technology*, 48(11): 1104–14.

Kling, B. (2000). Information Technologies and Social Change: The Contribution of Social Informatics. *The Information Society*, 16(3): 217–32.

Kraemer, K.L., and Dedrick, J. (1997). Computing and public organizations. *Journal of Public Administration Research and Theory* 7(1): 89–112..

Kumar, R., and Best, M.L. (2006). Impact and sustainability of e-government services in developing countries: Lessons learned from Tamil Nadu, India. *The Information Society*, 22: 1–12.

Kusek, J.Z., and Rist, J.C. (2004). *Ten Steps to a Results-Based Monitoring and Evaluation System: A Handbook for Development Practitioners*. Washington, DC: World Bank.

Ladouceaur, P.A. (1979). *Chiefs and Politicians: The Politics of Regionalism in Northern Ghana*. London: Longman.

Layne, K., and Lee, J. (2001). Developing fully functional e-government: A four stage model. *Government Information Quarterly*, 18(2): 122–36.

Lengrand, L. (2004). *e-Maroc 2010: Propositions pour une e-stratégie mise à jour.* Final report. Mission financed by World Bank.

Lenk, K., and Traunmueller, R. (1999). Perspektiven einer radikalen Neugestaltung der oeffentlichen Verwaltung mit Informationstechnik. In *Oeffentliche Verwaltung und Informationstechnik, Schriftenreihe Verwaltungsinformatik.* Heidelberg: Decker's Verlag.

Macueve, G.A. (2007). *Evaluating the Outcomes of E-government Projects in Mozambique: A Case Study of Maputo, Sofala and Cabo-Delgado Provinces.* LOG-IN Africa Mid-term Review Report.

Marcelle, G. (2000). *Transforming Information and Communications Technologies for Gender Equality.* Gender in Development Monograph Series No. 9. UNDP.

Mayne, J. (2007). Challenges and lessons in implementing results-based management. *Evaluation,* 13(1): 87–109.

McKinley, J.C., and Hathaway, S.R. (1944). A multiphasic personality schedule (Minnesota): V. hysteria, hypomania, and psychopathic deviate. *Journal of Applied Psychology,* 28: 153–74.

Minges, M. (2005). *Evaluation of e-readiness indices in Latin America and the Caribbean.* Santiago: ECLAC. www.eclac.org/socinfo/publicaciones/default.asp?idioma=IN.

Misra, D.C. (2006). Defining e-Government: A citizen-centric criteria-based approach. In *Proceedings of the '10th National Conference on e-Governance, Bhopal, Madhya Pradesh, India'.* http://unpan1.un.org/intradoc/groups/public/documents/UNPAN/UNPAN025373.pdf.

Misuraca, G.C. (2006). E-Governance in Africa, from theory to action: A practical-oriented research and case studies on ICTs for Local Governance. *ACM International Conference Proceedings Series,* 151: 209–18.

Mitullah, W.V. (2004). Participatory governance for poverty alleviation in local authorities in Kenya. *Journal of Regional Development Dialogue (RDD),* 25(1), Spring.

Mitullah, W.V., and Odek, W. (2002). Impact and potential of ICTs in micro and small enterprises (MSEs): A study of Kenya and Ghana – Kenya case study. Paper prepared for the United Nations University/Institute of New Technologies, Maastricht, The Netherlands.

Mitullah, W.V., et al. (2005). *Management of Resources by Local Authorities: The Case of Local Authority Transfer Fund.* Nairobi: Claripress.

Mitullah, W., and Waema, T.M. (2007). *ICTs and Financial Management in Local Authorities in Kenya: Case Study of Mavoko and Nyeri Municipal Councils.* LOG-IN Africa Mid-term Review Report.

Mogale City (2003). *Masters Systems Plan Management Report.* Mogale.

Mogale City (2007). *Integrated Development Plan 2007–2011.* Mogale.

Moon, M.J. (2002). The evolution of e-government among municipalities: Rhetoric or reality? *Public Administration Review,* 62(4): 424–33.

Muthee, M.W. (2004). Urban residents' associations and the management of services in Nairobi: A study of the Karen and Langata District Association.

Institute for Development Studies Master's Project Paper, University of Nairobi.

Mutula, S.M. (2006). Knowledge management-based approach to e-governance: A model for East and Southern African Countries. Paper presented at 'The XVII Standing Conference of Eastern, Central and Southern Africa Library and Information Associations', 10–19 July, Dar es Salaam, Tanzania.

Nairobi City Council (2004). *Report on Decentralization Program.* Nairobi: NCC Town Clerks Department.

National Computer Board (2003). *ICT Outlook 2002 – ICT Penetration within the Mauritian Society.* http://ncb.intnet.mu/mitt/ministry.

National Computer Board (2006). *Current State Assessment of E-Government in Mauritius (Draft Version 4.0).* http://ncb.intnet.mu/mitt/ministry.

National Office for the Information Economy. (2003). *E-government Benefits Study.* www.agimo.gov.au/__data/assets/file/16032/benefits.pdf.

Navarra, D., and Cornford, T. (2003). A policy making view of e-government innovations in public governance. In *Proceedings of the 9th Americas Conference on Information Systems,* Paper 103, http://aisel.aisnet.org/amcis2003/103.

Ndou, D.V. (2004). e-Government for developing countries: Opportunities and challenges. *The Electronic Journal on Information Systems in Developing Countries,* 18(1): 1–24.

Nicoll, P., Robinson, J., and O'Hanlon, B. (2004). *Measuring the Efficiency and Effectiveness of E-government.* Canberra: Auditor-General. www.anao.gov. au/WebSite.nsf/Publications/2C3CDF64278872A9CA256FA2007F445E.

Nugent, P. (1995). *Big Men, Small Boys and Politics in Ghana.* London: Pinter.

OECD (2003). The *e-Government Imperative. Oecd e-GovernmentStudies.* www1.oecd. org/publications/e-book/4203071E.PDF.

Okong'o, V. (2005). *The E-Government Experience in Kenya: The Story So Far.* www. idrc.ca/en/ev-93058-201-1-DO_TOPIC.html.

Orlikowski, W., and Boroudi, J. (2001). Studying Information Technology in organizations: Research approaches and assumptions. *Information Systems Research,* 2: 1–28.

Osborne, D., and Gaebler, T. (1992). *Reinventing Government: How the Entrepreneurial Spirit is Transforming the Public Sector.* New York: Plume Books.

Osborne, D., and Plastrik, P. (1997). *Banishing Bureaucracy: The Five Strategies for Reinventing Government.* Reading, MA: Addison-Wesley.

Osterweil, L.J., et al. (2004). Analyzing processes for e-government application development: The emergence of process definition languages. *Journal of E-Government,* 1(4): 63–87.

Pacific Council on International Development (2002). *Roadmap for E-Government in the Developing World, 10 Questions E-Government Leaders Should Ask Themselves.* The Working Group on E-Government in the Developing World. Los Angeles. Pacific Council on International Policy. www.pacificcouncil. org/pdfs/e-gov.paper.f.pdf.

Pentland, B.T. (2003a). Sequential variety in work processes. *Organization Science,* 14(5): 528–40.

Pentland, B.T. (2003b). Conceptualizing and measuring variety in the execution of organizational work processes. *Management Science*, 49(7): 857–70.

PNUD (2003). *Maroc: Rapport de Developpment Humain 2003, Gouvernance et Acceleration du Developpment Humain.* http://hdr.undp.org/docs/reports/national/MOR_Morocco/Morocco_2003_fr.pdf.

Polidano, C. (1999). *The New Public Management in Developing Countries.* IDPM Public Policy and Management Working Paper No. 13. Institute for Development Policy and Management, University of Manchester.

Pozzebon, Marlei (2004). The influence of a structurationist perspective on strategic management research. *Journal of Management Studies* ,41(2): 247–72.

Republic of Kenya (2003). *Economic Recovery Strategy for Wealth and Employment Creation, 2003–2007,* Nairobi: Government Printers.

Republic of South Africa (1998). Local Government Municipal Structures Act, No. 117 of 1998. *Government Gazette* no. 19614, 18 December, Cape Town.

Republic of South Africa (2000). Local Government Municipal Structures Amendment Act, No. 33 of 2000. *Government Gazette* no. 21652, 13 October, Cape Town.

Riley. B. (2004). *E-government: The Digital Divide and Information Sharing: Examining the Issues.* Ottawa: Commonwealth Centre for E-Governance.

Rockcliffe-King, J., and Mitullah, W.V. (2003). *Support to Local Government Program Components: Output to Purpose Review.* Nairobi: DFID

Rose, J., and Scheepers, R. (2001). Structuration theory and Information System development – Frameworks for practice. In *Proceedings of the '9th European Conference on Information Systems'.* http://folk.uio.no/patrickr/refdoc/Rose-structuation.pdf.

Rowan, M. (2003). Lessons learned from Mozambique's ICT policy process, Maputo. Paper for the International Development Research Centre (IDRC). http://198.62.158.214/geh/ev-46223-201-1-DO_TOPIC.html.

Rummler, G.A., and Brache, A.P. (1995). *Improving Performance.* San Francisco, CA: Jossey-Bass.

Sahay, S., and Walsham, G. (2006). Scaling of health information systems in India: Challenges and approaches. *Information Technology for Development,* 12(3): 185–200.

Saxena, K.B.C. (2005). Towards excellence in e-Governance. *International Journal of Public Management,* 18(6): 498–513.

Scholl, H.J. (2003). E-government: A special case of ICT-enabled business process change. In *Proceedings of the 36th Hawaii International Conference on System Sciences (HICSS'03).*

Sedibeng District Municipality. (2007). *Growth and Development Strategy.* Sedibeng.

Seifert, J.W., and Bonham G.M. (2003). The transformative potential of e-Government in transitional democracies. www.maxwell.syr.edu/maxpages/faculty/gmbonham/Transformative_Potential_of_E-Government.pdf.

Sheridan, W., and Riley, T.B. (2006). Comparing e-Government vs. e-Governance. Commonwealth Centre for Governance. www.electronicgov.

net/pubs/research_papers/SheridanRileyComparEgov.doc.

Siau, K., and Long, Y. (2005). Synthesizing e-government stage models – a meta-synthesis based on the meta-ethnography approach. *Industrial Management & Data Systems*, 105(4): 443–58.

Society for the Promotion of eGovernance and Price Waterhouse Coopers India (2006). *Government@24/7; Overcoming Contextual and Cultural Challenges*, Report and recommendations on egovWorld 2006, South Asia e-Government Summit, http://egovstandards.gov.in/events/egov-world-2006-south-asia-e-government-summit.

Songsore, J. (2003). *Regional development in Ghana: The Theory and the Reality*. Accra: Woeli Publishing Services.

Spender, J.C., and Grant, R.M. (1996). Knowledge and the firm: Overview. *Strategic Management Journal*, 17: 5–9.

Statistics South Africa (2001). *Census 2001*. Pretoria: StatsSA.

Statistics South Africa (2007). *Community Survey 2007: Municipal Data on Household Services*. Pretoria: StatsSA.

StatsSA (2007). *Community Survey 2007: Basic Results Gauteng*. Pretoria: Statistics South Africa (StatsSA).

Swiss, J.E. (2005). A framework for assessing incentives in results-based management. *Public Administration Review*, 65(5): 592–602.

Tiamiyu, M.A. (2000). Availability, accessibility and use of information technologies in Nigeria federal agencies: A preliminary survey. *Information Technology for Development*, 9(2), 91–104.

Tufte, E.R. (2001). *The Visual Display of Quantitative Information*. Cheshire, CT: Graphics Press.

Tusubira, F. (2004). Rural communications development. Paper presented at the 'International Seminar on ICT Policy Reform and Rural Communications Infrastructure', 23 August – 1 September 2004, Fujisawa and Tokyo, Japan. www.ictseminar.org/Doc/TusubiraUniversalAccessUganda%20Case.ppt#257,1.

Uganda Communications Commission (2001). *Rural Communications Development Policy for Uganda*. www.ucc.co.ug/rcdf/about.html.

UN DESA (2003). *Report of the Workshop on Poverty Alleviation and Decentralization for Ten West African countries*. Dakar: UN DESA and Government of Senegal.

UNDP (1997). *Governance for Sustainable Human Development: A UNDP Policy Document*. New York: UNDP.

UNDP (2002). *Handbook on Monitoring and Evaluation of Results*. UNDP Evaluation Office. http://stone.undp.org/undpweb/eo/evalnet/docstore3/yellowbook/documents/full_draft.pdf.

UNDP (2003). *Human Development Report 2003*. New York: UNDP.

UNDP (2004). *Morocco Country Profile*. www.arabgov-initiative.org/publications/egov/countries/morocco-e.pdf.

UNDP (2006a). *Human Development Report 2006 – Beyond Scarcity: Power, Poverty and the Global Water Crisis*. New York: UNDP.

UNDP (2006b). *Governance for Sustainable Human Development: A Policy Document.* http://mirror.undp.org/magnet/policy/default.htm.

United Nations (2002). *Benchmarking E-Government: A Global Perspective.* United Nations and American Society for Public Administration. www.unpan. org/e-government/Benchmarking%20E-gov%202001.pdf.

United Nations (2004). *Global E-government Readiness Report: Towards Access for Opportunity.* New York.

United Nations (2005). *Information and Communication Technologies and the Millennium Development Goals.* New York: UN ICT Task Force.

United Nations (2008). *UN E-Government Survey 2008: From E-Government to Connected Governance, Economic & Social Affairs.* New York.

Unwin, T. (2009). *ICT4D: International and Communication Technology for Development.* Cambridge: Cambridge University Press.

Verginadis, G., and Mentzas, G. (2004). A light modelling framework for e-government service workflows. *Electronic Government,* 1(4): 420–38.

Waema, T.M., (2004). *Final Report for the Universal Access to Communication Services: Development of a Strategic Plan and Implementation Guidelines.* Nairobi: Communications Commission of Kenya, November.

Waema, T.M. (2005). A brief history of the development of ICT policy in Kenya. In Etta, F.E., and Elder, L. (eds), *At the Crossroads: ICT Policy Making in East Africa.* Nairobi: East African Educational Publishers, pp. 25–43.

Waema, T.M., (2006). *Kenya ICT Sector Performance Review.* www.researchictafrica. net/old/modules.php?op=modload&name=News&file=index&catid=&topic=31&allstories=1.

Waema, T.M., and Bowman, W.N. (2005). *The Institutional Structures and Models for Implementing the Kenyan National ICT Plan.* Nairobi: Ministry of Planning and National Development.

Waema, T.M., Kashorda, M., and Kyalo, V. (2007). *Internet Market Analysis Study.* Report submitted to the Communications Commission of Kenya, May.

Waema, T.M., and Mitullah, W. (2007). E-governance and governance: A case study of the assessment of the effects of integrated financial management system on good governance in two municipal councils in Kenya. In Janowski, T., and Pardo T.A. (eds), *Proceedings of the 1st International Conference on Theory and Practice of Electronic Governance, ICEGOV 2007, Macao, China, December 10–13, 2007,* ACM International Conference Proceeding Series 232, pp. 263–8.

Waema, T.M., and Mitullah, W. (2008). e-Governance in local authorities in Kenya: Policy and institutional elements of implementation. In *Proceedings of 'LOG-IN Africa e-Local Governance 1st Conference, June 5-6 2008', Cairo, Egypt,* pp. 67–78.

Walsham, G. (1993). *Interpreting Information Systems in Organizations.* Chichester: John Wiley .

Wauters, P., and Colclough, G. (2005). *Online Availability of Public Services: How is Europe Progressing?* Brussels: Capgemini. http://europa.eu.int/information-_society/soccul/egov/egov_benchmarking_2005.pdf.

Weiss, T.G. (2000). Governance, good governance and global governance: Conceptual and actual challenges. *Third World Quarterly*, 21(5): 795–814.

West, D. (2002a). State and federal e-government in the United States. www.insidepolitics.org/Egovto2us.html.

West, D. (2002b). Urban e-government. www.insidepolitics.org/egovto2city.html.

Woldehanna, F., et al. (2004). *Proposal for the Establishment of Centre of Excellence in ICT.* Report submitted to the Ministry of Capacity Building, ICT Authority, Addis Ababa, Ethiopia.

World Audit Organisation (n.d.). www.worldaudit.org/democracy.htm.

World Bank (2003). *Better Governance for Development in the Middle East and North Africa: Enhancing Inclusiveness and Accountability.* MENA Development Report. Washington, DC.

World Bank (2007a). *World Bank Development Indicators.* http://data.worldbank.org/country/ghana.

World Bank (2007b). *World Bank Development Report 2007.* Washington, DC.

World Wide Worx (2008). *Internet Access in South Africa 2007.* www.worldwideworx.com/archives/150.

Work, R. (2002). Overview of decentralization worldwide: A stepping stone to improved governance and human development. In *Proceedings of the '2nd International Conference on Decentralization: Federalism: The Future of Decentralizing States'*, Manila, Philippines. www.decentralization.ws/icd2/papers/overview_decent.htm.

Wyssusek, B., et al. (2001). Business process modelling as an element of knowledge management – A model theory approach. Paper presented at conference on 'Managing Knowledge 2001: Conversations and Critiques', Leicester University, 10–11 April.

Yeebo, Z. (1991). *Ghana: The Struggle for Popular Power.* London: New Beacon Books.

Yourdon, E. (1989). *Modern Structured Analysis.* Upper Saddle River, NJ: Yourdon Press.

Zhang, P., et al. (2007). A hybrid e-government model: Case studies in Shanghai digital government. *Integrated Series in Information Systems*, 17: 697–718.

Ziani, B. (2003). *al-Tadbeer al-Baladi fi al-Magreb: Dirasat Tahliliyah liaadad min al-Halat.* Yemen: Mountada al-Dowal al-Arabiya llhokm al-Mahali, pp. 7–10.

Index

Tax Us If You Can:
Why Africa Should Stand Up for Tax Justice

Tax Justice Network-Africa

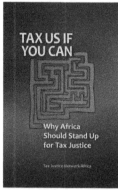

2011
paperback
978-0-85749-042-1
also available in pdf, epub
and Kindle formats

This lucid introduction to tax justice in Africa sets out the causes and consequences of tax injustice and offers options for a fairer future. Although tax revenues are essential for establishing independent states of free citizens, taxes in Africa are often regressive, tax administration ineffective and many commodity exports from Africa are tax exempt.

So what is the role of governments, parliaments and taxpayers? What needs to be done to achieve tax justice? The solutions suggested in this important book include raising awareness about tax issues, promoting a culture of tax compliance, increasing tax transparency and enhancing international cooperation on tax matters.

'This is an excellent study on a very important subject, on which both research and policy action have been extremely limited as well as clearly insufficient.'

**Professor Stephany Griffith-Jones,
Institute of Development Studies, University of Sussex, UK**

Women and Security Governance in Africa

Edited by 'Funmi Olonisakin and Awino Okech

2011
paperback
978-1-906387-89-1
also available in pdf, epub
and Kindle formats

When the path-breaking United Nations Resolution 1325 on women, peace and security was adopted in 2000, it was the first time that the security concerns of women in situations of armed conflict and their role in peace building were placed on the agenda of the UN Security Council.

In the field of international security, discussions on women and children are often relegated to the margins. This book addresses a broader debate on security and its governance in a variety of contexts while making the argument that the single most important measure of the effectiveness of security governance is its impact on women. But this is more than a book about women. Rather it is a book about inclusive human security for Africans, which cannot ignore the central place of women.

'In the first volume of its kind, some of the best and most engaging African intellectuals and activists have gathered to expose the fallacies of the current security paradigm to show how "security for women" must entail, at least in large part, "security by women".'

Professor Eboe Hutchful, chair of the African Security Network

'We need fresh perspectives and new ways of visioning governance in Africa so that women's security becomes an intrinsic measure of development and peace. This important collection of insights from across the continent leads the way.'

Winnie Byanyima, director of UNDP Gender Team

 Order your copy from www.pambazukapress.org